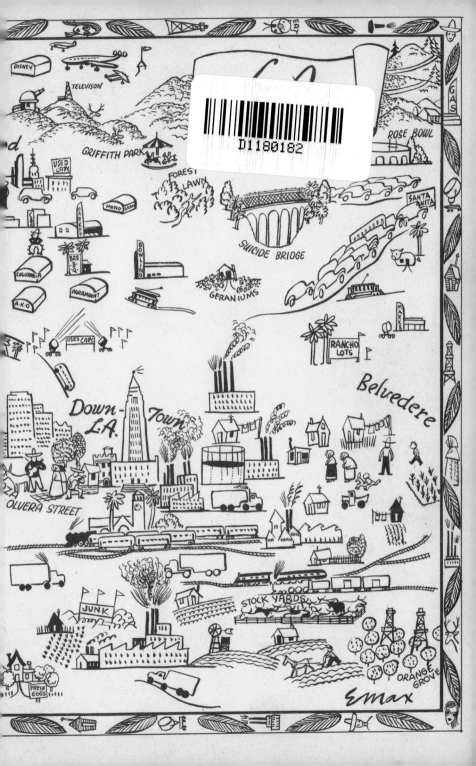

My L. A.

Marie Kaupp Feb.
1951

My L.A.

BY Matt Weinstock

Foreword by FRED BECK

NEW YORK
CURRENT BOOKS, INC.
A. A. WYN, PUBLISHER
1947

Printed in the United States of America
American Book–Stratford Press, Inc., New York

To Hilda

The kid on the bicycle slithers it into the petunias; Constant Reader unlimbers himself, steps off his stoop to retrieve it, settles himself back on the porch with his feet on the railing, eases his galluses, and, after a few grunts at the first page, he opens it up like a sandwich and eats the slab of solid and deftly seasoned meat that is Matt Weinstock's column.

Weinstock's column in the *Los Angeles Daily News* is the most widely read column west of the Gowanus, which happens to be a canal. Matt's daily piece reads as smooth as pie and thus Constant Reader, like all the readers of all the columns (except Howard Vincent O'Brien's in the *Chicago Daily News,* which is obviously brocaded rather than written) thinks that Weinstock approaches his typewriter and knocks out his charming and sometimes provocative articles in eight minutes flat.

And he's right. Matt Weinstock inserts the sheets in his L. C. Smith and jumps back. And there's his copy. He reads it over with a pencil in hand, poking commas into it in the manner of one poking cloves into a ham . . . and there it is; reading time two minutes, writing time eight minutes.

But:

Preceding that brief session at his L. C. Smith, which has been in use since the time of McKinley, Matt Weinstock has strained like George O'Brien playing the part of a sweaty-backed galley slave. He probably started writing the column in bed the night before. He and an idea probably snarled at each other until daybreak, when his day began.

Weinstock's prose may have the easy swing of easy writing, but each day's column is the result of digging and sometimes blasting. He eschews luncheons where the newest Viennese actress is presented to the press, but he sets out elaborate trap lines baited for local trivia. He might on occasion cover a literary tea for the purpose of investigating its stupidities for tomorrow's paper, but he's more likely to help bed down a wino in a Fifth Street flophouse, with a good ear tuned to the unfortunate one's story.

If he has a specialty, it's getting the significant out of the seemingly insignificant, and he's a master of the human-interest story. Matt can tell a sad one and a tragic one without getting it soppy with maudlin mawkishness.

There's one other ingredient that makes Matt Weinstock's column the best writing ever about Los Angeles. It's simply that Matt is one of the few writing men who knows Los Angeles.

At this point, I want to tell you a little secret. Forgive me if I appear to smirk, faintly, but once a long time ago I printed a false statement in a sort of a column that I write and which appears in the West's most polite daily. I stated that Matt Weinstock was writing a book about Los Angeles. Two things happened. First a lot of people wrote for a copy of the book. Second, a lot of publishers swooped down on Matt. He hadn't started the book, but these events caused him to do so, which is what I had hoped to see happen. I did it because there has been too much written about Los Angeles by Eastern journalists who come out, have lunch with Linda Darnell, and observe Los Angeles while relaxed in a cool breeze blowing across the surface of a Martini as served at Mike Romanoff's.

These boys write in the fine old tradition that Los Angeles, and/or Hollywood, is populated by screwballs. Most objective or facetious writings on the subject are influenced by what has been written before, and while the cults, and the Goldwyns, and the trafficking in cadavers, and the phonies and the damned geraniums will all appear in Matt's story of the town, all of them will be treated as you would expect by the one writer who can see the whole thing in its true light, not blinded by the bare midriffs in the Café de Paris, which is the name of the beanery on the Twentieth Century-Fox lot.

Matt started studying Los Angeles when he was a kid trapping 'possums on the present site of the May Company Wilshire. He went to U.C.L.A. for three years, ran out of money, and went to work for the *Los Angeles Daily News*. His study of his subject continued through the ensuing twenty years of Aimee, the earthquakes, the time the orange juice came rushing down the canyons to wash the foundations out from under the houses, and the time they tore down the little brick cribs to make room for the Moorish pile that is our depot.

As a newspaperman, he started covering high-school basketball, worked up to rewrite man, manned the city desk, and finally became managing editor of our town's only virile newspaper. The paper's star columnist left for a syndicate—it was Durling—and Matt talked to the publisher about taking on the columnist's stint and relinquishing the managing editor's job. He got the spot as columnist and remained on as editor.

That in time was corrected, and the column became his life. In its day-in day-out presentation it has told the story of Los Angeles. And that is what Matt Weinstock has now achieved between board covers.

Weinstock fans sometimes ask why his column isn't syndicated, like Bugs Baer and Barney Google. The answer is simple. Matt writes about Los Angeles for Los Angeles. This is all inside stuff, family secrets. Outsiders really shouldn't be allowed to read this book, which is written by the one writing man who knows every inch of his beat from where the swill meets the swells at El Sereño Beach to where it starts from the mechanical vegetable peelers in Old Mother Biltmore's third basement.

You will find Matt's book the gayest and wisest, the most readable and accurate story of Los Angeles ever written.

FRED BECK

July 1947

My L. A.

In Los Angeles you are conscious only of the present tense; there is no flavor of the past, no feeling for the future.—KATE BELL

IN THE minds of the cynical, there will always be some doubt that Juan Rodriguez Cabrillo did the world a favor when on October 8, 1542 he looked upon the shores of what is now San Pedro, or Los Angeles Harbor.

It wasn't a harbor at the time, for like much of the area, Los Angeles harbor is synthetic and cost sixty million dollars.

Cabrillo was unable to get a good look at the shore because a haze obscured it. Haze my eye, these same cynics will snarl, that was fog, just as now.

But Cabrillo, a good seaman and a calm, temperate man, knew better. This haze smelled.

Investigation disclosed that the haze was caused by fires along the shore, set to frighten superfluous rabbits from the tall grass. As the rabbits raced into the open, Indians flailed them with clubs. In one swoop they thus preserved their vegetable gardens, provided meat for their tables, and set a precedent for upcoming generations.

With some basis, Los Angeles has been described as a glorious climate wasted on an undeserving, vulgar, boorish people.

It has been compared to a freak exhibit at a third-rate circus sideshow, the one where the barker pounds his cane and shouts: "It walks, it talks, but is it human?"

Paul Schrecker, the European philosopher, called it a "conglomerate of disparate fragments." "Even the bad taste," he wrote, "seems to be fake bad taste."

George Sessions Perry termed it "New York in purple shorts with its brains knocked out."

Los Angeles is the most insulted city in the world. Its climate, its architecture, its people are worth a rib anytime. The magazines knock off an article a year on it as a matter of course. Their beaters incessantly pore over Chamber of Commerce files for new approaches, all emphasizing the crackpot phases.

But you don't have to read a magazine to learn about this horrible place. The most eloquent critics live here.

One faction was lured out by the ads showing the sun shining on a panoramic sweep of orange groves and snow-covered mountains, or of pretty girls in bathing suits posing provocatively at the beach. They liked the place and decided to stay. But they don't want anyone to get the idea they were pushovers, so they never let a day pass without saying something nasty.

The bitterness boys and girls from Sawdust Corners, Kansas, or Aching Back, Iowa, are something else. They considered themselves mighty sharp in a business way and came out to make a lot of money. The sunshine was secondary. The way they heard it, the hicks in L.A. were so full of the *mañana* spirit they didn't know what time it was. They were hardly off the train before they went for a smooth pitch on real estate, oil, or a rabbit farm. They got clipped good. When they gripe, it's with chimes. They're still around though, for the sunshine. It gets awfully cold, they remember, in the Midwest.

Then there are the slick boys from the Eastern culture centers. They come out expecting the aura surrounding them to diffuse magically and bring up the level of intelligence of the obviously ill-bred inhabitants. They meet a cold indifference, or even a few persons who say: "Don't let any of that stuff brush off on me, buddy." When their movie-contract or ad-agency chore is completed, they go away, still defiant egoists or saddened martyrs. Six months later they return to the disgusting place, willing to let bygones be bygones. A year later they wonder what it was they ever saw in the East. To explain this miracle: Los Angeles has brushed off on them.

Actually Los Angeles is the despair of journalists. They try to put their typewriter fingers on some identifying characteristic (after all, they had no trouble elsewhere with their identifying characteristics) and either rush into the night frustrated and brooding, or guiltily come up with the usual drivel about it being a crackpot town.

Ernie Pyle, when he was the Roving Reporter, before he became the greatest of the war correspondents, used to sneak into town, rent a quiet room at the homelike Mayfair Hotel, and catch up on his copy from places he had just been. He rarely used a Los Angeles date line. The city, he used to say, gave him a feeling of frustration. He found it lacking in warmth, honesty, and stability. He particularly disliked it for its vigorous Chamber of Commerce—he hated them all—and for what he considered the phoniness of Hollywood. On his final visit, before he left for his rendezvous with destiny on Ie Shima, he changed his opinion. For the first time he broke through the crust of publicity and found sincere, likable people in the film industry.

Only the fiction writers, especially the crime-story men, find Los Angeles a likely locale. Erle Stanley Gardner has six mystery novels laid in the area. A. A. Fair—reputedly one of Gardner's pseudonyms—has eight. Raymond Chandler has three. Their selection is understandable. The premises include some very convenient high, low, and medium-sized mountains, a desert, an ocean, all sorts of secluded canyons, and a well-established conviction that anything goes.

Hollywood has been done to death too, as the scene of what are known as fast-moving novels of satire, sex, and disillusion. Outstanding of these is Aldous Huxley's savage *After Many a Summer Dies the Swan*. James M. Cain's Mildred Pierce lived a few miles away in Glendale. W. R. Burnett's *Nobody Lives Forever* is set in Los Angeles.

But at the Public Library, where the shelves sag with hundreds of such books, even the janitors who sweep out will tell you that there isn't a first-class novel in the whole list.

The reason might be, conceivably, that Los Angeles doesn't hold still long enough for literary ideas to jell. Carey McWilliams names only four novels that suggest what Southern California is really like: John Fante's *Ask the Dust*, Frank Fenton's *A Place in the Sun*, Nathanael West's *The Day of the Locust*, and Mark Lee Luther's *The Boosters*.

Ironically, dozens of famous writers live in or near the city. Thomas Mann resides in Santa Monica, Upton Sinclair in Monrovia, Rupert Hughes, Jim Tully, James Hilton, Lewis Browne, Alfred Neumann, Lion Feutchwanger in Hollywood, Beverly Hills, Westwood, or San Fernando Valley. As a matter of fact, you can hardly go to the store without bumping elbows or fenders with someone who has just "hit the *Post*," "planted one" with a film studio, finished a play for Broadway, or been signed for thirteen weeks on the radio.

There's certainly no shortage of written matter about Los Angeles, not counting the thousands of travel folders distributed annually by the All Year Club of Southern California, the organization which changed the first letter of "Southern" from lower to upper case. Not too much of it, however, is a true or even a fair picture.

The legend is that Los Angeles is a hastily thrown together smear of pink and blue stucco dollhouses inhabited by long-haired men and short-haired women, clairvoyants, swamis, herb doctors, chiropractors, nature lovers, depraved motion-picture actors, psychopathic murderers, painless dentists, bond salesmen, gunmen, winos, radio announcers, and people who open every conversation with "What's doin'?"

These people, so goes the tale, are vulgar beyond belief. They put ketchup on their doughnuts. They can't engage in business without erecting their shops in the form of ice-cream freezers, crouched frogs, huge hats, gargantuan oranges, blimps, sphinxes, and windmills.

Their manners are atrocious. They drive their cars wildly, notching their steering wheels for each pedestrian killed.

They're lazy and consider the WPA the greatest thing that ever came along.

When they murder each other, the trials are fantastic spectacles, with the slayer claiming that he was enveloped in a white, purple, or polka-dotted flame at the moment he pulled the trigger.

They wear the damnedest clothes at the damnedest times: open-throated polo shirts and sports coats to opera first nights, gaudy slacks to funerals.

Furthermore, the streetcar service is terrible, everybody is always trying to chisel everybody else, the city streets are overrun with bums, a girl isn't safe out at night, and there are awful earthquakes and floods.

This is the picture painted time and again. And there's ground for the suspicion that the writers are all somewhat like the journalist assigned to do an article on sardine fishermen at San Pedro. He assembled his facts, then decided to blow a little color and romance into his piece with a visit to the harbor. On the waterfront he came upon a Slav about to ship out for sardines.

After a few minutes of unsatisfactory conversation, the writer asked: "What do you think about as your boat goes bobbing along in the phosphorescent glow?"

The Slav frowned and shrugged.

"All right then, what does your lookout say—you have a lookout I presume—when he sights a school of fish? Does he say, 'Thar she blows'? Or maybe: 'Ahoy to the starboard'?"

The puzzled fisherman thought a moment, then smiled as if the answer were too silly to express. "He say 'Fish!'" he said.

The people of Los Angeles know they're typed as slightly

nuts. They don't care; they laugh too at each newly discovered instance of screwiana. If the article writers only knew it, they've not begun to tap the surface on irregular behavior. A sign in a Seventh Street restaurant stated: FIRST VICE PRESIDENT WANTED—ABLE TO WASH A FEW DISHES. Western Avenue runs north and south. A Fairfax Avenue store advertised GLAMOUR PEANUTS. Drive-in eateries are everywhere and for years they tried to outdo each other with concoctions they called Nutburgers, Cheeseburgers, Chickenburgers, Idealistic Hamburgers, Chiliburgers, and Wimpies. Then along came Arnold Pressburger, the film producer, to put a stop to that sort of thing. A Ramona Boulevard repair shop soothes: AUTOMOBILE GASOLINE TANKS WELDED. NO EXPLOSIONS. All manner of crazy things happen on streetcars and busses. A woman on the Alhambra bus asked the driver why he didn't take a different route: "We passengers get awfully tired of the same scenery every day." Hale & Rain are builders on Atlantic Boulevard. Read & Wright is a real-estate concern in Beverly Hills. No, Los Angeles is no prosaic mosaic.

Intercity wrangling is going on between Detroit and Los Angeles as to which is the nation's fourth largest city, behind New York, Chicago, and Philadelphia. The 1940 census gave the spot to Detroit, but the office boy at the Chamber of Commerce will assure anyone that the tremendous influx of population since then has put Los Angeles safely ahead.

There's no question, however, about Los Angeles being the country's largest city in area. Its meandering city limits include 452.607 square miles, or at least they did when we went to press.

The three figures behind the decimal point are interesting. One day in 1943, in a surging passion for accuracy and column material, I checked an unofficial source to learn if the town had grown in size or was still 450 square miles, the round figure generally used. I was told it had indeed: it was 451.27 square miles.

The day after I printed the figure I received a formal communiqué from the inner sanctum of the inner vault of the city clerk's office, wherein such matters are writ on stone. My figure was wrong, I was told. A great deal had happened since *that* figure was correct. Tiny parcels of land had been snapped up right and left, with the result that I had short-changed the city 0.405 square miles. Not only that, the use of three decimal points instead of two had become standard operating procedure.

I firmly resolved never to let such a thing happen again. Since, I have carefully tabulated each little nudge onward and upward. Since 1943, ten more tidbits of acreage have been welcomed into the city. The largest was Angelus Mesa Addition No. 4, a matter of 0.409 square miles. The smallest was Lomita Addition No. 2, 0.008 square miles. I repeat, the city of Los Angeles has 452.607 square miles, including the 0.205 comprising Mar Vista Addition No. 3, annexed January 29, 1947. But the city clerk's office has promised not to sue me if another few decimal points come roaring in between this date and the time of publication.

During the war, my meticulous care in handling this matter bore fruit. Soldiers from Los Angeles detained in such places as Attu, North Africa, the Persian Gulf, and New Guinea took the cue and planted a new crop of LOS ANGELES CITY LIMITS signs.

This little game, by the way, has been going on for a long time. Fred Coffey, a Los Angeles newspaper photographer, had a large part in getting it started. Some years ago, he took a job on a round-the-world steamship cruise, photographing as he went. He took along an assortment of LOS ANGELES CITY LIMITS signs and not only planted them but photographed them in front of the Buddha of Kamakura, the Great Wall of China, the Taj Mahal, the Pyramids, Mount Vesuvius, and the Rock of Gibraltar. While returning to New York he fastened one of them to a large cork float and dropped it into the Gulf Stream. When last seen, it was heading northeast into the horizon.

Within the city limits are scores of miles of sun-baked waste-land, bosky dells, a reckless splash of neon, the Pacific Ocean, too many automobiles, some pretty good places to eat, and a few tired little rivers, which work only a few months of the year, then go underground. The Los Angeles River, which is a bare trickle most of the year, has been given careful treatment by the municipality. Along part of its route it has been supplied with a cement trough so that it won't disappear underground until the city so desires.

El Pueblo de Nuestra Señora La Reina de Los Angeles de Porciuncula—the city's real name, meaning the Town of Our Lady the Queen of the Angels of Porciuncula—was founded in December 1781 by forty-four somewhat reluctant colonists from Mexico. The town was ordained by royal decree after Felipe de Neve, governor of California, recommended to the viceroy of Mexico that it was an ideal spot for a mission.

Prospective settlers, approached by government agents, were indifferent. Months were required to assemble the group, mostly from Sonora, despite inducements of land, money, livestock, and implements. When the eleven men, eleven women, and twenty-two children in the group reached San Gabriel Mission, ten miles from Los Angeles, they were weary and depressed. Two of the adults were of Spanish origin; the remainder included one mestizo (half breed), eight mulattos, nine Indians, and two Negroes.

Early in the morning of September 4, 1781, the forty-four colonists, led by Governor de Neve and surrounded by soldiers and mission priests, arrived at what is now the Plaza in downtown Los Angeles. The padres invoked a blessing, de Neve spoke, and the city came into being. The Yang-na aborigine Indians, who were there first, looked on impassively.

Magazine writers have no trouble depicting the Los Angeles of today as a crazy hodgepodge, planned and populated by daft folk. Certainly a great deal happens to keep the screwball reputation alive. But it's only a trickle compared to the twenties, when the saga of Aimee Semple McPherson alone attracted such a fantastic press, and to the depression thirties, when economic panaceas based on something for nothing sprouted like geraniums. The truth is that the article writers are preserving a phony legend.

Los Angeles today is conservative. Actually it was always conservative, but this characteristic was obscured by the volcanic whims of a few exhibitionists. There is nothing particularly newsworthy about a million people quietly trying to figure out how to double their leisure by working as little as possible—and, of course, eat regularly.

Except in real estate, the old speculatve spirit is gone. Film tycoons and shoe clerks alike now play their holdings close to their vests, or rather, sports shirts.

They're troubled, though. All along they plugged for Los Angeles to become the largest city in the world. They thought in terms of increased valuation for their houses and lots. Now they can name their price but they've gone into a period of brooding. They never bargained on the fact that becoming a world metropolis involved bringing in strange new attitudes and new breeds of people who, if asked, would probably say the Mayflower is a doughnut shop on South Broadway, which it is.

Even in its present state of indecision and flux, Los Angeles is unbelievably underestimated. It is well on its way to being the most democratic city in the world. It has no caste except that of money and even in cash surrender value the line is very thin.

There's a temptation to get fancy, trying to describe what living in Los Angeles is like, because of the glib manner in which superlatives are thrown around. Put it this way. You do what you want to do and to hell with convention, with tradition, with taboos. There's a slight danger, of course, that this utter freedom means saying "To hell with other people." That happens too; but generally people are too busy arranging their share of what they consider their heritage: having fun in the sun.

For the land's sake!—Slogan in fertilizer ad in *Orange Daily News*

A small, wide-eyed boy in knickers, I came to Los Angeles in 1911. It was a cracker-barrel town.

People trusted each other. You could get credit at the corner grocery store. If you were late with a payment on the piano, a truck didn't suddenly back up to the front door to remove it.

Neighborhood drugstores employed messenger boys on bicycles to deliver prescriptions and purchases of more than fifty cents, even ice cream.

Merchants were distrustful of paper money. Silver dollars and five-, ten- and twenty-dollar gold pieces were all the rage, with the result that pants pockets needed a retread every thousand dollars.

The Chamber of Commerce, which now occupies most of the main floor of a huge building of the same name at Twelfth and Broadway, was virtually a hole in the wall on Broadway near First.

Downtown street corners had hitching posts and watering troughs. Palm trees lined the curbs on Broadway, mounted in large concrete boxes.

During the summer, a jovial fellow in a baseball uniform rode a horse slowly through the downtown streets: Main, Spring, Broadway, waving at friends and occasionally blowing a bugle call by way of announcing the baseball game at 2 P.M. at Washington Park, Washington and Hill Streets. The home teams were Los Angeles and Vernon. Washington Park has disappeared. The site remains an empty lot, used in the spring by visiting circuses. Baseball-minded folk now go to Wrigley Field, at Forty-second and Avalon, to see the Los Angeles baseball team play and to Beverly Boulevard near Fairfax, which is not strictly in Hollywood, to watch the Hollywood club, successor to Vernon in the Pacific Coast League.

Anything west of Western Avenue was considered out in the sticks. Hollywood was a quiet residential section. Some homes along Hollywood Boulevard had lemon and orange trees in their yards.

A person could stand at Santa Barbara and Western Avenues and see Saint Mary's Academy at Crenshaw and Slauson, with only open fields between. Leimert Park, now a modern, carefully planned residential district near Crenshaw and Santa Barbara, was a huge Chinese garden where a heaping lug box of tomatoes could be bought for five cents.

West Adams was Millionaires' Row. Beverly Hills, Bel-Air, Westwood, Brentwood, and Pacific Palisades were unheard of. West Pico, Olympic, and Wilshire Boulevards were barley fields. They were, of course, being subdivided and people were moving west from Boyle Heights, the old section of town on the Eastside, which was even then deteriorating.

The big treat was a trip to Venice, or Ocean Park, or Redondo Beach on Sunday on the big red Pacific Electric trolley cars. On ideal days, the P.E. ran three- and four-car trains, an awe-inspiring event to the juvenile mind. The thrill of thrills at Venice was a ride on the Race through the Clouds, a diabolically contrived roller coaster. From the top of its highest dip, passengers could see most of Venice, patterned after the Italian city, even to canals and gondolas. On a balconylike platform near the entrance to the Race through the Clouds, a four- or five-piece band, Dave Snell's I believe it was called, thumped out something called jazz music to lure the customers. The coaster has long since been dismantled as unsafe and the canals have been mostly filled in. Meanwhile Los Angeles is being spoken of as the jazz capital of the world.

On Saint Patrick's Day, everyone who knew about it made a pilgrimage to the Hibernian Bank downtown and received a tiny flowerpot with a growing shamrock.

As now, the kids were very movie-conscious. I personally was a "Perils of Pauline" man, attending Saturday matinees at the Sunbeam Theater (now the Sun) on Pico Street near Valencia. With companions, I used to bicycle out to Mack Sennett's studio on Glendale Boulevard and dabble a slapstick comedy. We stuck around all day in the hope that the director, who usually also acted, would decide suddenly to throw in a crowd scene. Our services, naturally, were available gratis. We also spent some time around the carbarn at Pico and Georgia Streets where Roscoe (Fatty) Arbuckle, John Bunny, Flora Finch, Charley Chaplin, Mabel Normand, and Gloria Swanson used to do their "chase" scenes. The carbarn is still a carbarn, much larger, of course.

I lived in a five-room house at Twelfth and Union for which my father paid sixteen dollars a month. Each year at Christmas the owner, an avid hunter, brought us a few ducks. One year, as my father wished him a merry Christmas, he said: "After this fifteen dollars will be enough." Our house was a mile and a half from downtown. We thought nothing of walking the distance and saving the nickel fare for candy or ice cream. Now no one would dream of such a thing. People get in their autos to go half a block. And the fare is now a dime.

My generation in those days was in its wildlife stage. We used to fish for carp in Westlake Park. We rolled bread into balls for bait and sometimes caught fifteen-pounders, which we sold. On a good day we made enough for popcorn, crackerjack, and, by pooling the money, an hour's rowboat ride. The filthy-rich youngsters, who had their own money, rented canoes and looked down upon us.

When the park attendants weren't looking, the more daring of the boys snared goldfish in the small display pond for their private aquariums, usually—large water jars. They used bent pins to avoid tearing the goldfishes' mouths.

Now Westlake Park, renamed MacArthur Park during the war, has been bisected by a causeway, fabulous Wilshire Boulevard, on which motor traffic pours day and night.

On occasions we'd hike about three miles to the Bimini Stream, near First and Westmoreland, to take a whirl at the wildlife there. If lucky, we'd bring home a few tired frogs, pollywogs, and minnows. An added inducement to the Bimini safari was the overhead trestle spanning the stream. It was quite a game to walk across the trestle, between streetcars, without falling through the ties. The streetcar service was bad then too, but one time a reckless friend was caught in mid-trestle by a car. The motorman stopped in time but was very unhappy about the boy. Today the Bimini Stream is gone. The gulch has been filled in and the space is occupied by used-car lots and houses. Only Bimini Baths, a swimming pool, remains as a landmark.

My companion on these jaunts was a kindred soul named Ed Zimmerman, who owned a four-cylinder, single-gear Henderson motorcycle. On weekends we'd go to Long Wharf, north of Santa Monica, or to Pier One or Pier Two at Redondo Beach, all long since casualties of tide and storm. We used to catch barracuda, smelt, mackerel, halibut, croaker, sea trout, sharks, and that nuisance of nuisances the inedible tomcod. All these are still caught by pier and offshore fishermen. But we also brought up herring, pompano, and Spanish mackerel, now virtually gone from these waters, and, of course, I used to catch a dull ache in the rear from sitting tandem on the rack of Ed's motorcycle.

To vary the monotony we'd bicycle out to a sun-baked wilderness somewhere near Slauson and Central Avenues, to trap horned toads and lizards for pets. Today this is a dense industrial section, though occasionally a lizard is seen racing for its life across the highway.

A few primitive automobiles roared and smoked through the streets, but Los Angeles was still a horse-and-buggy town. The slowest, most leisurely of these vehicles were the Chinese vegetable wagons whose happy, wise oriental owners brought fresh produce and fruit to the doors of customers. Scores of them toured routes throughout the city, first loading up with freshly picked goods at the immense Chinese gardens out West Adams way, around Crenshaw, now a thriving business and residential community. Carrots, beets, and turnips were three bunches for a nickel. Lettuce and radishes were thrown in free. For half a dollar a housewife could buy enough of everything for a week.

These Chinese vegetable men became friends of the families they served and on Chinese New Year's they brought the kids firecrackers and lichee nuts. Nevertheless they were considered fair game for the young hellions of the day. The gang to which I belonged systematically swiped grapes, apricots, peaches, and apples from their wagons after adroitly whistling from behind a house, causing the drivers to stop and go to the door to see what the lady wanted. When the Chinese saw they were duped, they rushed at us, screaming something horrible in their native language. We always saved a tomato to throw at them, from a safe distance.

Stealing fruit was assumed to be a prerogative of the teen-agers. The boys all cased their neighbors' fig, apricot, peach, and loquat trees so that the fruit could be quietly removed as it ripened and before the owners could get to it. Today many backyards have fruit trees which bear in season despite lack of care but their owners hardly bother with them. Everything is supermarkets.

I attended Tenth Street Elementary School, a small frame building on a quiet street. But Tenth Street became Olympic

Boulevard and now traffic swirls past it. Later I went to Sentous Intermediate School, a stucco triumph in its day, now a supply base for the city school system, encircled by bars and small shops. My sharpest recollection of Sentous is that in woodshop I somehow carved out and glued together a solid-oak chair, which I still sit on while at the typewriter. Any such ambitious project today would be frightening.

Next I attended old L.A. High, the city's first high school, a somber red-brick affair high on North Hill Street, just off the downtown section. The boys all played handball and on frosty mornings it was a test of hardihood to slap at the ball, knowing the impact would be painful. When the new L.A. High was built far out in the west part of town, at Olympic Boulevard and Rimpau, high adventure came to the students. A stately, castle-like structure, L.A. High was the only building for miles. After the streetcar left Western Avenue it weaved through miles of open fields, with only an occasional house to indicate this was part of an expanding city. Its rumbling noise flushed rabbits who ran from it and it was quite a trick for the boys in the back of the car to add to their terror by jerking the bell cord without the conductor taking drastic steps. Now this wasteland is one of the city's most desirable middle-class residential sections. Old L.A. High has long since become known as Central Junior High.

This was at the outset of the Terrible Twenties, when Los Angeles' destiny as an automobile town became clear. Boys with jobs, or means, got hold of Model T Fords and put bulletlike racing bodies on them. They were barely able to thresh and quiver up to forty-five miles an hour but their streamlined appearance at least gave the sensation of great speed. If they went dead or only hit on three cylinders, every boy knew all he had to do was stop, pluck out the offending coil box, and bang it on the curb. Presto, he had his missing cylinder back again. Today the high-school boys are engineers who build their own 110-mile-an-hour "hot rods" with special carburetors, engine heads, and pistons.

The twenties hit with explosive effect. Buildings were felled and new ones went up like magic. Spring, Broadway, Seventh, and Hill Streets were difficult for pedestrians as the sidewalks were covered over by the wooden superstructure that meant steam shovels were ripping into the earth for what were to become the basements of stores and office buildings. More buildings were started or completed in 1923 than ever before or since in a single year. New population was flooding in too and the boom extended to home building.

Tourists disembarking from transcontinental trains were handed folders inviting them to free bus rides to Culver City, Venice, Santa Fe Springs, Glendale, Compton, or Signal Hill, with a free lunch thrown in. Under a tent they heard a spiel on real estate, usually with the broad hint that oil might spurt from the tract any day.

Like other old residents, I could have bought a few acres of Wilshire Boulevard frontage for peanuts, business property now valued at five thousand dollars a front foot. They didn't and neither did I, a missed opportunity that has become a great communal bond, calling for crying in beakers of beer.

About this time—I was attending U.C.L.A. and nudging the newspaper business—I became aware of strange stirrings. The city was slipping into the beautiful, spectacular chaos which, on the surface, has become its outstanding characteristic.

Barefoot, white-bearded world savers roamed the streets. In the farce of prohibition, a bootlegger was undistinguishable from a police officer. Rococo movie palaces were springing up. Women were appearing on the streets with bare midriffs, slacks, high heels, and fur coats. Sex scandals were rocking the motion-picture colony. The cafeteria on Olive Street with the waterfall out in front, of course, hadn't yet been erected but eccentricity was in the air. Furthermore, the beachcomber point of view which came to a head in the depression thirties was festering.

But even then it was apparent to an objective observer that the thing to do was to be tolerant of erratic behavior and remember that the people in Los Angeles are no different than the people anywhere else. Their wants are simple: a couple of cars, a home with a patio and a barbecue pit, a few movie starlets for playmates, a bankroll. With the ocean only half an hour away, no one really insists on a swimming pool.

But that's enough reminiscing. I wanted merely to establish the fact that, having been exposed to the hot L.A. sunshine for thirty-five years, I have reached the well-done stage which is supposed to put all sorts of authority into anything I write about the place, but doesn't, and that I still think it's wonderful.

· 3 ·

NEWCOMERS usually have a difficult time getting used to Los Angeles. They are awed by the miles and miles of miles, and troubled by the fact that, as cities go, it doesn't seem to make sense.

The hard losers among these newcomers suffer most grievously. They set out, guidebook in hand, determined that no nuance, no bit of atmosphere, shall escape them. Only a brief safari through the environs is necessary to get them gibbering plaintively: "But which, or rather where, or rather what, is Los Angeles?" A good question.

My advice to the newly arrived is simply to stipulate that Los Angeles is one hell of a big place and to reconcile yourself to the fact that it starts and stops, it fuses, it disappears, it disintegrates: it consists of dozens of seemingly unrelated but nevertheless amazing communities. As Grandma used to say, there's nothing a body can do about a crazy quilt.

For sanity's sake, let's start at the beginning. Let's assume you are a tourist. Your train, the Southern Pacific, the Union Pacific, or the Santa Fe, after dragging maddeningly through the interminable maze of back alleys that seem to be part of the approach to every city, finally lurches to a stop at Union Passenger Terminal.

You tip the porter, walk down a ramp, then through a long, cavelike, but well-lighted passageway into the station, one of the city's newest and finest buildings.

If you arrive in the daytime your first look at Los Angeles is a delight: the station is a quiet, sunny patio with trees, benches, flagstones, and people saying hello or good-by. It could be the garden of some Spanish grandee's palatial hacienda except that no grandees have been around for a century or so.

If you have a few minutes, a look at the rest of the station is worth while. The architecture is modified Mediterranean and early Californian, a combination resulting in a stucco paradise with palm trees. The ticket room is quite a thing. It's immense, with a high, colored mosaic ceiling and inlaid, matched-stone floor. The waiting room is a little dream with leather chairs, much too good for the bums who try to sleep in them. Despite the hurrying crowds found in every terminal, Union Station gives a feeling of simple, sound-proofed, efficient grandeur.

Assuming Darryl or Louie B. isn't waiting for you for lunch or cocktails, a little snooping about the area is a good idea too. It's made to order for browsers who don't mind things that are old and people who don't keep up appearances.

The orientation lesson should rightly begin at the Plaza, reached by crossing Alameda Street, on which the station fronts, and walking a few steps west.

The Plaza today is a beaten-down, block-long patch of lawn, pigeons, palms, and huge spreading magnolia trees. Gray-haired Mexicans in dungarees sit on benches, staring into space or sleeping, although romanticists would probably insist they are enjoying a siesta. Bleary-eyed, toothless, ragged drifters sit on the fencelike, outward-facing bench which circles the Plaza, discussing their moments of triumph, their false teeth, or where they go from there. On Sundays, loud and impassioned Bible babblers roar at whoever will listen, their gospel lost on amused tourists or evangelical colleagues who already know what it means to be saved.

Here Los Angeles was born and here the shabby relics remain. Across the street to the east is a listless remnant of old China-town. It consists of a row of curio stores and restaurants and, farther down the street, a cluster of buildings known as "Old Los Angeles." They represent a futile attempt to identify the section with its past in terms of merchandising of today. But they're on borrowed time. Eventually they'll be removed to make way for parking lots, which is what happens to buildings that don't pay off, or perhaps may be swallowed up in the projected freeway and civic-beautification plan still on the drawing boards.

To the north is Olvera Street, a bazaarlike lane created in the alleged mood of an early Los Angeles market place. In a slow, five-minute stroll from end to end, the tourist may buy or at least smell perfumed candles, tacos and enchiladas, pinon nuts, Mexican candy, huaraches, and other leather goods. The street was deliberately made to order for the tourist trade. There is an artist who instantly draws profiles, a puppet theater, and, on occasion, musicians from one of the cafés shuffle through the walk, singing soft Spanish songs. Sturdy, noisy, black-haired, and flashing-eyed children, offspring of the Olvera Street merchants, race between the stalls. Midway along the thoroughfare is the Avila House, best-preserved of all the old adobes. It was built by Don Francisco Avila, head of a famous early family, and in 1846 it became the headquarters of Commodore R. F. Stockton, who conquered California for the United States. The first house in Los Angeles to fly the Stars and Stripes, it is now open for inspecton for a small fee.

To the west is La Iglesia de Nuestra Señora la Reina de Los Angeles, the Old Mission Church as it is better known. It was dedicated December 8, 1822, a marker states, which makes it the oldest church in Los Angeles. On its restored adobe walls the current generation has chalked its contempt for tradition, including KILROY WAS HERE.

To the south, a square, solid-looking three-story building, painted battleship gray, is identified by a landmark sign at the curb and a metal marker on the wall as the Pico House, built by Governor Pio Pico in 1869. As history goes in Los Angeles, this is considered fairly ancient. The blare of a juke box and a curious clicking noise come from the open door and as you get closer you identify the sound: it is a pool hall.

The old and the new clash and blend in a gentle apathy at the Plaza but traffic surges madly around it. A few steps away, at Sunset Boulevard and Main Street, a highway marker states that Hollywood is seven miles west, Santa Monica seventeen.

By now, you will have discovered a group of large buildings two blocks to the south, overshadowed by a white, spikelike tower. This is the City Hall, Los Angeles' one outstanding landmark. When the downtown section is but a smudge on the horizon from Palos Verdes, twenty-five miles away, or from Pasadena, half that distance, the City Hall tower is usually visible, prodding the sky.

You see it plainly from the top of the Memorial Coliseum in Exposition Park. It has a fairylandlike quality when viewed from the Baldwin Hills, especially when framed by the V of the LaBrea Boulevard canyon. It confronts you suddenly and surprisingly from Third and Bixel. It may be detected as a tiny needle in a haystack of buildings from Pico and Beverwil, ten miles west.

It looms ubiquitously because it is the highest structure in town, twenty stories. Other buildings are restricted to thirteen stories on the theory that anything higher might be allergic to earthquakes.

Alongside the City Hall are the new, modern Federal Building, the Hall of Justice, the Hall of Records, and the State Building. They house the jail where Grade A felons are quartered and the courts where Charley Chaplin and Errol Flynn have their trials and where actresses, knees crossed, get their marriage licenses, approval of their contracts, their citizenship papers, and their divorces.

As part of this orientation lesson, you should know that First and Main Streets, distinguished by the presence of a bubbling fountain, civic statuary, and a cool walk through trees, flowers, and shrubbery on the City Hall lawn, is the starting point for Los Angeles' house-numbering system. First Street divides the north and south, Main the east and west. It might be helpful also to keep in mind that the thirteen blocks south of this intersection and nine blocks west of it form a rectangle generally known as the downtown section.

Twenty-five miles to the south are San Pedro and Wilmington, parts of the city. Long Beach, a few miles farther down the coast, is a separate city. So are Glendale, eight miles north; Burbank, twelve miles northwest; Pasadena, eight miles northeast; Huntington Park, seven miles southeast; Compton, ten miles southeast, and Santa Monica, seventeen miles west. All of these are in Los Angeles County, but then so is Pomona, thirty-five miles east. Confusing? The thing to remember is that Los Angeles grew by accretion, subdivision by subdivision. Wherever real-estate exploiters could entice unwitting strangers into a down payment, on dry river beds, oil fields, vegetable gardens, nooks, crannies, new communities burgeoned. In some of these isolated sections, residents at one time or another must have wondered precisely why they were there. They were ripe for annexation when a well-dressed visitor stopped by to tell the glorious advantages of being part of Los Angeles: fire protection, low water rates, improved roads, a sewage system. Weary of digging their own cesspools, the suburbanites jumped at the opportunity.

For sanity's sake, consider the downtown section the head of an octopus, linked to its outposts by thin, tentaclelike highways. In between are bulging, independent cities which have resisted annexation and retain their own jails, courts, cops, and councilmen. Beverly Hills, self-styled wealthiest city in America, is the prime example. Located ten miles west of the downtown section, it fiercely preserves its autonomy. Los Angeles traffic flows through and around it, en route to Westwood, Brentwood, Bel-

Air, and Santa Monica, but motorists know they better behave. Beverly Hills will have no trifling with its ordinances. Its police officers relentlessly track down speeders and signal jumpers. A nonresident with a patch on his pants better not venture into Beverly Hills at night, either: he'll be invited to remove himself from the city limits. Economic security is the thing. Lack of it is frowned upon.

More and more, Los Angeles is considered a metropolitan area rather than a city. The area includes some forty-five cities and twice that many unincorporated areas. They're known, for one thing, by their Chambers of Commerce. Relatively close in are Angelus Mesa, Crenshaw-Vernon, Eastside, Firestone Park, George Washington, Greater East Los Angeles, Highland Park, Lincoln Heights, Ninth District, Pico Boulevard, Southside, University, Westlake, Wilshire, and the Miracle Mile Association. In the outlying sections there are Bel-Air, Canoga Park, Eagle Rock, Encino, Hollywood, North Hollywood, Northridge, Pacific Palisades, Pacoima, Reseda, Roscoe, San Fernando Valley, San Pedro, Sawtelle, Sunland-Tujunga, Tarzana, Van Nuys, Venice, Watts, West Division, Westwood Village, Willowbrook, and Wilmington.

The last time Uncle Sam took a census, in April 1940, Los Angeles County was given a nose count of 2,785,643. By January 1, 1947, the Regional Planning Commission estimated, the figure was 3,703,903. With the population still rising steadily, the Commission predicted in February 1947 that the total would reach 3,747,962 by April 1, 1947, a gain of nearly a million over the 1940 census.

The Commission predicted an April population of 1,890,202 for the city of Los Angeles, as compared with the 1,504,277 residents in 1940. Other predictions for April 1: Long Beach 252,748, Pasadena 103,354, Glendale 98,782, Santa Monica 70,053, Burbank 68,059, South Gate 46,977, Alhambra 46,853, Inglewood 44,054, Huntington Park 31,809, Pomona 29,728.

But any normal tourist by now is practically hysterical trying to put the question "What about Hollywood?" I've been leading up to that, friend, in slow, easy stages—to soften the blow.

Somehow the idea has been conveyed, possibly by the movie columnists, that Hollywood is set apart from Los Angeles and, for that matter, from the rest of the so-called civilized world. The legend prevails that the studios are identified by a glamorous technicolor aura which hangs over them daily except Sunday, that they are surrounded by high, thick walls and moats containing the bodies of luckless film-crazed aspirants who threw themselves futilely at the portals, that pictures are shot regularly at Hollywood Boulevard and Vine, that the stars stroll the boulevard on regular schedule, nodding politely to swooning thousands, that Hollywood is the center of beauty and culture, marred only by the fact that it is surrounded by vulgar, uncouth, dirty old Los Angeles.

Let's get it over quickly. The contrary is true. Hollywood is not the octopus that wags Los Angeles. It wags only itself—very expressively, of course—but actually it is only a flicker of one of Los Angeles' tentacles.

As outlanders hear it, Hollywood is the place where movies are made and celebrities hang out. True, up to a certain point, but only Columbia, Paramount, and R.K.O., of the big film factories, are in the movie capital and the last two stretch it pretty thin. Let's not quibble. Throw in United Artists and a dozen or so small independent studios.

But M.G.M. is in Culver City; Warner Brothers is in Burbank. Universal is in Universal City. Republic is in Studio City. Fox is on the fringe of Beverly Hills. Selznick is in Culver City. Disney's is in Burbank.

And the stars? They live in San Fernando Valley, Coldwater Canyon, Benedict Canyon, Beverly Hills, Brentwood, Bel-Air.

The live-wire Hollywood Chamber of Commerce, naturally, wants you to believe Hollywood is in itself an ecstatic entity bounded by Doheny Drive, Beverly Boulevard, Mulholland Drive, and Barham Boulevard, forming a rectangle approximately twenty-five miles square. Post-office officials downtown in the Federal Building insist with somewhat more firmness that Hollywood has no identity, it is merely a post-office station.

The Chamber of Commerce has for years pressured to have the post-office cancellation in the disputed bailiwick printed as HOLLYWOOD. The government has remained adamant in its refusal. Thus letters mailed in the alleged magic-lantern land are canceled with the familiar coin-sized circle containing the hateful name LOS ANGELES, along with the date and the time of day. Only the adjoining wavy-line "killer bars," as they are called—they "kill" the stamps in the canceling machine—identify the place of origin, a branch post office called Hollywood. Sometimes, because of the machine's speed, the killer bars don't print HOLLYWOOD at all.

Furthermore, as far as the post office is concerned, the Hollywood station includes a much smaller boundary: Western Avenue, La Brea, Melrose, El Cerrito, approximately ten square miles as against the Hollywood Chamber's claim of twenty-five.

Well, that's life. If Hollywood doesn't exist except inside a post-office branch, it doesn't exist.

It does, of course, but on different terms. Hollywood is a bustling business community. The boulevard is alive with neon-lighted shoe stores, drugstores, department stores, dress shops, millinery shops, curio shops, hotels, restaurants, theaters, and bars. They are the type of commercial enterprise found everywhere, even to the display windows, the showcases, and the advertised products.

There is something else, though. Undeniably, Hollywood is a magic word. Stroll the boulevard and you are conscious of an eager, almost feverish quality. The gossip columnists and the publicity boys have done their work well. Everyone looks at everyone else. Who knows but what the laughing girl in slacks who passes by may be next year's screen discovery, or that the solemn, pipe-smoking man in the sports coat may be this year's Academy Award screen writer? It's just as likely, of course, that she may be an unemployed waitress or somebody's fifth wife. And he could be a curbstone bookie or a fourth-rate agent wondering where his next meal is coming from. The point is that they have acquired, by careful study, the informal, slouchy look characteristic of celebrities.

Oddly enough, the big thing in Hollywood, at least in the Vine Street sector, is not motion pictures, but radio.

N.B.C., a modernistic, three-story, pastel-green building at Sunset and Vine, is more or less the showcase. It identifies itself importantly as Radio Center, a slight poke at C.B.S., another streamlined glass-and-cement microphone haven a block away, on El Centro Street.

It may well deserve the name, for N.B.C. in Hollywood sends out thirty-five big commercial evening network programs—in comparison to New York's eighteen. C.B.S. does all right too. A.B.C., a former affiliate, still has some space in the N.B.C. building, but other offices and studios are scattered throughout Hollywood.

The fact is that Hollywood's radio industry has busted its britches. The broadcasting stations have long since been inadequate to handle the load and many shows and rehearsals are conducted from former playhouses and night clubs, taken over for the purpose. In radio, audience participation is very important. Jokes may die miserably as they filter out over the air, but their perpetrators, alert to popularity ratings, like to be comforted by audible hand clapping, rehearsed or spontaneous.

The witching hour in Hollywood is noon. Ever conscious of the inexorable second hand, radio producers, announcers, writers, stars, ad-agency men, and publicity men swarm out of their offices to the Brown Derby. There, under the frowns of the caricatures of what are loosely known as celebrities which fill all available wall space, they perform the important kibitzing and make their big deals. The stampede has become such that the Derby, for lack of space, some time ago inaugurated the policy of refusing admittance to just ordinary people who came to gawk. It's almost as difficult to get a table at Lyman's, Chi-Chi, Musso Frank's, Brittingham's, Billingsley's, Breneman's, Les Comiques, or the dozen or more other restaurants which prepare food, but not all of which have caricatures.

The gawkers and autograph seekers are not to be denied. They line up outside the Derby and the artists' entrances of the radio stations for a glimpse of a "name." As for the broadcasts, no tourist considers his stay in Los Angeles complete without crashing a few of them. As a result, tickets to the top-bracket shows and those on which refrigerators, radios, sets of silverware, and kitchen utensils are given away are in great demand.

The most obvious way to reach Hollywood is by way of Sunset Boulevard, which though a direct route is a devious one. It meanders through the Silver Lake section, forming at Silver Lake Boulevard another of the city's interminable business communities, and probes through miles of former residential property converted in recent years to small business. At Vermont Avenue, some four miles west of downtown, Sunset Boulevard takes a new lease on life. Though a little more than halfway to Hollywood, the folks here have long considered that they live in "East" Hollywood. The jolt to the newcomer is that he eases into Hollywood proper without restraining walls, a fanfare, or a view of a movie set. Perhaps ironically, Sunset Boulevard becomes one of the city's finest thoroughfares after Hollywood has been passed. West of Fairfax Avenue, you drive through the fabulous Sunset Strip, with its rococo restaurants, intimate night clubs, and glaring white, dollhouselike antique shops, actors' and writers' agents' offices, publicity offices, and real-estate offices. It would be foolish to name them here. They change management and location so often any mention would be dated. West of the

Strip the scenery again changes. Sunset Boulevard winds through beautiful, palatial estates, heavily overgrown with trees and shrubbery. You pass through Beverly Hills, Westwood, Bel-Air, Brentwood, and, as the ocean comes into view, Pacific Palisades. To the north the Santa Monica Mountains cast a shadow. Out of them, dozens of extensive canyons feed into Sunset Boulevard. Some extend over the mountains into San Fernando Valley. Others come to a dead end somewhere up the canyon. In these cool, shaded retreats live the celebrities and the wealthy, amidst their swimming pools, citrus orchards, *Lebensraum*. Their choice of seclusion is deliberate and, unless you know where they are, they're hard to find. A story is told of a tourist who set out to visit a friend in Benedict Canyon. Forewarned, he stopped at a gas station and asked directions. The attendant obligingly routed his course out Sunset Boulevard, then added: "But God help you if you miss Benedict Canyon!"

Hollywood, to get back there for a moment, can also be reached directly by Beverly Boulevard, similar to Sunset in that it is zoned for business. It has, however, another distinction. In recent years Beverly has become a center for pest eliminators. Near Alvarado, the Paramount Pest Control has a large illuminated sign with a figure of Old Doc Killzum, a Krazy Kat-like man with a top hat, and the startling caption HIS PATIENTS ALL DIE. Farther along, at Virgil, the Los Angeles Termite Control advertises that WE TERMINATE TERMITES. Western Exterminator, near by, states: WE LIVE TO KILL BUGS. Beverly Termite frankly calls itself THE BUG HOUSE, owner John M. Roach styles himself "The Bug Man," and over the entrance driveway is painted THROUGH THIS PORTAL PASS THE DEADEST TERMITES IN THE WORLD.

But any way you figure it, Hollywood is only a highly publicized way point in a community of way points. After a tourist reaches his own verdict as to whether it "sends" him, he still has a long way to go to get the rest of the picture.

First he must have an automobile, without which life in Los Angeles is almost unbearably restraining. Then he can sneak up on the scenery from vantage points thoughtfully provided by nature.

For a starter, get the grand sweep of the city from the City Hall tower, the roof of the Federal Building, or, if necessary, from the County Jail, high in the Hall of Justice. Another good view can be had from Pico and Beverwil. Or linger for a moment at the crest of Normandie at Clinton. Go up Micheltorena Hill and look down. Park along Sunset Boulevard in the Strip at night and study the twinkling lights. Get a view of the setting sun plunking into the Pacific from the Baldwin hills.

Another adventure is to set your sights on the Hollywoodland sign above Beachwood Drive. The letters are forty-five feet high and are mounted on telephone poles. The thirteen letters extend 548 feet horizontally. The sign has been posted for twenty-four years and, with the City Hall, is the most observed landmark in the city. Above the sign is Mount Lee, seventeen hundred feet, highest peak in the Hollywood hills. From the plateau, on which the Don Lee television station W6XAO is located, a sight-seer lucky enough to arrange a visit can get the best of all possible views of Los Angeles, a full 360-degree panorama, including a beautiful tile swimming pool alongside the television station. When the visibility is good, the ocean may be seen glimmering in the sun from Santa Monica to Palos Verdes. Off toward San Fernando, there is the huge Hanson dam. Airplanes flying at a thousand feet seem suspended in mid-air below. Hollywood and Vine is merely a cluster of pimplelike buildings. The southwest and the harbor areas are merely a smudge. Downtown, the industrial district seems shrouded in its own white-and-gray smoke. And you become aware that the City Hall has competition as the highest structure, from the huge, unsightly gas tank near by.

Don't miss the wonderful Arroyo Seco Parkway to Pasadena.

Drive through Laurel, Coldwater, and Beverly Glen canyons to San Fernando Valley, stopping at the crest for a moment of awe. Mount Hollywood, Outpost Estates, and Mulholland Drive are worth while too.

Griffith Park, with its observatory, zoo, golf courses, picnic grounds, bird farm, hiking trails, and picturesque Fern Dell alone is good for a dozen visits.

If you're in a mood for miles, drive from Redondo to San Pedro through the Palos Verdes coastline, stopping at Lookout Point for a marvelous view of San Pedro Harbor. Pack a lunch and drive through Topanga Canyon, or Mint and Bouquet Canyons above Castaic, or up San Gabriel Canyon above Azusa, or up Angelus Crest Highway above Montrose, or take Highway 101, Roosevelt Highway as it is called, from Santa Monica to Oxnard or Santa Barbara.

Remember, after you've done all this, and also visited the publicized tourists' spots, you've hardly seen anything.

For instance, not half a dozen persons in Los Angeles know that three minutes from M.G.M. studio, a mere turn off Washington Boulevard in Culver City onto an unimproved road that seems to head into the Baldwin hills, there is rolling countryside that could be France or Italy or New Zealand. It's farm country, with horses and cows grazing and rows of corn and beans growing, though airplanes taking off from a near-by field barely miss the weatherbeaten farmhouses and stables.

At one of these farmhouses, if you know your way around, several vicious-looking dogs will jump out and bark at you, if you stop your car. In a moment an aged, unshaven Italian comes out of the house, recognizes you, quiets the dogs, and welcomes you.

The farmhouse is old but scrupulously clean and you notice a new electric stove and a huge electric refrigerator. You are directed to a chair at the kitchen table. The aged host disappears and returns soon with a large bottle of wine. He has been down in the cellar, filling it from one of many barrels. He grew the grapes, he made the wine, the same as he did in Italy many years ago. His wife brings out fresh jack cheese, made from the milk of the cows in the barn. She cuts off huge slabs and slices French bread.

The old man tells you he is tired, he has been plowing all morning. He doesn't work as hard as he used to, though, he says, smiling, not since he rented the twenty acres to some movie cowboys who board their horses there. He insists on taking you out to see a three-weeks-old colt.

The aged Italian came to California forty-five years ago and worked until he had enough money to buy some ground far away from the city. Later he bought more and more. Now he could retire, but the idea never occurs to him. He will do his own plowing until he dies.

He is interested in what you are doing and is delighted that things seem to be coming along all right in the outside world. He doesn't get away from the place very often, though he has a new car. Before you know it, he has made three more trips to the basement to replenish the wine. It's good, solid Burgundy, nothing more, but with the cheese and the bread it's ambrosia. If you do not drink and eat what he considers your share as a grown man he growls that you are in danger of becoming a sissy as a result of the soft city life.

He could as well be a Greek, a Chinese, a Basque, a Rosicrucian, a member of Aimee Semple McPherson's church, a Japanese, a Russian, or a Vermonter. He isn't concerned that Los Angeles may some day be the largest city in the world. He is oblivious to the political and economic tensions that get men to snarling at each other. He works hard and lives simply and he likes it that way.

But his generation is declining and his point of view is disappearing, perhaps in a few years his farm and the already encroaching airfield and movie cowboys will disappear. In their place will be a new stucco subdivision or a ladies' ready-to-wear garment factory. Until that happens, however, he's part of the picture.

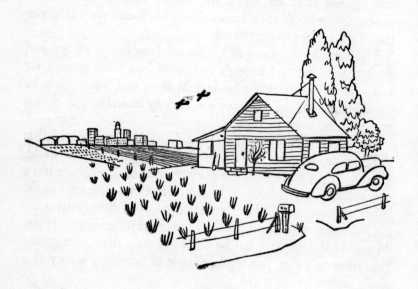

• 4 •

*No matter how cold it gets at night, the vacuum
cleaner next door is always running in the daytime.*
—COMPLAINT OF WARTIME SHIPYARD WORKER, A
DAY SLEEPER

RAIN is taken for granted elsewhere, but not in Los Angeles.
Except for a little wintry cold, it's the only real change in
the weather there is.

At the slightest patter on the roof, ordinarily complacent
citizens become soothsayers and witch doctors, loaded to the
nostrils with the right answers.

After half an hour of heavy rain, an old timer is likely to cock
an eye heavenward and predict: "If it keeps on like this, I'll give
it an hour before Culver City is flooded." At a flash of lightning
and a roll of thunder, every able-bodied man considers it a duty
to deplore: "Never used to have that kind of stuff out here, the
climate's sure changing."

Arch Republicans used to blame excess rainfall on Roosevelt.

When a real rainstorm hits, it's an A production. Los Angeles
grew so fast, its drainage system never caught up with the population. After a hard, steady downpour, poorly drained streets are
flooded from curb to curb with a foot of water. Cars plow
through it with a speedboat effect, but sooner or later some of
them stall and trouble begins. Traffic is liable to become tied up
indefinitely. Shoppers and office workers may be marooned for
hours. Basements are flooded. If a wind accompanies the rain,
trees are uprooted and fall on power lines, throwing areas into
darkness. Lazy little streams become raging torrents, ripping out
bridges and cutting deep gorges. Houses built on the banks oc-

casionally are undermined and topple into the drink. Such deluges have one saving grace: they recede as rapidly as they come. Actually the flood water settles in the low area near Del Rey, where the residents are all superior mudders.

The most feared storm is the cloudburst in the near-by mountains, creating a flash flood. Torrents of water suddenly cascade down canyons, tearing at houses and grounds, and spreading over the towns at the base of the mountains.

New dams and improved flood-control measures have lessened the menace, but if a storm is heavy enough, residents of Montrose, Tujunga, and Glendale expect to get their socks wet. San Fernando Valley usually takes the worst beating. Many new residents who never suspected it suddenly discover they live on an old river bed.

The storm of recent date most vividly remembered occurred early in March 1938. Metropolitan Los Angeles couldn't have been more completely paralyzed if an earthquake had hit. More than three hundred police flood calls went out, three times the normal load. The broadcaster was rarely off the air, keeping his flock of radio cars busy aiding stranded children, guarding retaining walls about to collapse, roping off live wires that were down, and straightening out traffic blocks. The most fascinating call was about a man who fell in the Los Angeles River. His progress was reported as he was swept toward the sea. He turned out to be Byron Summers, the famous distance swimmer, testing his strength. A barber on Grand Avenue found a four-inch fish on the street, put it in a pan of water, and displayed it for his customers' entertainment. The average streetcar speed downtown was twenty feet every five minutes. Telephone traffic was five times the normal load. The best remark, by a man in a stalled car greeting a repair man, was "For a while I thought of sending out a dove." Inevitably, husky youths appeared downtown, offering to carry trapped citizens across puddles for a dime. If the girls were pretty enough they got a free ride.

In the same storm a film actress was marooned in her home on Lookout Mountain in the Hollywood hills without food and an actor friend volunteered to brave the torrent coming out of the canyon with a supply. He mudded laboriously to the house, only to find a party in hilarious session. "We were all out of food all right," she explained, "but I had a couple of cases of Scotch so I called in the neighbors and we're just letting it rain."

After the flood subsided, workmen set about digging half a dozen cars out of the mud in Santa Monica. A bystander, noticing several officers watching the operation, asked: "How come the cops?" "Aw," he was told, "they're just waiting to put parking tickets on them."

If a storm lasts any length of time, the United States Weather Bureau is besieged with calls from persons who ask disgustedly: "Say, how much longer is this rain going to last?"

One meteorologist tells of the time he heard a bus driver whisper confidentially to a passenger: "No question about it, the Weather Bureau is in cahoots with the Chamber of Commerce. How else could there be so much more rain in Glendale than in Los Angeles?"

After a particularly violent rainstorm, which was described in the papers as having originated in the Northwest, a Seattle paper retaliated beautifully. It told of the arrest of an itinerant who had fled there to escape the Los Angeles rains and who had a strange type of thermometer in his pocket. Police were baffled by the instrument. Put on a radiator, the mercury went up only a few degrees. Dipped into a pitcher of ice water, it fell only two or three degrees. Finally the itinerant confessed. It was a Los Angeles Chamber of Commerce thermometer. The temperature was fixed to register a low of seventy-six, a high of eighty.

Another apocryphal story deals with an old timer's explanation of a siege of surplus dew.

"Those rain clouds," he said, "were heading for Florida and got off the track."

A newcomer, pointing skyward, said: "Is that so? Then what are those up there?"

"Oh," countered the defender, "those are just the empties coming back."

No two winters are alike in Los Angeles, but occasionally it gets darn cold. Newsboys on corners keep warm with fires in large open cans. Resourceful boys on Wilshire Boulevard wait for busses to stop at their corners, then stand with their rears to the exhaust. Each time a thin layer of ice appears where a faucet has dripped on the cement, some shivering, thin-blooded resident will tell everyone he sees that day: "I've lived here twenty years and I never saw any weather like this!"

Each year a controversy arises over the smudging in the citrus areas, which causes a layer of gray, impenetrable smoke to settle and blot out the sun. One school of thought is that the smoke protects the crops. The other is that the smoke or smudge, which results from imperfect combustion, is unnecessary; what really saves the oranges, lemons, and grapefruit is the heat. Until the point is settled, no one blames the poor beleaguered farmer who loses his sleep and uses the only equipment he has. I personally string along with the theory that an orange's best friend is its smudger.

Then there's fog. Some years it won't go away, even in summer, until the sun breaks it up around noon. Other years, as 1946, there's hardly any. Asthma and sinus sufferers hate it the worst.

Since industry came to Los Angeles, one of the major problems is smog, a corrosive layer of industrial gases. It is worst when, due to atmospheric conditions, it hugs the ground. On these occasions it settles around the City Hall, where municipal workers have worked out this patter: "How are your eyes this morning?" "Right smart, right smart."

A man who works downtown but lives in La Canada told his

fellow workers he was going to take a few days off and sit in the sun at home: the smog was getting him down.

One asked, "How about that fog and stuff out where you live?"

"Oh, we don't have fog," he replied.

"You don't? That's strange, I live near you and we do."

"Oh no, that isn't fog, that's high *velo*."

"High *velo*, what's that?"

"Well, when we bought our place the real-estate man assured us there was no fog out there. It was something that looked like fog and I asked him about it at the time. But he said we wouldn't have to worry about it, it was high *velo*."

His friends broke it to him gently. *Velo* is a Spanish word meaning veil, or, to be bluntly atmospheric, fog.

But there are, as advertised, three hundred beautiful, sunshiny days each year. There are blue skies, or at least there were until the smog came, and gentle breezes and little or no humidity in summer. It's no wonder that people from everywhere, once bitten by the sunshine bug, never want to go back where they came from. Those who do go back usually plan to return.

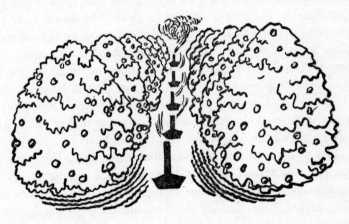

· 5 ·

Southern California is a retreat for all failures.—SIN-
CLAIR LEWIS, *Los Angeles Herald-Express*, OCTOBER
11, 1943

PERHAPS the greatest misapprehension about the city has to
do with cults. Because of the emphasis visiting writers have
given a minute phase of local effluvia, the notion has spread that
turbaned swamis sit cross-legged on street corners, pondering
upon their navels, and suave crystal-ball gazers lure frustrated
old maids into bosky dells and remove them from their money
and other possessions.

The fact is that, except for an occasional upsurge of the Holy
Roller spirit, Los Angeles is very, very pagan. There are too
many other things to do on Sunday.

All discussions of cults and evangelists, of course, begin and
end with Aimee Semple McPherson. She was quite a gal. Unquestionably she cast a spell over those who heard her. Few
persons can project themselves and keep an eye on the collection
plate as she did. She thoroughly understood showmanship; she
had daring and imagination. One time the marquee on her
Angelus Temple listed THE HOUSE OF UNCLE SAM. VIVIDLY
ILLUSTRATED. Once she put on her own version of "Snow White
and the Seven Dwarfs." A favorite number of her tambourine
band was "Cheer, Cheer, for Old Notre Dame."

She toyed with her audience like a magician. Even scoffing
tourists, who visited Angelus Temple for the sight-seeing value,
came away impressed. Aimee brought down the house any time
she wanted. One Sunday she had the congregation hilarious,
remarking as she found one of the Thirty Dollars Every Thurs-

day I O U pension certificates in the collection plate: "Someone better keep that one until next Thursday." Each year she put on a special program to celebrate her birthday. She told her life story and how she received the call. She never mentioned which birthday it was.

When Aimee died in September 1944, the papers naturally reviewed her career, including her spectacular disappearing act. Some of her followers resented this. Telephone calls flooded my paper. Her flock always felt that the papers misused her. In a sense they were right.

But these followers never appreciated to what extent Mrs. McPherson was publicity-conscious and how the exploitation that built her power and fortune later helped tear them down. She hired one newsman after another: Ralph Jordan, Jim Kendrick, Reg Taviner, Jim Bolger. They didn't last long. She expected the same miracles of her publicity men as she performed at Angelus Temple.

Mrs. McPherson never achieved the co-operation she would have liked from the papers. She couldn't understand that after her disappearance, with the accompanying rumors of illicit romance, she had a standard thrill value.

It was literally true that an Aimee headline was good for an additional twenty-five thousand circulation on one paper. Her marriage to David Hutton, her divorce, her trip to the Holy Land, her squabbles with her mother, and her legal disputes were thus all grist. She pleaded for the papers to give space to the good work done at the Temple but in vain.

During her disappearance and so-called escape from her kidnapers, I was city editor of the *Daily News*, which did not go maudlin on the case. We felt free to treat her escapade lightly. Always, the morning after a story with a little bite in it appeared, Mrs. McPherson telephoned. "This is Sister Aimee," she said. "I don't think your story about me is very nice." She always called more in sorrow than in anger. Sometimes she said she prayed for all newsmen.

Part of the Aimee story came during the depression. Families were being evicted; jobless men walked the streets; children were found destitute. Frequently desperate men and women came into the newspaper office, begging for help in obtaining a job or food. In many cases they had been refused aid by welfare agencies because they couldn't qualify. A call to Angelus Temple by any newsman, even by those who wrote bad things about Mrs. McPherson, was always good for a basket of food, clothing, or a helping hand, no questions asked.

But Sister Aimee belonged to a time that is gone, or, rather, to a time that never existed except as a headline frenzy. She rests today in a ten-thousand-dollar bronze casket at Forest Lawn Memorial Park. Meanwhile Angelus Temple, led by her son Rolf, carries on quietly, its flamboyant days gone.

The I Am Case was quite another matter. The bubble burst in July 1940 when Mrs. Edna W. Ballard, her son Donald, and twenty-three associates were indicted by a Federal Grand Jury for three-million-dollar mail-fraud conspiracy.

The first trial ended with a hung jury but in January 1942, after a long second trial, the Ballards were found guilty. Mrs. Ballard was fined eight thousand dollars and given one year's probation. Donald, whose real name was disclosed as Edona Eros Ballard, was fined four hundred dollars and given a thirty-day suspended sentence.

The verdict was appealed on the ground that religious issues had been injected into the trial. The Circuit Court of Appeal upheld the conviction but the United States Supreme Court reversed it and sent the case back to the Circuit Court for determination of other questions raised by the Ballards. Months later, in December 1946, after a second review of the convictions, the United States Supreme Court by a five-to-four vote threw out the indictment against the Ballards—the cases against

the others had been dismissed—because women had been ex-
cluded from the jury. There is some question that another trial
will ever be held as the witnesses have scattered.

The trials were fraught with fantasy. The government charged
that the Ballards controlled the Saint Germain Foundation,
through which they distributed books and pamphlets. The books
contained divine discourses with the shadowy Saint Germain,
who, it seemed, could be summoned whenever the Ballards put
in a call and through whose ministrations disease, poverty, mis-
fortune, and death could be conquered. For these books, the
Ballards accepted "love gifts."

Mrs. Ballard was charged with representing herself as having
attained a state of supernatural immortality. She was said to
have told followers she could ascend to heaven at will. She
stoutly denied the accusation in court, though she admitted that
she had personal healing powers. Throughout the trial, she
termed the case as persecution. She blamed the I Am involve-
ment with the Federal Government on Nazis and Communists.
One witness related that at one service she had hexed Franklin
D. Roosevelt.

A former business manager of the cult testified that the founder, Guy W. Ballard, who died six months before the original
indictment, had assured him that a painting of Jesus Christ he
had had been painted from life. Another witness declared the
Ballards warned I Am followers of an impending geological up-
heaval. Another witness, however, denied the government al-
legation that Mrs. Ballard had told followers to sell everything
except what they would need for the next two years and give
the funds to the movement, because the earth was to be destroyed. One woman testified Mrs. Ballard had told her to leave
her husband because he used tobacco.

Much of the testimony centered about a so-called violet con-
suming ray which had strange mystical powers. In the I Am
belief, evidence disclosed, green and purple were sacred colors

with supernatural powers. Red, according to Saint Germain, was a carnal color, and church workers were forbidden to wear red dresses. All through the trial, Mrs. Ballard wore a completely violet ensemble, from hat to stockings and shoes.

Perhaps the high point was the testimony that on one occasion Donald Ballard claimed an invisible power known as K-17 which came to him through certain ascended spirits. K-17 was so powerful, the story went, that it had been used to sink a flotilla of enemy submarines bent on attacking the United States.

The I Am Temple, where the ten thousand followers gathered, was a huge, glaring white, barnlike building with incongruous minaret gingerbread on its tower, and was located on a slight hill at 123 North Lake street, above busy Beverly Boulevard. The words I AM were emblazoned high on the tower and were illuminated at night. The temple has been remodeled and is now occupied by a less spectacular religious order.

Another departure from the norm made the papers in October 1946. The good folk of suburban Baldwin Park complained indignantly to county authorities that the quiet, rural nights were being disturbed by loud singing, hallelujahs, and moans and groans. They came from the home, or rather the back yard, of a neighbor, George Whyman, seventy-seven.

Seemingly a new cult had sprung full-blown from the chicken coops and rabbit hutches of Whyman's back yard.

The leader of the cult was disclosed as the Reverend Joe Jeffers, who had a long record of brushes with the law. Reverend Jeffers admitted that the prayers and songs may have been noisy at times, but he explained Whyman was hard of hearing and wanted to hear what was going on. As for the report of two neighbors that they saw persons rolling on the ground and, on one occasion, a blond woman wearing a white gown: pure fantasy, said Reverend Joe.

He even volunteered information about himself since his trouble in 1939 when he and his former wife, Joy, were tried on morals charges. The trial proved a sex orgy for the papers when dictaphone records of the couple's love-making were introduced as evidence. Nevertheless, they were acquitted.

After the trial, the couple broke up and Joe went to Florida. There he got into a jam over stealing Joy's car and he was sentenced to Atlanta Penitentiary. While in prison he did a great deal of research, confirming a belief that he had long held that Yahweh was the true name of the Creator. He quickly established a direct, two-way beam over which he communicated with the Deity.

When he returned to Los Angeles with his blond wife Helene to spread the word on Yahweh, Whyman offered him a place to live until a site was selected for the permanent temple. That's all there was to the noise.

Bible in hand, smiling confidentially, Reverend Joe confided to newsmen on the front porch: "Russia is going into Palestine and the world will soon end atomically. Only a few believers will be saved, these people among them." He nodded toward his followers.

"Thank you, Father," said the followers. "Amen."

Reverend Jeffers, of course, is considered a bad boy in the soul-saving racket. Almost all the religious exhorters in Los Angeles today are conservative. They work out of established churches, or rent auditorium or theater space on Sundays. Some key their sermons to the current events of the day, with such titles as "Beware! The Truce of the Bear," "Has Decontrol Started the Boom and Bust," and "Consider Communism Calmly." They're salesmen, peddling little blocks of amnesia and Valhalla, but they're a far cry from the world savers, health faddists, table pounders, and brimstone boys of an earlier era.

When I was a city editor some years ago a woman and a little girl came in and the woman asked that the paper print a story about the revival services the child, her daughter, was conducting in a tent on South Broadway. The woman was all mother, as the saying goes, and the girl was a particularly poisonous specimen with blond curls and a vacuous expression that could easily have been mistaken for having seen the light. I said I was sorry, such an announcement came under the heading of advertising, not news, and I couldn't use it. The woman went into a semi-fit, demanding to see the publisher and talking boycott by her parishioners. Her tirade ended with the snarling question: "Young man, where do you expect to go after you pass on?" I said it didn't matter much, though I was a cremation man myself. She went into a horrible wail at such blasphemy. Quickly recovering, she cried: "Gertrude dear, pray for this poor lost soul," and Gertrude got down on her knees alongside the city desk and did what she could for me.

Evangelists still drop by and pitch their tents, hoping to do an Aimee, but they attract only a few hundred of the eager in outlying sections and near-by towns. The most recent of these was Rosa Mae, a pretty teen-age girl. When she appeared in Long Beach, a four-column ten-inch newspaper ad warned LAST CHANCE TO HEAR THE TEXAS CYCLONE, CHILD EVANGELIST, IN LONG BEACH, BEFORE LEAVING FOR GREAT REVIVAL IN SAN DIEGO. Describing Rosa Mae as STUPENDOUS, ASTOUNDING, CONVINCING, the ad invited the public to "Bring the sick and afflicted to be prayed for. Come and hear the secret of divine healing explained. Broken bones, Cancer, Blind Eyes, Deaf Ears, Tumors, and many other afflictions healed in answer to this child's prayers." But Rosa Maes are a rarity.

More numerous are the psychics of one sort and another who advertise in newspaper classified sections. One regular advertiser gives as her qualifications that she is the seventh daughter of a seventh daughter and was born with a veil. As a result, she unhesitatingly gives "Egyptian egg readings."

But there's no pattern to the procedure followed by the different groups. One sect, in keeping with the times, has adopted the theory of carrying its message to the public. Two persons, usually a man and a woman, ring doorbells in the residence sections on Sundays and ask permission to play a phonograph record, religious in nature. The man carries a portable machine. One hearty fellow, full of good will from sipping beer, invited them in. The couple wound up their machine and played the record, a sonorous, admonitory message telling of the peace that comes with getting right with the Lord. When it was finished the host announced cheerily: "All right, I listened to your record. Now you've got to hear one of mine." He selected a low-down barrel-house number that had them pale.

A downtown store hired a seer to fasten attention on its book department. He offered to answer anyone's problems: three questions for a dollar. One day a woman telephoned the book section and asked for him. He was out at the moment, retreading his ouija board, or something. The woman said it was urgent and the book-section girl offered to take the message. "Tell him," panted the caller, giving her name, "that I want to change my Question Number Three. I asked if our hot-water heater would last much longer. Well, it just blew up."

The Embassy Building at 843 South Grand Avenue is the major downtown outpost for free-lance oratory depending on catch-as-catch-can audiences. The building houses a hotel and a veritable maze of auditoriums. There is a full-size church with stained-glass windows, an organ, and a pulpit and there are countless other halls, large and small, reached by side doors and alley passageways. A stranger is just as likely to walk in on a touring evangelist hurling metaphysical thunderbolts as he is to sit down at a quiet CIO union meeting.

After one health meeting at the Embassy, two elderly women ambled to the powder room, where this conversation was overheard:

"Did you enjoy the meeting?"

"Well I don't know, I'm not sure I'll waste any more time coming to these meetings, what with the atom bomb and all."

One of the better-known pastors who holds regular Sunday services and keys his sermons to the political or economic crises of the moment was revealed in an unholy role by a newspaper reporter. The reporter was interviewing a visitor from the Pacific Northwest, who had achieved considerable notoriety on his contention that he could predict earthquakes. When the quake man asked about the pastor, the reporter said he didn't know anything about him but asked the reason for the question. "Aw the guy's always bothering me for advance dope on earthquakes," the quake man replied. "I guess he wants to tip off his flock to what's coming, sort of a scoop I guess you'd call it."

Not all true believers, naturally, find it necessary to belong to something. One woman appeared at work one day with a bad toothache. Next day she was bright and chipper. A fellow worker asked how she felt. "Fine," she said. "I gave the tooth to the Lord yesterday afternoon."

Another woman visited a turbaned seer on Whittier Boulevard on the Eastside to verify her suspicion that such things were phony. Half through her reading she said: "Aren't you ashamed of yourself, taking gullible people's money? Even if it is only twenty-five cents?"

The seer was momentarily disconcerted at being unmasked but rallied to his own defense. "No I'm not," he said, "they come in worried about their financial matters or their health or their love affairs. I give them courage and hope and they go out happier for what I tell them. Yes, I take their twenty-five cents but I think I do them at least that much good!"

· 6 ·

The name of this city is in Spanish the city of angels, but with much more truth might it be called at present the city of the Demons.—FROM THE DIARY OF THE REVEREND JAMES WOODS, NOVEMBER 12, 1854.

As THE traffic signal at Temple Street and Broadway changed to STOP, an elderly woman looked devoutly skyward, crossed herself, and ventured out into the pedestrian zone. By her gesture she proved herself a veteran of the traffic wars.

Approximately five hundred persons are killed and fifteen thousand wounded each year on Los Angeles city streets. The annual toll for both city and county usually exceeds one thousand dead.

Considering that one person of each 2.6 has an automobile, which means that something like a million cars rove the avenues, the miracle is that the figure isn't twice as large. For motor traffic in Los Angeles is more inconsiderate, more vicious, than anywhere in the world.

All day long, especially in late afternoon, the air is rent with the sound of skidding tires and metallic crashes and, in a little while, the approaching police-ambulance siren.

A strange psychological frenzy takes hold of normal citizens when they get behind the wheels of their cars. They fight for position, scramble from lane to lane for the slightest advantage, and swear or glare at each other as they wait for signal changes.

Out-of-state drivers or, for that matter, out-of-city drivers, are terrified by the motorized rodeo they encounter. They have three choices. They can continue to drive slowly and carefully, in which event they must submit to street-corner snarls of "Is that the way they drive in Kansas?" They can throw caution to the winds and join in the jolly game of Wrinkle Fender. Or they can become pedestrians, the category most likely to meet sudden death.

In their way, curiously enough, home-town drivers are competent, though reckless. They simply have exaggerated ideas of their judgment of distance, or the efficiency of their brakes, or their chances of beating a signal.

When a collision or an accident occurs, it's always the other guy's fault, and frequently the gendarmes have to intervene to prevent the two aggrieved parties from putting their opinions into violent action. The rate of collision was such early in 1937, incidentally, that the insurance companies drastically increased their accident rates.

Traffic-safety men assemble regularly and deplore the me-first attitude which impels home-town motorists. Sometimes they feel that the answer is a new educational program to make drivers conscious of motoring hazards. This answer may take the form of a slogan, as "Don't let death take your holiday," which newspapers, radio, and billboards flung at the public in 1946 during the Christmas and New Year's season, when mortality is high. Sometimes they conclude despairingly that the only answer is instructing police officers to give out more citations for the violations which, their surveys indicate, are most responsible for accidents. The one thing they're certain of is that, basically, motorists in Los Angeles have very bad manners.

An example of motorist's inhumanity to motorist took place at an outlying shopping center where cars park at a forty-five-degree angle to the curb. A driver backed out suddenly into the front of a streetcar. The impact knocked him back into his parking place, over the curb, and onto the sidewalk. He was unhurt and had the presence of mind to turn his wheels so his car didn't strike a building, but before he could back off and before he could get out of his car, another auto swiped the parking place out of which he had been bumped.

All traffic is mad but the crush at Los Feliz Boulevard and Riverside Drive on Sunday afternoon is the most consistently insane. Cars pile up at all four approaches for several blocks. No one gives an inch. Anyone trying to make a left turn is a saboteur or a leper. Into this maze came a young man in a convertible coupé, determined to turn left. When it became apparent no one would let him by, and horns blared behind him, he leaned out, wagged a finger at each grim driver coming from the opposite direction, and shouted: "Ooh! You're naughty!"

When motorists figure in too many accidents or are reported for reckless driving, they are remanded to the Motor Vehicle Bureau for re-examination. A woman who had been in three accidents in one year was ordered to take another driver's test. She passed all phases of it so easily the examiner was puzzled and asked about the accidents. "Well, it's like this," she said. "My husband has a wooden leg. He can't sit comfortably in the front seat, so he sits in back and puts his wooden leg up on the back of the seat while I drive. It's when I turn around to talk to him that the accidents always happen." The examiner recommended they get a coupé.

A woman's car went dead at the 5 P.M. rush at Seventh and Hill Streets. She tried with a kind of frantic dignity to get it going. Meanwhile, the man behind her sounded his horn very irritatingly. After about three minutes of stepping vainly on the starter, the woman stuck her head out—it was a very haughty, richly groomed head—and told the noisemaker: "You're the kind of person that makes this world very difficult to live in."

A paradox of Los Angeles traffic is that despite the heavy death and accident toll, autoists and walkers are severely regimented. Pedestrians have been slow to accept the dictum of a mechanical robot but since policemen lurking in the intersections have made it a practice to hand out citations for jaywalking they have mended their ways. And motorists for the most part obey traffic signals out of habit.

One time I was riding with a publicity man and he drove boldly through a stop signal at a busy intersection. I called his attention to the red light.

"Oh, I never pay attention to that signal," he said, "I'm mad at it. I never come past this corner but what it says stop. It's the most unco-operative signal I ever saw."

"Yaw but—" I gasped.

"You see," he went on, "traffic signals have personalities. Now look at those boulevard stop signs we're coming to. They're friendly. People are glad to stop for them. They smile and nod each other on, like Alphonse and Gaston."

"A very interesting philosophy," I said, huddling in my seat, listening for a siren.

He may have something, but the only signal I know with a personality is at the northeast corner of Adams and Hauser. As the GO sign drops into position, passersby may observe that someone has written in crayon on it TO HELL.

A man pulled his car, in reverse, out of a driveway directly in front of a beelining LaBrea bus. The lady driver efficiently jammed on her brakes, then said to her passengers: "Now ain't that just like a man driver?"

On crowded Hollywood Boulevard, a man going against the flow of sidewalk traffic bumped into a writer, then said: "Why don't you look where you're going?"

The writer studied him. The bumper was around forty-five, and looked fairly intelligent. "It's too late," the writer said. The bumper asked what he meant. "Well, if you haven't learned left from right at your age, I'm not going to take on the job of teaching you. But sidewalk traffic stays on the right, just like motor traffic."

The offender was thoughtful. "You know," he said, "I never thought of that."

A visitor from Colorado stopped for a signal on Wilshire Boulevard and when he failed to take off rocketlike at the green light the driver behind gave him the horn. The Coloradan, a large man, got out of his car and asked: "Did you want me?"

"No," said the honker mildly, "I just wanted to get going."

The Coloradan put his foot on the running board. "Well, a fellow never knows when he'll run into some people he knows," he said slowly. "I'm from Colorado. Lots of people here are from Colorado. I thought when you blew your horn you wanted to see me. Large world, isn't it?" He made his nonsensical garrulity last for three signal changes, by which time, he figured, he had got over his point.

A similar instance occurred on Florence Avenue in Huntington Park when a motorist in a 1934 Chevy coupé stopped for a red light. A fourth of a second after the light changed to green, the man behind, in a long, snooty speed job, saw red and leaned on his horn. The man in the Chevy didn't grind into low gear and start nervously in kangaroo leaps, as some persons might have done. He calmly climbed out of the car, sauntered around to the back, and made a great show of shaking his bumpers and spare tire. As the light turned back to red, he said cheerily: "Thought I heard a noise. Guess not." With that he got back in his car.

A motorist stopped for the red of a red-orange-green light. For him it was no mere pause that refreshed. He had been trying for blocks to isolate a haunting knock in his motor. Thus absorbed, he failed to start with the green. When the horns behind reoriented him it was too late, the light was red again. A motorcycle officer drew up alongside from nowhere and asked: "What are you doing, mister, waiting for your favorite color to turn up?"

A slight case of bumper bashing on Figuerora Street was followed by the usual harsh words between drivers. The older man monopolized the conversation and the youngster, losing ground every minute, shouted: "Aw why don't you take a load off your tires?"

Traffic stopped with a bang at Sixth and Broadway, the reason a seven-ply pile-up. The front car, which had stopped suddenly, was driven by a woman; the other six by men. Five of them kept their peace, but the sixth, an old fire eater, yelled: "Why didn't you stick out your hand?"

"I did," she yelled back.

"No you didn't," he retorted.

"Funny thing about you men," she mused. "You can't see a woman's arm. But if my leg had been sticking out you'd have seen it a block away!"

Some sort of milestone in policeman-motorist relations was reached when a motor cop motioned Gib Brush, news photographer, to the curb on Los Angeles Street. Gib was not surprised. He may or may not have made the signal at Third Street. The officer dismounted, put his foot on the running board, and asked: Where's the fire?"

"At 501 Temple Street," said Gib, reading from a scrawl on an envelope.

"Are you kidding?" asked the officer.

"No," said Gib, flashing his credentials, "and it'll be out if I don't get there right away."

The officer, a beaten look on his face, waved him on.

A doctor driving along an isolated stretch of highway near Los Angeles was passed by a topless old car, speeding and weaving. Horror-struck, he watched it somersault into a ditch and come to rest upside down. He hurried to the spot and was met by a very muddy drunk. The doc, who had seen two men in the car, asked where his companion was. The drunk insisted he was alone in the car. A quick look disclosed a second man face down in the mud, out cold. The doctor worked on him and got him breathing. The drunk said: "Well well, if it ain't old Joe! How'd you get here?" The physician loaded them both in his

car, took them to a hospital, and patched them up. As he was
leaving, the first drunk came over and said, "Well, so long, doc,
I want to shake your hand and let you know there aren't any
hard feelings. That accident was just as much my fault as it
was yours."

· 7 ·

The tourist in search of urban pleasure will find himself thwarted by some ordinance, the primary object of which is to force Middle West moralities upon all inhabitants. Puritanism is the inflexible doctrine of Los Angeles.—WILLARD HUNTINGTON WRIGHT (S. S. Van Dine), 1915

THE CITY COUNCIL and the mayor on one occasion wrangled long and violently over a trivial municipal issue. A newspaper editorially deplored their schoolboy conduct and ascribed the matter to "peanut politics."

A tongue-in-cheek subscriber objected. "The peanut is a valuable agricultural commodity," he wrote the editor, "and should not be slandered."

If he didn't score a bull's-eye in describing Los Angeles officialdom, he was close.

It is said that the citizens get the kind of government they deserve. There's some question that the population of Los Angeles is so undeserving.

Municipal affairs seem always to be run by willful amateurs. Certainly the men who get elected seem uninspired, defensive, and generally mediocre.

As elsewhere, politics have traditionally moved in a monotonous pattern from corruption to reform and back again. For many years, the racket men in charge of gambling, brothels, bookmaking, and slot machines operated cozily in a pleasant profit-sharing basis with law enforcement authorities. These bad boys were known as the Combination or Syndicate.

In return for their largesse, they expected and received the usual "protection" and an assurance that no Eastern or Midwest racketeers would be permitted to muscle in on their exclusive hunting grounds. Many a big-name outsider was met at the train on his arrival and escorted to the ticket booth to purchase a stub for the next train Eastbound. These polite services were always accompanied by righteous quotes from the District Attorney or the Police Chief assuring the suckers that he was keeping Los Angeles pure.

One day in 1927, Al Capone and his entourage came to town, allegedly to sniff out the prospects. The gendarmerie buzzed. One rumor was that Capone had purchased an immense seaside ranch and planned to land contraband whisky from Canada. Another was that he and his playmates decided they were tough enough to depose the hometown hoodlums.

After a nervous week, the Chief of Detectives told the press: "Eastern gangsters will not be tolerated in Los Angeles." He sent two detectives to call on Capone. Capone greeted them cordially in his hotel suite and offered them drinks. The cops were obsequious—after all they were in the presence of royalty —but managed to blurt out that the chief wondered what their intentions were in Los Angeles.

Capone assured them he was merely vacationing. "I just came out to see what California looked like," he said, "that's all."

The cops said that his visit had started some speculation and if it was all the same to him, he better cut it short.

Capone eyed them tranquilly. "O.K.," he said, "I intended to leave for Chicago tomorrow. Is that all right?"

The cops said that would be fine.

"Now that we've finished with business," smiled Al, "let's have a drink."

Scotch was poured and chitchat exchanged. One cop asked how Chicago was and Public Enemy No. 1 said everything was fine. "Oh we have our troubles," he qualified, "lots of bad boys in town. We try to keep things down—it's bad advertising—but it isn't as bad as the papers make it out. We've got too many punks with ten-cent brains who want to be big shots."

Next day, true to his word, Capone took the train for Chicago. The newspapers made much of the Police Department's prompt action in ridding Los Angeles of the nation's top menace. One headlined CAPONE TOLD TO BLOW; GANG CHIEF ROUSTED. With sighs of relief, the gamblers went back to their card and dice games.

Inevitably, during the reign of Mayor Frank L. Shaw, some men who pulled the strings got too greedy. It was said that they collected a dime for each towel used in the bordellos.

What happened is best illustrated by an incident at a reunion of E.T.O. veterans. They reminisced about the strange customs they found in France. One veteran recalled that the man with the biggest manure pile in the village was always elected mayor. Judge Leroy Dawson, a noted wit, broke in. "We have the same system over here, of course," he said, "except that when the pile gets too smelly we recall the mayor."

The manure pile, estimated to have been worth fifty million dollars a year to the criminal empire which for twenty years dominated Los Angeles politics, assailed the nostrils to the point of nausea in 1938.

Until this time, the handful of men known as the Combination or Syndicate had a beautiful, foolproof, going concern. They did business openly and paid off where they had to, whether to a man sworn to uphold the law or to a shady citizen who had the knack of building up nuisance value.

Some individuals and organizations, and the newspaper on which I worked, had fought them sporadically, with no permanent effect. On the other hand, some papers abetted the Syndicate.

But the Combination boys, slick as they were, flunked in psychology. A tide was rising and they didn't see it.

In an unprecedented recall election, a superior court judge, short, dumpy, graying Fletcher Bowron, defeated shorter, dumpier, but black-haired Mayor Frank L. Shaw. It was one of those rare occasions when voters became so aroused they acted.

The blow-off started innocently enough. A real-estate man named Ralph Gray sued Harry Munson, a former police commissioner, for $2900. Gray charged he hadn't been paid for services he rendered in Shaw's 1933 campaign. The suit hinted at the sources of underworld money used in municipal elections. In fact, Gray accused Munson of being a front man for the Combination.

As the trial date approached, Gray's friend, Harry Raymond, a private investigator and former policeman, advised him to secure A. Brigham Rose as his attorney. Rose already was attorney for Clifford E. Clinton, the cafeteria man, who as a county grand juror had become appalled at civic graft and had formed a purity group named CIVIC, Citizens' Independent Vice Investigating Committee.

Soon spokesmen on both sides were calling each other names. One snarling clash involved Raymond and Earle E. Kynette, chief of Mayor Shaw's police spy squad. The fury continued through the trial, at which Gray won a judgment. Munson immediately filed bankruptcy proceedings.

Then came the incident that tipped over what may have been the most solidly entrenched graft system in the nation. Harry Raymond stepped into his car and pressed the starter. A bomb exploded, throwing more than a hundred metal slugs into his body. Miraculously, he wasn't injured fatally.

After a long trial, Kynette was convicted of placing the bomb and sentenced to a twenty-year term in San Quentin. Public indignation lasted up to and including the recall election and Los Angeles had a new mayor.

When Bowron took office he announced a wholesale purge of bad boys was upcoming. The gamblers and their stooges on the public payroll didn't believe he meant it. They thought it was a fancy play to quiet the church vote, after which he would do business with them.

Instead he became tougher. The final blow to any hope of continued graft was the forced retirement of twenty-three officers who had been key men in the Shaw administration setup. Recognizing reality at last, the Combination dispersed, mostly to Las Vegas, Nevada, where gambling is legal.

Now the town is relatively clean. Bookmakers and other gambling entrepreneurs who operate do so on a "sneak" basis: that is, they take their chances on being raided; they cannot buy protection.

Nevertheless, Mayor Bowron is continually heckled. Whatever his personal point of view, he is forced into the position of being a reformer. Many persons who clamored for the cleanup now think they like things better with a smear on them.

The case of Councilman Harold Harby is another sample of Los Angeles politics. In August 1941, Harby was accused by Clifford Clinton's CIVIC committee of using a city car on a two-week, five-thousand-mile pleasure trip to Montana. Harby's reply was a lame admission that he had used the car but had made the trip to study the Great Falls park system.

A few days after the accusation Harby, to indicate his humility, rode to the City Hall from his home in Palms, some twelve miles, on a bicycle. Clinton promptly accused him of not having the proper registration for the bicycle. Harby said he didn't think Clinton was observing the golden rule.

A newspaper furor arose over the auto trip, however, and on September 4 Harby took the floor in the City Council to justify the trip. He gave a complete travelogue, which his colleagues found boring.

The city attorney's office wasn't impressed either. It issued two criminal misdemeanor complaints but withdrew them with the suggestion that Harby reimburse the city the cost of the trip. He jumped at the chance, writing a check for $122.12 as full payment. Some observers thought the figure should have been nearer a thousand.

But Clinton would have none of this. He petitioned the county Grand Jury to take action to oust Harby. The accusation was voted, charging misconduct in office, a charge rarely used, which subjected Harby to dismissal from office if found guilty.

A delegation appeared a few days later in City Council chambers and filed a petition in support of Harby. His actions were beyond reproach, it stated, and the unfavorable publicity was to be deplored.

Nevertheless, he went to trial in January 1942. Again he tried to justify his junket as a study of Montana parks and again the jurors were unimpressed. He was convicted and removed from office.

He appealed the verdict but the Appellate Court upheld the ouster in May and condemned him for abuse of public office. His job was declared vacated and he was formally suspended from the Council. Nearly a year later, February 9, 1943, his last hope of regaining his seat legally, a writ of mandate, was denied.

But in the primary election in April 1944, the voters re-elected him to his position. In their minds, clearly, a man who joyrides in a car at the taxpayers' expense is no criminal. If they were councilman, obviously they'd want to do the same.

Along with lack of real leadership, Los Angeles has a sad political heritage. A tight, conservative little group seems to hold the copyright on progress. It's in favor of progress if it's the right kind of progress, if it doesn't upset the status quo, and if it is what is known as good business.

As a result, Los Angeles is in a deplorable condition. Traffic is out of hand. The sewer system is a public disgrace. Transportation is outmoded. Downtown parking is hopelessly inadequate. The stalling on smog control has become a scandal. The crime and juvenile delinquency curves are getting steeper. In short, Los Angeles is years behind in its planning.

Many of these problems can be attributed to the war and the tremendous influx of population, as well as lack of foresight by officialdom, but there's evidence that as the city's traffic facilities and sewer system are outmoded, so is its constitutional framework. Dr. C. E. Hawley, of the University of Southern California, told the Kiwanis Club in March 1947 that, "from the point of view of the political scientist, the city charter of Los Angeles is an inequitable monstrosity, an impediment to getting things done, a conspiracy against good government, something that should never have happened. Of the many criticisms that could be levied against its more than five hundred sections and 350 pages, the most devastating is that it violates the basic principle of simplicity. Little wonder that citizens throw up their hands in despair. On the basis of past experiences of this and other cities, one cannot be very hopeful of a basic change in the charter. Normally such changes come only after major disasters such as floods, earthquakes, or truly scandalous scandals. Short of such events, the best one can hope for are piecemeal changes such as those being proposed at the next election."

During the depression thirties, Los Angeles politics directly reflected the urge for a better life. Candidates for local as well as state offices had only to disclose their love for President Roosevelt or Upton Sinclair and they were swept in on the tide.

By 1940 the voters' attitude had changed. Economic panaceas were out. Candidates went back to their old tightrope act titled "All Things to All Men." Today most municipal-office holders are conservative and unfortunately the dull rather than the eager type, and being susceptible to the usual political pressures, office-holders in L.A., as anywhere else, obviously will pay more attention to the men who put up substantial campaign funds than those who opposed them or contributed nothing. It would be naive to assume otherwise.

Perhaps the best sample of the city's chaotic and haphazard approach to politics was the mayoralty election April 3, 1945. Mayor Bowron, running for re-election, had thirteen opponents. They included Clifford E. Clinton, the cafeteria man who originally backed Bowron but has since repudiated him. Others were a county supervisor, a councilman, a former assemblyman, a war veteran, a woman whose campaign literature established her as "the Trotskyite candidate for mayor," a man named O. K. Jones, and a fiery woman named Dolores Gunn who drove around the city in a Packard limousine emblazoned with lurid personal opinions of Bowron. The payoff though was the appearance of an organization calling itself Common Sense Volunteers, with the motto "Anybody but Bowron or Clinton." Yes, things get confusing, especially to people who don't care very much about politics anyway and more particularly to the thousands of new-comers who don't even try to make sense of them.

This apathy was frivolously speared in one election campaign. A worker for a certain candidate asked a Japanese if he would kindly place a placard in his store window. The Japanese didn't seem to understand. The worker went into his pitch, extolling his candidate. The Japanese listened intently, politely concealing his lack of comprehension. After ten minutes, the worker thought he detected a gleam of understanding in the merchant's eyes and wound up his argument with a ringing finale. The Japanese, greatly relieved, took a nickel from his pocket and said: "Hockay, here fi' cents, go get cup coffee!"

· 8 ·

*Car 73! Change broadcast number 14 from indecent exposure to rape. That is all!—*CALL HEARD OVER KGPL, POLICE RADIO STATION.

AN INTERESTING relic at the police homicide bureau is an old, corduroy-covered ledger known as the murder log. In it, every killing since the turn of the century is recorded in memo form.

The first entry has to do with the strange death of Simon Christensen September 9, 1899. Other entries are written in the formal manner of the times. The stabbing of a man named Gonzales is attributed to "outlaws." Another death is believed the work of "highbinders."

The entry for February 1, 1922 is one of Los Angeles' major unsolved crimes. It is the fatal shooting of William Desmond Taylor in his home on South Alvarado Street. The case has been reopened again and again, sometimes on legitimate clues, more often by a district attorney who needed the publicity. In recent years it has become dormant, yet veterans in the homicide bureau will confide that the murderer has been known for years and, and far as they know, walks about free in Hollywood. They have reconstructed every detail of the crime, its motive, and why it has not been solved. As the years pass, chances of an arrest and prosecution become increasingly remote. Witnesses have died, or disappeared. It's a long time since 1922.

Many other unsolved murders are also listed: Siever, Tallman, Katz, to name some of the more prominent. But murder in Los Angeles has dropped down in class. Today the men most likely to be found dead are beer-joint brawlers, "other men" in family triangles, and third-rate bookmakers.

Los Angeles police officers have come in for their share of notoriety over the years but considering the untamed spirit of some of the citizens they deal with, they are no better or no worse than the policemen elsewhere. There are simply good ones and bad ones.

The city of course added several notches to its reputation for screwiana at one oral quiz given police-officer candidates for chief. Asked "Do you want to be chief of police?" one officer, thinking it a catch question, said: "No, the chief isn't independent, he takes orders. Someone else collects the money and he collects the beefs."

Another candidate, asked "Do you think there are others better qualified than you for chief?" replied: "Yes, but they didn't pass the written exam."

Another officer was asked if he, as chief, would devote more attention to traffic or prostitution. He replied he would consider traffic first because if there were too many traffic accidents there wouldn't be any men to patronize the bordellos.

The classic q. and a. in a police examination occurred at a different time. Asked "What would you do in case of a race riot?" a candidate for promotion replied: "I would take down the number of both cars!"

One time two policemen brought a nickel slot machine into court, a routine matter, as the man in whose place it was discovered had already been fined. The judge ordered the machine destroyed and the contents, amounting to $4.91, given to a local hospital. A reporter asked one officer how the machine happened to have the odd cent. "Oh," he said, "there are always some dishonest persons trying to play the nickel machines with pennies. And many's the time I've worked those two-bit machines with nickels."

A man serving thirty days on a misdemeanor charge became

a trusty, which he liked much better than just sitting there. Life really opened up for him when a big shot was jailed as a suspect in a forty-thousand-dollar fur robbery. "Hey pal," pleaded the big shot from his cell, "read me that part in the paper where it says I had the police baffled."

In running down and capturing an erratic motorist in El Monte, highway patrol officer Larry Lee recognized the offender as the same man he had arrested the day before. Officer Lee's memo to his captain was as follows:

At about 1:30 A.M. this date we duplicated our work of yesterday. We picked up the same drunk, same place, same time, same way, put him in the same jail to be arraigned before the same judge. At the suggestion of my partner, Officer McCarty, I would like to request that in the future this man be required when drinking to leave his false teeth at home, as he has a habit of carrying them in his hip pocket. Yesterday while frisking him, Officer McCarty was bitten. This morning it was my fingers.

Ralph Graham, who earned the title "The Phantom Burglar" in a series of depredations in the expensive Bel-Air section, told police when captured: "I would like to register a beef against the movie boys and girls whose playthings I swiped. All of them except Fanny Brice exaggerated the amount of stuff taken. I mean they really got out the old multiplication table."

For a certain scene, a move studio needed five hundred moths. The assignment was given two prop men, to whom the impossible is routine. So there they were at 11:30 P.M. at Wilshire and Western. Net in hand, one climbed on the other's shoulder under a street light. The top man whipped efficiently at the little beasties. He was doing very well, with a growing audience, when the law arrived. The cops asked what was going on. The bottom man explained they were catching moths.

"Very cute," said the law. "For a moment I thought the moths were catching you."

With their equipage, they were taken to jail. They asked permission to phone the studio. The cops said no. They were clapped into the clink for the night. Next morning they were in court.

"According to this report," said the judge to the top man, "you were standing on your friend's shoulders with a butterfly net and you told the officers you were catching moths. This is highly irregular."

In the nick of time, studio emissaries roared to the courthouse and retrieved them, and, more important, the moths.

Motorists don't always know it but when they are given citations for traffic-law violations the gendarmes write additional comment for the guidance of the judge when the case is heard. Usually judges look for such information as "admits guilt," "surly attitude," "unco-operative," or "had been drinking." One judge was delighted to get a note stating "This man very unhappy."

On a hot day, a court attaché met Judge Leroy Dawson at a recess and said: "This is a good day for a Tom Collins, Judge. Did you ever try one?"

"No," the judge replied, "but I've tried a lot of fellows who have."

One of the town's long-standing feuds was between two well-known attorneys, Colonel William H. Neblett and S. S. Hahn. Neblett represented Pearl Canfield when she sought to retrieve a share of the two-million-dollar Scripps newspaper properties of which her husband, Byron Canfield, had been part owner. The trial lasted three months and almost daily the two attorneys debated bitterly. One day Hahn complained to Judge Walter Gates that he was being discriminated against. Whenever his legal opponent's name came up, he said, he was called "Colonel"

Neblett. Neblett's associate counsel defended the military title as authentic and appropriate.

"All right," retorted Hahn, "but I insist if Mr. Neblett is called 'Colonel,' I be called by my military title." He placed his honorable discharge paper on the judge's bench as if it were a court exhibit.

"What is your military rank?" asked the judge.

"I was a corporal," said Hahn, and he was given this rank throughout the remainder of the trial, which he won.

A full-blown swami, replete with turban, was picked up off the sidewalk acting strangely. The police report stated he was drunk. He pleaded not guilty and asked for a jury trial. In court he confided to his attorney: "I'll hypnotize the jury. I may not get them all but I'll get eleven anyway. That won't be so bad, eleven to one for acquittal." Throughout the proceedings he transfixed the jurors with a cold eye. It worked nicely. The jury disagreed and he was freed. Afterwards, the jurors were found to be angry. They had stood eleven to one for conviction, but one woman had remained unshakable. The blow to the swami's vanity was severe, but he comforted himself by saying: "I hypnotized one of them anyway." A reporter heard this boast and asked the adamant juror if she had been hypnotized into her decision.

"Don't be redic," she said. "I just didn't think they proved it on him."

A vacuum-cleaner salesman and a housewife who resented each other took their brawl to court. The woman testified she told the salesman she didn't want a vacuum cleaner but he put on the pressure. Indignant at his gall, she asked the name of his boss. He shouted, she testified, "None of your damn business." One juror, hand cupped to ear, asked a repeat of the testimony.

"None of your damn business," the judge repeated.

"Gosh," mumbled the juror, "I thought we could ask a question. That's a deuce of a way to talk to an old man."

· 9 ·

The only thing you can definitely predict about earthquakes is, the farther you are from the last one, the nearer you are to the next.—Dr. Edgar K. Soper, U.C.L.A. Geology Professor

No one who experienced it will ever forget the big quake of March 10, 1933. It caused the deaths, more or less indirectly, of a hundred persons. They died of fright, heart attacks, getting in the way of falling cement, but mostly accidents. The traffic between Los Angeles and Long Beach, where the quake centered, was frightful.

Heading away from Long Beach were terror-stricken residents who had seen buildings crumble. En route there were rescue squads, police and sheriff's deputies, anxious relatives. Long Beach was cut off from the world for hours.

Supposedly solid buildings collapsed like anthills. School buildings especially fell apart, revealing a scandal somewhere in their construction that was never fully investigated, or made public. Had classes been in session—the quake struck in late afternoon—thousands of children may have been crushed.

The greatest damage, though intangible, was done to people's nerves. An earthquake of fairly major intensity, such as this one, is a personal reminder from the unknown that you too are mortal and don't forget it. To this day, people haven't.

Quakes don't come very often but when they do they receive top priority with the natives. There are two kinds, the sharp jolt that gives the sensation that a giant has picked up the house and is bouncing it, and the gentle, swaying motion.

At the first awesome rumble of the kitchen dishes and the

window panes, the hysteria boys and girls run to the phone for train or plane reservations to anywhere. Some jump in their cars and drive wildly eastward. Old timers usually hold rigid a moment and say: "I wonder if that's an earthquake?" Likely as not, someone will reply: "Naw, that's the fleet at battle practice out in the channel." Or, "They're probably testing those sixteen-inch guns at Fort MacArthur."

People unanimously confess to a momentary feeling of utter helplessness. They put it this way: "If you're up in a plane you figure you can get back to the ground. When you're at sea you can take to a lifeboat if something goes wrong. But when the earth shakes under you there's no place to go."

One night I was dozing against the competition of a gay party down the street. Someone was saying good-by in Scotch or bourbon dialect. I wagered mentally on his chances of getting home without being arrested for drunken driving. A breeze had been ballooning the curtains away from the window. I was faced away from the window when I experienced a floating sensation. The wind, I thought, was very strange. But when I looked at the window the curtains were still: there was no wind. Then came the anxious moment. Should I lie still and perhaps let the roof drop in on my lap? I didn't have to make the decision. At that moment, the alcoholized gentleman down the street got his car started and took off in a flurry of farewells. He didn't know it, but he was very reassuring. What was an earthquake to him? The moral is, of course, stay drunk during quakes and they won't hurt you.

Since 1933, people are earthquake-conscious. On days when an ominous stillness hangs in the air, they say: "This is regular earthquake weather." There's no such thing. A tiny temblor, the polite name for them, makes medicine men of ordinary citizens. They talk knowingly of sunspots and blood on the moon.

Everyone too has his own prescription for safety, though at best this is whistling in the dark. A story is told of a situation in

Tacoma, Washington, when it was rocked in 1939. Guests in a hotel ran about in wide-eyed, terror-stricken panic. One fellow remained calm. He made for a doorway, took a stance, and shouted above the din: "I'm from Los Angeles. *We* always stand in doorways!"

A nervous bystander said: "I'm from Chicago. What the hell do I do?"

Actually, most quakes come and go without people knowing of them. When a light swaying motion was recorded in 1937, Lee Arvidson, manager of the Regent Hotel on Hollywood Boulevard, where a number of boxers, wrestlers, and actors live, flung down his pen in irritation. "I thought I told those wrestlers to quit practicing on the roof!" he said. He called a bellboy and instructed him: "Go see if Whiskers Adams is up there jumping rope again!"

A woman spent the afternoon of Sunday, June 18, 1944, prettying the family burial plot of an Inglewood cemetery. She was tired when she finished, so tired she overcame her natural objections and sat for a short rest on a headstone in the next plot. At that moment, the quake which centered in the Inglewood area almost moved the headstone out from under her. She didn't realize immediately what was happening and had a few bad minutes. She'll never sit on another headstone.

By and large, Los Angeles takes its earthquakes the way it takes its weather: with a great deal of conversation and not much else. There's none of the mass hysteria that is conveyed in some newspaper stories that get printed in the East and Midwest. After the 1933 quake, the stories clearly indicated that the end of the world was at hand. They told of herculean rumbling in the distance, of huge cracks opening in the earth swallowing hills, of papier-maché homes crumpling into dust, killing uncounted scores. They hinted that the Chamber of Commerce was dictating policy on the coverage of quakes and making them sound less catastrophic than they were.

If a poll were taken, Los Angeles would preponderantly prefer an occasional quake to the tornadoes, hurricanes, and zero weather elsewhere. As a matter of fact, the feeling has been expressed that what Los Angeles needs to keep out the population overflow is a good substantial earthquake.

10

*The famed climate has one major flaw—you can't
eat it.*—DICKSON HARTWELL, *Liberty*, SEPTEMBER
21, 1946

UNTIL World War II, the measure of community progress,
or, more appropriately, the holy shrine before which the
builders of the city worshiped, was population. The general
theory was that Los Angeles could never have too much. Now
they wish they hadn't said that.

Los Angeles' first population burp—they didn't become booms
until later—took place in 1869. The Southern Pacific Railway in
that year completed the first transcontinental line, to San Francisco, and some of the voyagers overflowed southward. They
looked like the start of a great, wonderful sucker crop and real-
estate men began breathing heavily. Sensing profits from the
outside, they prettied up the city, tearing down old decrepit
structures and erecting new hotels, churches, and warehouses
and improving the streets. By 1873 they knew they had guessed
wrong. The boom failed to materialize.

Boom No. 2, considerably more spectacular, derived from the
completion of Santa Fe's transcontinental line and a bitter rate
war. The S.P.'s fare from the Missouri Valley in 1886 was
around $125. When the Santa Fe came in it was lowered to
a hundred. It was the Santa Fe's turn, then the S.P.'s. On
March 6, 1887, Santa Fe got down to twelve dollars and Southern Pacific met it. Within a few hours, they squared off at eight
dollars, then six dollars, then four dollars and by noon Santa Fe
announced a rate of one dollar. The two railroads must have
suddenly realized the futility of their throat cutting, for the fare

soon returned to fifty dollars, but the bargain had not gone unnoticed. During 1887, Southern Pacific hauled more than a hundred thousand persons to Los Angeles, Santa Fe almost that many. Among them were a high percentage of boomers, riffraff, bunco steerers, and ilk. A frenzy of speculation took hold of newcomers and natives alike. Everyone was selling something. A story is told that an Easterner attending church was approached by the pastor after the service, asked if he were a newcomer, and sold a lot in a new tract. More than a hundred towns were blueprinted in Los Angeles County between 1884 and 1888. Sixty-two of them have no present identity. Before 1890 the boom was no longer even an echo, an estimated fourteen million dollars in property values having gone down the drain. On the asset side, boom towns such as Glendale, Alhambra, Monrovia, and Azusa thrived, university sites had been designated, water pipe, sidewalks, and transit line, though unused, were installed—ready for the next boom.

While residents who met on the street still cracked: "I had half a million dollars wiped out in the crash and, what's worse, five hundred dollars of it was cash," the fuse was ignited on Boom No. 3. It is known as the boom of 1906, but it had its inception with the creation of the Chamber of Commerce, October 15, 1888. In the three years after it started business, the Chamber sent out more than two million pamphlets and circulars. It sent beaters eastward with scenic displays, charts, agricultural exhibits, models of homes. Smooth talkers organized excursions for blocks of Midwesterners, willing but not quite sold on the trip westward. In 1901, sixty thousand winter tourists arrived.

From 1910 to 1918, there was no outright explosion, but rather a steady growth. This period saw the growth of what is known as the California bungalow, perhaps the ugliest type of architecture ever designed. Los Angeles is filled with them, especially in the Wilshire and southwest districts. They stand as a strange paradox: the newcomers who came westward for the sun built homes in which they get practically none.

The real big boom took place in the twenties and it is probably better described as a bacchanalian revel or clambake. More than 1,272,037 persons migrated to Los Angeles County, creating the cities of Tujunga, South Gate, Lynwood, Bell, Hawthorne, Torrance, and Maywood. "They camped on the outskirts of town," wrote Mildred Adams, "and their camps became new suburbs." This influx, called the greatest migration in American history, was attributed to the automobile. The one-way stream of rattle-trap cars with bedding, washtubs, and baby carriages lashed to the tops and sides that moved westward in 1924 has been described as not unlike a swarm of invading locusts. More than 90 per cent of these invaders settled in the city, which added 661,375, a gain of 114.7 per cent, to its population for the decade. The lure may have been oil, which had begun spouting at Huntington Beach, Long Beach, and Santa Fe Springs or it may have been the burgeoning motion-picture industry, but the best guess is that it was the climate and a hope for the best.

For twenty years, outlanders had heard a faint tapping about the climate. In 1921 it was being hammered into their consciousness by a new organization, the All-Year Club of Southern California, Ltd. During this year, as the story goes, Los Angeles was having an epidemic of postwar profiteering. Fearing such a scandal would give the city a bad name, the Chamber of Commerce high command took action to clean house. One step was to obtain the co-operation of the *Los Angeles Times,* in printing the names of those found charging extortionate prices. One day a woman hotel operator charged into the office of publisher Harry Chandler, who was always accessible to the public. She waved a copy of that day's newspaper, in which she was named as a profiteer. In highly colorful language, she said the charge was unfair. The way things were, she said, she had to make enough out of her hotel in the two tourists' months to compensate for the rest of the year and naturally her rentals were high. Chandler was impressed. He called together a brain trust and after some discussion decided that what Los Angeles needed was a new type of promotion to stimulate travel westward the year around. The result was the All-Year Club.

In 1941, the peak tourist year, 1,800,000 out-of-state visitors made the trek, spending $202,000,000 of which nineteen million went into taxes. A spot check in the fall of 1946 indicated that tourists were spending twice as much as in 1941 and the figure might reach five hundred million, putting the tourist business in the upper brackets with agriculture, oil, and aviation.

But by 1946, many other things had happened, all bad. There had been the depression and its outcropping of movements, John Steinbeck's *Grapes of Wrath*, then the war, with the payroll bonanza of Southern California's airplane factories and shipyards bringing new thousands West. When the war shut off, so did much of the factory work. Few of the horde, estimated at approximately a million persons, showed any inclination to return home.

Now wherever you turn, out in the desert, in remote canyons, at distant shorelines, you find people. Around the city they've broken down the doors and are coming in the windows and the transoms and out of the woodwork. At Blythe, the entering point to Southern California for out-of-staters, cars line up for two or three miles, waiting to be checked to see if they have any Mediterranean fruit flies in, say, a bag of oranges or peaches or apricots, which, after all, are for sale in California too.

In November 1945 border inspectors at Blythe conceded the greatest coastward trek in history was under way. Their figures showed that during the month 27,369 automobiles carrying nearly seventy thousand persons funneled through their station.

But cars were also leaving California in increasing numbers. In January 7903 cars left California. This increased to 10,811 in June, then swelled to 24,282 in November, making only 3087 more cars entering California than were leaving. The number of passengers in the Eastbound cars was not available.

Most of the out-of-staters who streamed into the state in November looking for sunshine or jobs were middle-class residents of Illinois, Michigan, Kansas, or Ohio, inspectors said. Texans were few and far between. The migrants included 31,457 former war workers and other Californians coming back after vacations in the East.

Six months later, in May 1946, 457,324 persons from other states spilled through Blythe into California. Newsman S. A. Desick, sent by the *Los Angeles Examiner* to take a sociological sampling of the newcomers, found a feeling among the invaders that they were entering a new land.

A musician said, "I've always wanted to come to California." To him, California was the "Promised Land in High C." He knew about the Los Angeles housing shortage, so he placed his widowed mother, Julia, and their belongings on a trailer and left Cleveland, Ohio.

A man from Menomonie, Wisconsin—"Don't remind me of the place"—had a more specific reason: "I've been in every state west of the Mississippi and wouldn't want to live anywhere but in California. It has the finest educational system in the land." He was stationed here while in the Army, started to build a home several months ago in Santa Ana. Then he ran out of nails. Back to Wisconsin he went and bought a half ton of nails: "So I'll stick it out."

Trailers are the modern covered wagon as the "California fever" runs its benign course through the nation. A young man from Pittsburgh took a general engineering course at the University of Southern California and liked the "elbow room here" so well he went back and returned with his parents in a large trailer, "to beat the housing shortage."

Another engineer, from Youngstown, Ohio, visited here three

months before, found "industry young and greater chances for young people." His choice was Long Beach. Another Youngstowner also liked "elbow room." A writer, he had his heart set on some property at Big Bear Lake. "This proves I was determined," he said, pointing to the two-place motor scooter on which he and his wife made the trek.

A serious, mild-mannered father of four children decided that Southern California was where he wanted to bring them up.

"I knew the climate was wonderful," he said. "And I knew the opportunities were wonderful. My own firm opened a plant here. So I asked for a transfer and got it."

The family will live in a trailer house in Anaheim until he can take time out from his mechanic's job to build a home.

Farmers, young and old, are also in the montage of humanity settling here. A young man of twenty-eight from Victoria, Texas, "liked the living" while stationed here as a Seabee. He will cotton farm in Porterville, in the San Joaquin Valley, with his in-laws.

A sixty-five-year-old New Yorker said if it hadn't been for the war he would have escaped the harsh Eastern climate "long ago." A butcher said he wanted to retire. Last fall he came here from Chicago, found a home in West Los Angeles, and went back and brought his family, including four young daughters.

"The blue haze captured me," he said. "Here you can live leisurely and dream of better things."

Concluded Desick: "That was the kaleidoscope as it shifted through persons and families who are embarking on the country's greatest adventure—California."

All this has resulted in an odd situation. Let's skip the native sons; according to legend, traces of some have been discovered, but this has never been verified. Start with the old residents who have been here thirty years and are considered pioneers. For years they've been deploring the stiff, formal newcomers who have been here a mere twenty years. They consider them unassimilable. The two-decade group frowns on the ten-year residents as greenhorns. The single-decade invaders are very sad about the unlikely crop of outlanders who swept in during the war. And the wartime arrivals, many of them out of work now, view with alarm the postwar hordes arriving with their mad money, buying their houses out from under them at thrice inflated prices.

On August 8, 1946, a newspaper printed this story:

Floyd Heagle, 33, a painting contractor, and seven relatives including five small children, yesterday were found living in an automobile parked at the curb alongside Echo Park. They have been living, or rather existing, in the car for three weeks. For several nights they slept in the park but they were evicted when a nearby resident complained to police. Heagle, his wife, their three children, Geraldine 10, Floyd jr. 7, Adrian 1½ and his cousin, Mrs. Dorothy Johnson, 28, and her two children Priscilla, 9, and Jimmy, 2, were evicted from their home in Highland Park three weeks before. They had lived there three and a half years. Mrs. Johnson's husband was reported missing in action during the war. "I've traced down every lead I could for a house," Heagle said, "but when I get there it's always gone. It's incredible but there isn't a house for us anywhere." The two families were staying near Echo Park lake, where cooking and sanitation facilities were available. The children played during the day in the park.

Heagle's case sounds exceptional, but even in 1947 it was typical. So much so that on February 6 Representative Helen Gahagan Douglas told the House that 162,000 families lived in tents, garages, stores, hotel rooms, and trailers, or doubled up: more than were made homeless by the San Francisco Earthquake or the Johnstown Flood.

Much of the blame for this overcrowding is placed on the All-Year Club, which continued to place ads in the magazines painting Southern California as an alluring vacation land. As the housing crisis grew, however, it warned potential newcomers of the shortage.

The All-Year Club justifies its position by pointing out the half-billion-dollar tourist "take" for 1946 and other satisfying rewards for what has been called "enlightened community self-ishness at work." The club bluntly calls its work the "tourist industry." It makes no mystery of the fact that it coldly and deliberately sold Southern California as a play spot without comparison. If the wrong kind of people or too many of them have danced to this Pied Pipering, it's one of those things.

The All-Year Club has all sorts of figures, statistics, and breakdowns. Generally they prove that tourists spend their money like little gentlemen and get not only value received but more for their money than elsewhere. Unquestionably the Southland offers a wider choice of places to go than any other community can. Furthermore, tourists are sent questionaires after they return home, asking how they liked things. The All-Year Club receives replies from 20 per cent of them, a very high figure even with self-addressed stamped envelope enclosed, and practically all of them say nice things. If they weren't satisfied customers, selling would make no difference.

Early in January 1937, the Hearst-owned *Herald-Express* had an editorial giving the statistics on tourist travel for 1936, stating that 1,517,864 out-of-staters had visited Southern California (more than the city's resident population) and spent $188,891,-100. It concluded, "They are welcome, not alone for their spending power, but for themselves as well." A contributor, T. R. L., rebutted as follows:

> Dear Lord, send guests with spending power,
> And we will praise thee every hour.

For while we fleece the Eastern swell,
We love him for himself as well.
But keep from us, we beg of thee,
The shiftless sons of poverty,
(Thy tin-can tourists are the worst)
And thine the glory, Willie Hearst.

Every Hamburger and hot-dog stand, of course, considers
itself a tourist attraction, but, by their own statements, vaca-
tioners enjoy most the climate and the beaches. A survey of
winter visitors in 1938–1939 disclosed the pleasure quotient as
follows: Climate 57 per cent, beaches 21, "Everything" 15, good
roads and driving 14, broadcasts and studios 13, Catalina Island
12, Huntington Library 11, scenery 10, Tournament of Roses
10, Hollywood 9, Forest Lawn 9, movie theaters, stars, and
studios 8, mountains 8, horse races—Hollywood Park and Santa
Anita—8. ("Wonderful hospitality," incidentally, registered 2.)

Summer visitors in 1939 became ecstatic as follows: beaches
79 per cent, climate 65, mountains 64, groves and vineyards 58,
cities 58, cultural attractions 52, missions 46, movies 38, desert
33, night life 29, sports 16, fiestas and pageants 11, Catalina 7.
(The Huntington Library, as uncultured visitors appraised it,
scored a 1, tying tours to movie stars' homes, Gay's Lion Farm,
and unusual sights such as Olvera Street, Chinatown, flying
fish, and oil derricks.)

Winter tourists (722,364 in 1941) on an average are slightly
past forty years of age, stay approximately forty days, and in
their carefree way spend something like $350 per person. Sum-
mer tourists arrive in larger numbers (1,147,250 in 1941), are
younger, stay only seventeen days, and spend slightly less than
two hundred dollars per person.

Another thing: tourists carry away with them a new idea of
living. Many of them become inadvertent salesmen for Los
Angeles' now gigantic apparel industry, specializing in playsuits,

sports shirts, and phony Hollywood labels, or for California wines. The least they do is demand of their corner druggist back in Axhandle Junction why he doesn't have avocado sandwiches, with lettuce and mayonnaise, as they do in Los Angeles. What can the druggist do but order some?

In 1946, the city's unhappiest year in terms of housing, the full impact of all this propaganda, planned and inadvertent, had Los Angeles bulging at its seams. All tourist records were blown to pieces: 2,944,545 persons from other states came to Southern California, a 70 percent increase in volume over the record set in 1941.

The All-Year Club was quick to point out that they spent $509,926,355 while here, which "helped cushion the effects of the quick cutoff of the huge sums in war contracts." The influx also provided 81,843 jobs, with a payroll of $130,000,000, and swelled the area's sales and gasoline-tax revenue by nine million dollars and the city's sales tax fund by five hundred thousand. The club stated also that "these visitors were accommodated without aggravating our housing shortage problem," its survey disclosing that 62 per cent stayed in hotel and resort accommodations, 32 per cent with friends and relatives, six per cent in trailers and camping tents.

Among the unhoused, these figures were met with a deep, almost vicious growl. Even those to whom housing is no problem have become defensive on the subject of more people.

No, the rose-colored glasses aren't being worn any more. The suspicion is getting around that population alone may be a false idol. The problem, however, is usually stated another way, something like "Gad, where do they all come from?"

But having turned on the faucet, the population plus stimulators have discovered they may have broken the washer and can't turn it off; not only that, the ocean is likely to sweep in. Three or four million persons from elsewhere in the nation, many of them veterans who got a taste while they camped in the vicinity, are said to be planning to come to California.

One of the most interesting weathervanes has been a series of billboards on the roof of the William May Garland real-estate office at Olympic and Grand Avenue, in downtown L.A. In the decade following the turn of the century, the sign stated 300,000 POPULATION BY 1910. Successively, the sign has been changed to state 1,000,000 POPULATION BY 1920, 1,500,000 POPULATION BY 1930, and 2,000,000 POPULATION BY 1940. The present sign, dimmed by sun and weather, states 2,500,000 BY 1950.

Where they're going to live and what they're going to use for money is a little matter that will doubtless be taken up at the next meeting.

11

When the last McKinley is uttered,
When the last, last tears have been shed,
And the last, last candle has guttered
O'er the defenceless dead;
O waft me on wing of fairies,
Uprising to greet the dawn
To the singing of caged canaries,
As featured at Forest Lawn;
Where a family grave is rented
'Neath a sky with never a rift,
And the corpse of the late lamented
Is wrapped as a Birthday Gift.
—ARTHUR WIMPERIS

IF, AS HINTED in All-Year Club folders, life in Los Angeles can be beautiful, death is an exquisite, almost unbearable delight. As nowhere else in the world, newspaper, radio, billboard, and streetcar ads exhort people to take advantage of the opportunity to die gloriously, luxuriously, and cheaply, with special emphasis on the package deal. "Why live," they seem to state, "when we can bury you for practically nothing?"

More than one hundred firms are listed in the classified telephone directory under FUNERAL DIRECTORS. Most of these are small and appeal to their clientele on the basis of a quiet, dignified chapel service, with burial elsewhere.

Two concerns, Pierce Brothers and Utter-McKinley, have engaged in an expansion race and between them the scramble for corpses is fantastic. Pierce Brothers has eleven branches, Utter-McKinley twelve. The Pierce Brothers advertise they "conduct more funerals than any other firm west of New York." Utter-

McKinley advertise A FINE FUNERAL $68, $165, $225, $365, with a drawing of a handsome opened casket (minus the deceased) captioned YOU WOULD EXPECT TO PAY AT LEAST $250 FOR A COMPLETE FUNERAL WITH THIS RICHLY FINISHED ROUND-END HALF-COUCH CASKET. AT UTTER-MCKINLEY'S, ONLY $165. In another ad, Utter-McKinley announced a ten-strike: the services of Frank A. Nance, Los Angeles county coroner for twenty-four years, had been procured and, in his new capacity as vice president, he was available for "helpful advice." Pierce Brothers, in the immediate postwar period, advertised a "pledge to hold the line of funeral prices" with "funerals from $70, Budget terms." Utter-McKinley, in a smaller ad, designed for the common man, offered COMPLETE FUNERAL AS LOW AS $68. Edwards Brothers, one of the oldest firms, with ONLY ONE ESTABLISHMENT CENTRALLY LOCATED, a beautiful colonial-type building, met this competition in its ad stating FUNERALS AS LOW AS $70 with the added inducement, in large letters, UNDERSTANDING.

Over the years, as the competition between Pierce Brothers and Utter-McKinley grew, the trend in advertising changed. In the early days, thoughtful or despondent mortals pondering upon where they would all be a hundred years from now were invited reverently, almost wistfully, to plan ahead. Today they are admonished thunderously to pay attention to their futures. Some sort of precedent was achieved by Utter-McKinley with a beautiful girl staring irrelevantly from a billboard. She looked like the same handsome smiling miss who plugged cigarettes, tooth paste, nonfattening beer, or toilet soap on near-by billboards. With somewhat of a jolt, observers realized this Lorelei was plugging the guy with the scythe.

The titan among these dealers in death, of course, is Forest Lawn Memorial Park in Glendale. It advertises "Everything at the time of sorrow, in one sacred place, under one friendly management, with one convenient credit arrangement and a year to pay." Its eighty-seven-foot carved cement Tower of Legends, which actually houses a 165,000-gallon water tank, stands at the crest of its 303 acres, a landmark against the sky, visible for miles.

The entrance to the park is distinguished by an imposing set of wrought-iron gates, larger than those at Buckingham Palace. To the left, inside them, there is a beautiful lake, where white ducks and swans glide and a fountain splashes. To the right there is a picturesque little cottage with a large sign, FOREST LAWN LIFE INSURANCE Co. Polite, efficient attendants freely give information on the three methods of burial: Entombment in the mausoleum, inurnment in the columbarium, interment in one of the cemetery sections with such names as Dawn of Tomorrow, Sweet Memories, Everlasting Love, and Resurrection Slope.

Smooth macadam roads lead to Forest Lawn's three famous churches. Wee Kirk o' the Heather is a replica of the church in the village of Glencairn where Douglas proclaimed his undying love for Annie Laurie. In a tree-shaded forecourt, there is the Wishing Chair, built from stones brought across the sea from the little Scottish kirk, now in ruins. The Little Church of the Flowers was inspired by the church at Stoke Poges, Buckinghamshire, where Thomas Gray composed his "Elegy Written in a Country Churchyard." The Church of the Recessional, newest and largest of the three, is a reproduction of Saint Margaret's of Rottingdean, on the Sussex Down, portions of which date to the tenth century. It takes its name from Rudyard Kipling's "Recessional," for the poet lived in Rottingdean.

Visitors are reminded that Forest Lawn strives to be a "place of inspiration and enjoyment for the living as well as a noble resting place for the departed." It has no works of art showing sorrow, or suffering or death.

There is no Crucifixion.

Under Art Treasures are listed the majestic Memorial Court

of Honor in the Great Mausoleum; the Last Supper Window, renowned re-creation in stained glass of Leonardo da Vinci's great painting; America's greatest collection of large marble statuary; the Tower of Legends; Michelangelo's colossal ten-ton "David" in exact reproduction, enshrined in the hilltop Court of David; America's greatest collection of stained glass; Bouguereau's painting "Song of the Angels" in the Chapel of the Angels; the "Mystery of Life" group in the Mystery of Life Garden, a mammoth marble group of twenty-two infants, adults, and oldsters who gaze in wonder at the birth of a duck and the wooing of a pair of doves.

Forest Lawn ranks among Southern California's top tourist attractions. Something like one thousand persons visit it each week: twice as many, the employees' handbook makes note, as check in at the Metropolitan Museum of Art in New York.

It has been widely publicized in the magazines and the newspapers. Therein lie the remains of Jean Harlow, whose funeral and mortuary chamber cost sixty thousand dollars, par for the course; King C. Gillette; Will Rogers; Carole Lombard; Irving Thalberg; Tom Mix; John Gilbert; Florenz Ziegfeld; Joe Penner; Aimee Semple McPherson, and nearly a hundred thousand other persons.

Under the Tower of Legends, each year, Easter sunrise services have become a tradition. Twenty-five thousand persons congregate annually on a hillside to await the sometimes foggy dawn, the arrival of which is usually accompanied by the Philharmonic orchestra, a singer from a movie studio, and a spiritual message. A noted writer came away inspired at this mass rekindling of spiritual beliefs and expressed his amazement at the awesome spectacle of so many people standing thus, in, of all places, a cemetery. The article he wrote was mimeographed and given employees for study and reflection.

Cynical newspaper reporters and photographers unlucky enough to draw the assignment, which means awakening at

3 A.M., see only a tremendous exploitation idea grown into a nasty habit and a surging mass of people trampling the graves of the paying customers.

The founder and head of Forest Lawn is Dr. Hubert Eaton, known as "The Builder." Dr. Eaton was given an honorary LL.D. in 1937 from William Jewell College, Liberty, Missouri, from which he graduated with an A.B. degree in 1902—converted a fixation into a fortune.

As Dale Carnegie told the story, Eaton, when a boy, had to pass a graveyard one night to take an urgent message to the home of a relative. He heard a stirring and saw a ghostly form. Terrified, he ran as fast as he could. He learned later the "ghost" was one of several goats eating grass but the incident made so deep an impression on him he came to dread cemeteries, even when he was grown.

In time, he became a successful metallurgist and chemist and moved to California to retire. There he became interested in real estate and banking and, in 1917, on a mortgage foreclosure, his company acquired a fifty-five-acre cemetery. He was assigned to develop it. From the hilltop where the Tower of Legends now stands he stared down at a scene of desolation, filled with grotesque tombstones of all shapes and sizes, rotting trees, unkempt lawn. He was seized with the inspiration to rebuild it into a cemetery with the theme of hope instead of defeat. From this forlorn place of the dead he evolved his Builder's Creed: "I believe in a happy Eternal Life. I therefore know the cemeteries of today are wrong because they depict an end, not a beginning. I shall endeavor to build Forest Lawn as unlike other cemeteries as sunshine is unlike darkness, as Eternal Life is unlike Death."

He acquired an additional 150 acres and told his bosses he wanted to put in sweeping lawns, towering trees, splashing fountains, beautiful statuary, a pipe organ. They said he was crazy. He persisted and persuaded them to let him buy a fine piece of statuary that had been on exhibit at the San Francisco World's

Fair. He put a sympathetic landscape architect to work on his dream. He patiently hunted out the heirs of those whose bodies were buried in the old graveyard and obtained their permission to remove the gloomy headstones and substitute small artistic bronze plaques laid flat in the grass.

Today Forest Lawn has seven and a half miles of paved roads, twenty-eight buildings, eighty miles of underground water system and drains, and more than twenty thousand trees and shrubs. The undertaking establishment and the Great Mausoleum are built of steel and concrete, resistant to fire and earthquakes. The Mausoleum contains enough steel and concrete to erect a sixty-story office building and its foundations go thirty-three feet deep into solid rock. The memorial-park idea embodied in it is being copied extensively.

On the back fly leaf of one of the pamphlets his staff gets out is Eaton's key to success:

There is a master key to success . . . with which no man can fail. Its name is Simplicity. Simplicity, I mean, in the sense of reducing to the simplest possible terms every problem that besets us. That almost any man can succeed, if only he will simplify everything in his life to the nth degree, has been my working theory for 40 years. As a very young man, I stumbled across this great fundamental truth; that anything which is complicated is wrong. Simplicity rules everything worthwhile. . . . Whenever I have met a business proposition, which after taking thought, I could not reduce to simplicity, I have left it alone.

Forest Lawn employs more than five hundred persons, who gather monthly at meetings which have been described as "pious, punctual, perfect." Attendance is compulsory.

Employes are offered cash prizes for suggestions that might better the service. The "find" in this category was a man who in

1944 came up with the payoff idea that grave sizes be reduced from 33⅓ square feet to 30 square feet. The suggestion was immediately put into practice. It meant more bodies and therefore more money to the acre.

"Interment space," as it is called, is the ogre that plagues the management. If the present rate of body planting is maintained—approximately five thousand a year—space will be available in Forest Lawn for only twenty-five years more. These plots are sold for from forty-five dollars to $450 each, depending on the location, and the purse of the purchaser. They represent an impressive increase in value. When Eaton took over the rundown cemetery, the property was valued at around a thousand dollars an acre. On the basis of eleven hundred grave plots to the acre and assuming the average selling price to be $150 per plot, Forest Lawn has increased the value of its gently rolling hillsides from one thousand dollars to $165,000 per acre.

To a restless man such as Eaton, whose key to success is simplicity and who believes implicitly in planning ahead, it is clear that his statuary orchard will one day be full up. Already steps have been taken to alleviate this grave shortage. Forest Lawn had acquired the 486-acre Providencia Rancho, a beautiful section on the north bank of the anemic Los Angeles River in Burbank. Across the stream is Warner Brothers Studio. A brassie shot away is the expensive Lakeside Country Club, where film stars play. Near by is the handsome hillside Barham Boulevard residence section. When the plans were made known, opposition immediately formed and Forest Lawn's application for a zoning permit was turned down by the Planning Commission. One of these days, perhaps, Dr. Eaton's Dream No. 2 may come true—twenty-five years is a long time.

The feud between Forest Lawn and other Southern California undertakers began in 1933. The Memorial Park contended that it was not receiving its fair share of interments, that rival firms were granting commissions and other inducements which it would not duplicate. In its own defense, **Forest Lawn** established its own mortuary within its sacred grounds. No more, it advertised, need bereaved families endure the torture of weaving through Los Angeles' mad traffic, behind a hearse. The case was fought through the state Supreme Court before it could operate its own undertaking plant. The package deal it is now able to offer—"One telephone call in time of need"—is a deadly advantage over its rivals, an unbeatable exploitation point.

And to those who talk disparagingly of its statuary, of the obscenity and vulgarity and thinly cloaked unctuousness, there is another talking point. Residents of Los Angeles, in a large measure, revere their dead. And those who visit Forest Lawn to place flowers on the graves of loved ones, or those who are merely tourists, are awed and impressed with the lush, planned beauty and the planned reverence of the place. No matter how noisy the opposition, **a thousand weekly visitors to a cemetery can't be wrong.**

• 12 •

Do you know what Hell is? Come in and hear our organist.—SIGN ON WEST ADAMS STREET CHURCH

IN TERMS of what they might be, Los Angeles newspapers are undistinguished and uninspired. They do very well, by column and wire, with what is happening in New York, Washington, Moscow, and Upper Mongolia but they seem reluctant to tackle Los Angeles except superficially, in terms of the usual murders, plane crashes, freaks, floods, movie romances, riots, and sex crimes. Sex crimes, of course, are a house specialty. When an actor seduces a pretty girl who hollers or a wife chopper goes to trial, the papers bow to no others in the matter of blood and thunder.

But there is no awareness that Los Angeles is itself a big story. The papers rarely display any civic-consciousness free from political or economic taint. Seldom does a paper attempt to analyze the seething forces within the city, the attitudes of its people, or the points of view of the great men of science, art, writing, motion pictures, architecture, and medicine who live there, in relation to similar forces, attitudes, and points of view elsewhere.

Perhaps the editors have become touchy about the city's superfluous publicity as a crackpot paradise, now long outdated, and believe the answer is simply to play dead.

A better explanation, probably, is that they are bound by policy or their ideas of newspaper significance have become outmoded or dulled.

This sterility, happily enough, does not extend to working newsmen. They're a competent, alert bunch, fast with their facts and as imaginative as their colleagues in other cities; but they just work there, as the saying goes. They don't make the rules.

Los Angeles, however, isn't a good newspaper town. It has no press club, for one thing, and newsmen have no identity as a group. The excessive distances, rather than any lack of gregariousness, are the reason. They live in Altadena and Santa Monica and El Monte and Inglewood.

It would be wrong, nevertheless, to intimate that L.A. newsmen are a bunch of sissies who rush right home to the wife and kiddies after a hard day over a hot typewriter. They drink their quota and are driven by the same pixie spirit as all reporters. Over the years they've hung up as daffy a saga as you'll find.

A news editor named Ed was of the old school: tough, tyrannical, violent. One night after the home edition had gone to press, he penciled out or "killed" the type which would be replaced by later news in the next edition, then got up from his chair and disappeared. An hour passed, then two hours. The men on the rim became apprehensive. The deadline was almost at hand and no substitute copy had been set to replace the "kills." Should they risk Ed's temper, and being fired, by sending copy to the composing room to fill the holes? They didn't. Fifteen minutes before deadline Ed, roaring drunk, limped in, sidled into the slot, and slowly fed copy to the boys on the rim. One copy reader, more daring than the rest, noticed Ed wasn't himself.

"What's the matter, something wrong?" he asked.

"Aw, that God-damned wife of mine shot me in the belly," said Ed casually. "She's been threatening to do it for a long time and when I went over to the hotel just now she finally did it."

After being shot he had gotten into a cab and stopped at Georgia Street Hospital to get bandaged and taped up. But he made it plain he wasn't angry at his wife: "What I'm afraid of is I won't be able to hold my liquor now," he said. He grimaced, as though in pain. "Hey, I can feel it running out the hole now," he said in alarm.

Al Morrow was the night city editor on the lobster trick: midnight to 8 A.M. After a tough night in which he cleaned up a murder case, several suicides, and some traffic accidents for the "Late News" morning edition, he went home dead-tired and immediately fell asleep. Around 11 A.M. the phone rang. Mrs. Morrow explained to the caller that Mr. Morrow worked nights and that he was sleeping. The caller said it was terribly important so she roused him. Morrow stumbled to the phone and muttered a sleepy "Hello." The caller went into his dance. He was Mr. Jones of the Crystal Point Beach Club which was offering to a selected list of persons a greatly reduced rate in memberships which included many wonderful privileges—swimming pool, tennis and golf, horseback riding—and since Morrow's name had been highly recommended, did he want to take advantage of this amazing opportunity while he could? Morrow was about to make use of his extensive vocabulary but caught himself. He told Mr. Jones he was quite interested but wanted a day or two to think it over and see whether he could handle the financial end. He took Jones' number and promised to call. The next morning around 3 A.M. the phone rang at the Jones residence. Mrs. Jones told the caller that her husband was asleep and she hesitated about waking him as he was awfully tired. It was a matter of life and death, said Morrow. When Jones came on the line, Morrow said: "Hello Jonesy, this is Morrow—remember, you called me yesterday and I said I'd call you back. What's the matter, you sound sleepy? I'm at work now and I thought I'd give you a ring. I wanted to tell you that I don't want any of your God-damned beach-club memberships. But you sound sort of drowsy: tell you what, I'll call you back for the next two or three nights about this time so you get it straight. Good night!"

A managing editor had a daughter with theatrical ambitions

and one day she got a part in a play. The M.E. called Burrows, the drama critic, into his office and asked him to cover the opening performance. When Burrows returned from the theater around 11 P.M. the M.E., beaming over his glasses, asked "How was she?"

"She stinks," said Burrows, "and I'm going to say so in my review."

The M.E., thinking he was kidding, said: "Now I don't want to see the copy, of course." But he watched Burrows finish his review and send it to the composing room. He called an office boy to bring a proof and was aghast to read that Burrows had written scorchingly of his daughter's alleged acting. He waddled to the drama office and said: "You can't run this, I'm killing it." Burrows dejectedly poured himself another drink from the bottle he always kept in his office for such depressing occasions. But when the M.E. left for the night, Burrows sneaked into the composing room and put the objectionable paragraphs back into the form. Thus came to a close two promising careers: an actress' and a drama critic's.

One paper requires each of its beat reporters to turn in one feature story each week in addition to regular coverage. Now no one is more resourceful than a beat reporter, but there are days when the best newsmen run dry. On such a day, a hotel-beat man invented the colorful Sir Roger Wheebury, of Wheebury by the Sea, England. Sir Roger, ostensibly stopping at the Biltmore, consented to be interviewed on the alarming decline of the mustache cup. He was in America trying to revive interest in this stalwart, traditional male item. When the story appeared, with a cartoon, a sudden demand was created for these relics and one store, which had been trying to unload them for years, cleaned up.

During prohibition, Los Angeles was no better and no worse than other big cities. You couldn't tell the bootleggers or hijackers from the policemen without a program or a grand-jury indictment. This was the golden era of the police reporter, who went along on raids to obtain a proper share of the spoils and generally conducted himself like a king. One such reporter was John Malone, tough, forthright, smart, quixotic. One night after work he and Jack Fulton, a comrade made in the same mold, visited a place in the foreign section where liquor was not only obtainable but could be cadged gratis. They drank and talked the night through, mostly about what wonderful fellows they were. Fulton, though, kept interrupting to remark he was irritated with the police department. He had been given a citation for parking too long in one place. Around 9 A.M. they weaved out of the bistro. Malone went to his office; Fulton headed for the police station, then on First Street between Broadway and Hill Street. At First and Broadway, Fulton saw a policeman directing traffic and, without ado, stepped up and punched him in the face. The officer escorted him to jail. An hour later Malone learned of his dear friend's incarceration. He called on the Deputy Chief of Police and demanded that his friend, a peace-loving citizen who wouldn't hurt a tarantula, be released and the brutal officer who had assaulted him be sent to the sticks. The deputy chief investigated and said he was afraid the facts were against Fulton. Malone stormed. They couldn't do this to his pal. He went into the jail cell where Fulton was sleeping off what was wrong with him and tried to rouse him. Fulton abusively told him to go away. Malone persisted, trying to make clear to Fulton that they'd thrown the book at him. Fulton wanted only to be left alone. Malone pulled once more at his shoulder and Fulton, in a single loose-jointed move, got up snarling and threw a terrific uppercut. "Keep that man in jail!" shouted Malone, his lip bleeding. "Don't let him out; he's a vicious criminal, a menace to the public. He hit an officer and now he has struck me, his good friend. I'll sign the complaint."

I'll never forget an obituary ritual inaugurated on the copy desk by Jim Parent, the greatest news editor I ever knew. Short, broad, bald, and bespectacled, Jim belied the deep sense of irony that was within him. Suddenly in the city room, over the clatter of typewriters, the mumblings into telephones, the cries of "Boy!" there came a chant, led by Parent, a basso profundo. It meant that a piece of copy had arrived at the desk stating that some tycoon or captain of industry, or, as later, some local heel whose life had been an exemplary pattern of legal embezzlement, bigotry, or hypocrisy, had passed on. In chorus, the glum copy readers sang:

> He robbed the poor,
> He robbed the rich,
> And now he's dead,
> The son of a bitch!

There are times when honest reporters have to hold their noses over what they are unable to write because they can't prove it. Such an instance occurred at a coroner's inquest into the fatal shooting of a man in a beer joint. The evidence was all against the defendant, a bad boy around town, but the jury absolved him of blame. It seemed the defendant did the dirty work for a politician, who naturally didn't want his boy to get his reputation smeared, so when the coroner sent out a man, as is the custom, to pick six unknown citizens off the street to serve on the coroner's jury the politician was prepared. He had hired forty men to walk up and down the street on the block where the coroner's deputy picked his jurors. Six of the forty were selected and the hand-picked group unhesitatingly brought in a verdict of justifiable homicide. For their walk in the sun all forty received five dollars each. The jurors got a five-dollar bonus.

During the depression, the editor of a paper got hold of a new monthly magazine which had a wonderful article on technology. If the plan were put in effect, a new era of concentrated efficiency, leisure, and happiness was inevitable. Fired with enthusiasm, the editor called in his managing editor and asked that his most competent reporter be assigned to handle the subject. The reporter, a middle-aged veteran of rewrite batteries all over the land, was given the article to read, and instructed to hop it up into page-one stuff daily until further notice. Meanwhile, the editor wired the magazine for any additional material it had on the subject. The first few days the reporter bore up bravely and banged out sensational stories. Circulation climbed. Everyone wanted more money for less work and leisure. But no more material came from the magazine and after two weeks of rewriting the same tired article the reporter got a hunted look. Oddly enough, about this time he began to smell better, as if he were spending more time at the barber shop. Toward the end of the third week, he told the M.E. he better be taken off the assignment before he blew his top. He was told to stay put, boss's orders. A few days before the end of a month of rewriting the same article, though by now local clubs desiring the new leisure were forming, the reporter came roaring through the office, insulting one and all. He was fired before he reached his desk. Next day, as his successor was cleaning out the desk, he found forty-three empty bottles of fragrant Aqua Velva which, taken internally, had almost but not quite sustained the unfortunate reporter through his ordeal.

A certain city editor through the years has developed the theory that he got the best work out of his staff by bluntly insulting them, undermining their morale, and threatening to fire them. He doesn't know it but those who have had to deal with his diabolic sabotage have divided themselves into three groups. One small, aging, but compact unit readily admits he *was* a heel, although another phrase is used. A second group says firmly he *is* a heel. The third, by far the largest, contends he *was, is,* and *always will be* one, and have elected a president, vice president, and secretary to keep alive this vivid hate.

A man about town got off the beam and spent a quiescent evening in the Van Nuys Jail on complaint of his wife who claimed he beat her. One paper, reporting the incident, stated he was "sobering up" in the jail. Next day the playboy's attorney called the paper's M.E. demanding a retraction and talking libel. His client, he said severely, had spent a little time in the clink on a disturbing-the-peace charge but even the arrest report made no mention of intoxication. Furthermore, he asked that the retraction be read him over the phone before it was printed. The M.E. called in the reporter who had handled the story and said: "You got us into this, get us out." The reporter returned to his desk and wrote: "The *Daily Blat* stated erroneously yesterday that John Doe was sobering up in the Van Nuys jail after, according to her complaint, he beat his wife. This was incorrect and the *Daily Blat* is happy to make a correction. John Doe was not drunk when he beat his wife, he was in full possession of his faculties." The reporter dutifully called the attorney and read him the corrected version, stating it would appear on the identical page and position as the previous story. The attorney, catching on quickly, said maybe they better forget the whole thing. The reporter was reluctant to do so, explaining that this M.E., a hard man, was ordering him to make the retraction and he was going to make it, but when he got the desired plaintive note in the barrister's voice, he reluctantly agreed.

On the night before Christmas, some years ago, Jackson Berger, a city editor, discovered that the yuletide poem that ran traditionally on page one, second section, had not come in. It was to go with a picture of the Babe of Bethlehem for which a film studio had posed a glamorous star and an infant prodigy, both under contract. Jack telephoned John Steven McGroarty, California poet laureate, at his home in the green Verdugo hills, and said briskly: "Look, Mac, we've got to have a poem on the Nativity for the home edition. I'll switch you to rewrite. Let me have it in fast takes."

"But Mr. Berger," said McGroarty, a gentle old soul, "a poem, on the Nativity—that takes a little time."

"Hell, you've had two thousand years," said Berger. "Start dictating!"

During the war, as city editor of another paper, Berger figured in another episode involving Christmas and a snappy last line. Jack Carey, one of his reporters, in a Christmas Eve fit of despondency, drank a quart of tequila and decided to end it all, by inhaling monoxide fumes from the exhaust of his car. He started the motor, then stretched out on a pillow under the exhaust pipe. He lay there, according to his own estimate, for an hour and all he got was a premature hang-over, a shower of annoying gasoline and oil globules in the eyes, ears, nose, and throat, and proof that his car needed a valve-and-ring job. Next morning he went to work and approached the city desk where Berger was busy editing copy.

"You know," said Carey, "I tried to commit suicide."

"Yeah," said Berger, without the question mark, not looking up from his copy.

"I turned on the motor of my car and got in back and inhaled for a long time," said Carey.

"Yeah," repeated Berger, still intent on his work.

"I sucked up fumes for an hour and nothing happened," said Carey, trying frantically to impress the boss. "I'm still alive."

"Yeah," said Berger. "The God-damn gas you get nowadays isn't good for anything."

A woman called the city editor of one of the papers and said, in a worried voice: "I understand you have someone there who talks to alcoholics."

"Yeah," said the city editor, glancing at his staff, "we talk to our own but it doesn't do any good." Then he gave her what she wanted: the address of Alcoholics Anonymous.

While the eleven-million-dollar post-office and Federal building was under construction in 1938, the newsmen covering the beat from cramped quarters in the Pacific Electric Building got hold of a blueprint of their future quarters and let out anguished cries. It had no private plumbing. They rushed to their type-writers and wrote indignant tongue-in-cheek letters to F.D.R., cabinet members, senators, and congressmen. They deplored the aggravating situation they would face in the new building, making the point that after they'd sat through some boring Federal Court testimony, nature called loudly and suddenly and would not take "No" or "Maybe" for an answer. The letters inundated Washington and became a *cause célèbre*. The assistant to the secretary of the treasury, cornered, issued a "Can do." The Treasury Department procurement director, wondering what the fuss was all about, promised an adjustment. Wheels turned; plans were revised. Today the press room is the most palatial of any in the civic center, with chromium, tile, celotex, and air conditioning. The reporters, Jack Greenlees, Ray Hanners, Bill Keefe, Arthur C. Todd, and Taylor Trumbo, were very happy about the whole thing but they tried to keep their cozy nook a secret. Otherwise city editors might expect more glamour in their stories.

Police reporters are generally fellows who spend their lives around the press room. They talk tough but they aren't very. Joe Ross was an exception. Large and loose-framed, he kept in pretty good shape. One time, hearing that jiu-jitsu lessons were being given police recruits, he enrolled and attended classes diligently. Thereafter he was always trying out holds on his luckless press-room companions, beating his chest, and flexing his muscles. The instructor may or may not have eased up on Ross when the going got rough but when the day of graduation came, Joe also was given his diploma. It was a gala day for him, and to celebrate it he walked into the press room with a jug in one hand and the scroll in the other. Some hours later, still proud and happy, he went home. His wife, seeing his exuberant mood, reminded him that the Smiths, next-door neighbors, were coming in. That was fine, said Joe. When they arrived, Joe exhibited his scroll and he and Smith had a few drinks. Suddenly Joe realized that Smith was a tiny fellow, an admirable subject to test out his jiu-jitsu holds. After more drinks, Smith was agreeable. Joe lifted him aloft, whirled him around, and let go. Smith dropped behind the sofa, bumped his head, and went out like a light. Joe, recovering from whirling, looked around for him and was dismayed to find Smith had apparently walked out on him. He said something impolite about a fellow who would drink your liquor, then duck without even a thank you. Disgusted, Joe went to bed. Around midnight, Mrs. Smith, who had gone home, telephoned to inquire about her husband. She was told he had gone home an hour before. A search of the neighborhood was launched, then a reluctant check of the hospitals, the jails, and the coroner by Joe, still disgruntled by his guest's bad manners. At length Joe returned to bed. It was now around 2 A.M. He awakened, hearing noises. A burglar, perhaps, was in the house. Revolver in hand, he advanced on the living room and flashed on the lights. There was Smith, trying to extricate himself from behind the sofa.

A reporter on a beach paper stirred up a series of scandals by visiting water-front dives, eating and drinking with bad boys, and writing what he learned. Naturally his hot copy curtailed the activities of the wrong-money crowd. One night, to discourage him, a bartender slipped him a mickey finn. He became very ill—which is what mickeys are supposed to do, but he came back again and again. Each time he was given another mickey. He became sick each time but figured that was the penalty for getting his material and a little high. For though he's a sharpie otherwise, the reporter never heard of mickey finns.

One L.A. paper is hopelessly addicted to dog stories. The staff is briefed to ferret out at least one a day. The paper's police reporter telephoned his office one day that a dog had bit a boy's lip. Did the desk want to send a photographer to the receiving hospital for a picture? "Gosh, no," said the city desk man. "We're the friends of dogs down here, not the enemies!"

A police reporter was arrested at Seventh and Hill for spectacular, riotous drunken driving, a felony charge, meaning San Quentin if convicted. The reporter's friends rallied, decided the best was none too good in such a grave situation, and obtained the services of an attorney known as "The Great." At the trial sixteen policemen testified that the reporter was drunk. The Great called into play the suave courtroom technique that earned him his title and the reporter was acquitted. The reporter could scarcely believe it.

"My friend," said the Great, "you are not guilty of driving while intoxicated."

"But I thought I was," said the reporter, and he pondered on the awful majesty of the law. Why, a horrible injustice had been narrowly averted! He shuddered. Turning to the Great, he said: "Sir, you have proved beyond any doubt that I was not drunk on the occasion specified by the police. You have proved further I am a model of sobriety. Obviously, I have never heretofore been drunk, though these accusations have been made—wrongfully I now realize. Thank you very much. Now I am going out and get drunk for the first time."

An alert city editor became attracted to a story from San Diego about a girl there who had been roused from a sleeping-sickness coma by violin music, and assigned a reporter to whip up a local story of the same nature. The reporter located a six-year-old boy who had been in a coma for three months in Camarillo State Hospital. He arranged to take along the boy's mother, who lived near Los Angeles, and after some difficulty got hold of a lady fiddler who could make the trip. Darkness had settled when they got started. It was near midnight when the reporter knocked on the door at Camarillo. A stern woman opened it and said suspiciously: "Yes?"

"Lady," said the reporter, "all I want to do is play a little violin music for one of your patients."

"Oh, that's fine," said the stern lady, "come right in."

As he entered, two husky guards grabbed the reporter and hustled him to a private room. At length he convinced them he was indeed a reporter, not an escaped patient, and that the mother and violinist were outside. They came in and, as the violinist played, the boy became more fully awake than in weeks. The mother was supremely happy, to the point that on her return home she told a neighbor of the experiment. The neighbor caught the contagion and phoned an opposition newspaper which broke the story and the reporter's heart.

During the war, newsman Joseph Saldana went to Washington on a government assignment. On arrival there he wired an L.A. friend: "Next time you're browsing along Main Street, see if you can find me a cheap Phi Beta Kappa key. A guy is lost here without one dangling from a watch chain." He was shopping on his own, he stated, for a briefcase, in which he had nothing to carry except his lunch. He became excruciatingly aware of his great lack at a conference for fourth-, fifth- and sixth-string bigshots. He found himself encircled by a crush of watch-chain and briefcase boys. "That was a fine review the *New York Times* gave your new book," said one.

"Thanks," said the second. "How's yours doing?"

And so on. At length one asked Saldana: "Written anything lately?"

"No," he mumbled, swallowing cigarette smoke, "haven't done anything for a couple of years."

"What did you do last?" pursued the *littérateur*. "Oh, just light stuff. Chicago publisher," he said apologetically.

He didn't mention it was a detective-story magazine, but if he had had a fraternity key bouncing off his bosom, he could have turned this retreat into a counterattack. Because he used to be a police reporter. He can tell better true stuff than their lies.

While in a bar in Mazatlan, Darr Smith and his wife got to talking with a young Mexican. Soon they bought each other drinks and proposed toasts. These things are common in Mexico. But each time, Darr observed, the Mexican proposed the same toast: "Meestair Smees, friends until we have to be enemies."

"What's this enemy business?" he asked.

The Mexican explained he was a nationalist. Americans, he said, were traditional enemies. Someday his people would fight and take back all we stole from them. Pointing an accusing finger, he charged: "You stole from us California, Texas, New Mexico, and Arizona! I demand that you return them." Another beer cooled him off momentarily but soon he flared up again. "Meestair Smees, where you come from hah?"

"Los Angeles," said Meestair Smees.

The Mexican became dreamy-eyed. "Ah," he said softly, "Los Angeles was once Mexico," Then, pounding the bar: "Give it back!"

Meestair Smees disclaimed responsibility for the theft but the Mexican would have none of such honey-tongued equivocation. He turned somewhat viciously to Darr's wife and asked: "Meesis Smees, where you come from, hah?"

"Chicago," she said.

"Ah, you are good, you are fine American," he said happily. "You steal nothing from us."

In 1938, when Hitler grabbed Austria, a news editor yelled for the office boy to bring him whatever photos relating to the subject were on file. The boy brought a batch of them, including a magnificent picture of an Austrian consul lowering his nation's flag and a German consul raising the Nazi standard. The news editor heatedly discussed the picture with his colleagues a few minutes, then yelled at the office boy: "Haven't you got anything with women in it?"

There was the time an installment of a syndicated serial story failed to arrive by air mail. The managing editor called in the paper's top feature man and gibed: "You're always bringing in fancy angles; now sit down and bat me out an installment of this serial. You've got two hours before deadline." The reporter had read snatches of the story and, with his usual confidence, wrote the installment and it was printed. Next day the M.E., furious, summoned him. "Do you know what you did in that business you wrote yesterday? You sent the hero to Europe." The reporter was nonplussed. He explained weakly he thought the guy he'd given a typewriter ride to Europe was a minor character. "O.K., wise guy," said the M.E., dropping a handful of newly arrived installments into the waste-basket, "from here on it's your story. Finish it your way!"

In 1942, when the Japs were still pushing us around in the Pacific, a newspaperman dropped an attractive emblem into a metal salvage heap. It was the Order of the Rising Sun, famous Japanese decoration. Behind this simple act was a story. Some twenty years before, this newsman covered the state legislature in Sacramento. Domei, Japanese news agency, had a man there and the two became quite friendly. One day a Japanese baron visited Sacramento and the Domei man arranged a party in his honor for the correspondents. Each reporter found himself seated next to a Japanese. The newsman drew a navy lieutenant. Behind each chair was a Japanese girl. As toasts were proposed the lieutenant clinked glasses with the newsman and said "Bottoms up." Then the girls refilled their glasses. The dinner had fourteen courses and went on for hours. Between courses the lieutenant kept bottoms-upping with the reporter. After a while, through a heavy champagne fog, the reporter mused to himself: "Hey, what is this?" He didn't especially like the stuff, but the lieutenant persisted. Finally the meal was finished and everyone got up formally. The newsman somehow rose to his feet, only to see a waiter behind him with a tray. "Scotch and soda?" said the waiter brightly. The newsman, with champagne almost running out of his ears, was about to refuse when the lieutenant insisted. "Bottoms up," he muttered bravely, if unsteadily. By now, the newsman realized some kind of game was being played, but he was too far gone to remonstrate. The Jap lieutenant lifted the glass for his gulp but collapsed to the floor, out cold. The newsman was sipping methodically, studying this phenomenon, when the baron, who had been watching, rushed over, congratulated him on winning the drinking championship of the Japanese navy from the title-holder, then pinned on his breast the Order of the Rising Sun.

The Japanese invasion of the City Hall was quite another thing. It happened one spring night in 1944, when wartime restrictions were tight as could be. At night, only the Main Street entrance to the building is open and persons who have business there had to sign the register and be timed in and out. One day the checker-upper of the register discovered that seventeen Japs had entered the building the night before and had not checked out. Clearly they were saboteurs bent on giving the municipal seat a big swift kick. A fast sleuthing job uncovered the dirty work. Seemed the night police reporters had become bored. This is always a dangerous situation, for bored police reporters get playful ideas. The three of them, Pat Hogan, Walter Ames, and the Joseph Saldana mentioned before had signed in as usual, but, unobserved, had scribbled names like Tomo Yamamoto, Hidea Fujikawa, and Harold B. Nakamura. Then they sneaked out through a little-known basement exit and after a while came in again and signed different Japanese names. When they ran their score up to seventeen, they called it a night. The police, of course, called it something else.

The Iowa picnic is always a big news event of the year and the papers always cover it with story and pictures. One year the reporters came away with varying estimates of the attendance. The *Herald-Express* stated 100,000, the *Times*, 48,000, the

Examiner, 25,000. The *Daily News* wondered in print if the others were sending their circulation departments out to cover the event.

A seventy-six-year-old man, sitting on his front porch one night, was attacked and robbed by a bandit. He was rushed to the police hospital with a penknife imbedded in his head, penetrating his brain, necessitating an immediate operation. The flash went out to city desks and photographers were dispatched to the hospital.

At one office, the desk man said over the phone to his police reporter: "We won't have a photog available for at least half an hour. How long will that guy hold out?"

"Just a minute, I'll find out," said the reporter. He asked the patient, who was nonchalantly smoking a cigarette, how about it.

"O.K., he says he'll wait," the reporter said. He did, and recovered.

In the midst of fantastic informality, the mausoleumlike California Club retains an austere dignity. One of its regular events is the annual Lincoln Club dinner February 12. One year, as a city editor was about to assign a reporter to cover it, he noticed in fine print in the corner of the invitation DINNER COATS. Mockery seized the city room.

"I thought Abe Lincoln abolished sleevery," ranted one reporter.

"God must dislike dinner coats, he made so few of them!" misquoted another.

"General Grant, you are relieved of your command!" orated a third, talking to a blank wall. "Imagine wearing a soldier's uniform!"

The reporter who attended, wearing slacks, was admitted after long argument, only through the persuasive powers of the one newsman who appeared properly dressed.

The management of one paper, to combat dull copy, designated a staff member "The Sparkle Editor." His job was to inject brightness and gaiety into the eight-point type. He quit suddenly one day, after receiving, from a New York jewelry firm, some samples of silver polish. Fun-loving comrades had arranged it.

After a riotous weekend, two reporters stumbled into the police press room and pooled their resources, nearly a dollar, enough for half a pint of restorative. They dispatched a Saint Bernard to the nearest grog shop and were about to bend an elbow when a hot call came in: a shooting at Sunset Boulevard and Alvarado Street. They rushed to the address, only to find the call a false alarm. By this time they were shaking to pieces. Quieting his flutters, one reporter reached in his pocket for the bottle. It jumped out of his hand and smashed. Just then a woman came by, wheeling a baby carriage, and saw the heart-rending spectacle. "You poor boys," she said. From under the pillow of the sleeping infant she produced a pint of whisky. Each took a swig and instantly felt renewed interest in world affairs. The lady screwed on the top, replaced the bottle under the pillow, and wheeled off, her face lit up with the smile of the Good Samaritan.

During the Shaw administration, the palatial Clover Club, located on the Sunset Strip, was a gambling rendezvous, patronized by film people who liked to play for high stakes. Inevitably, a siege of righteousness gripped the city and it was raided. While the law took names and confiscated evidence, Casey Shawhan, a *Times* reporter, interested himself in the pretty poker and roulette chips. They were inlaid with the clover-leaf emblem and made a quiet, clinking, expensive sound. Casey remembered that the dime-store chips in use at the press-room penny-ante game were dog-eared and their color was almost obliterated, so he took a few along as souvenirs. Some weeks later he received a frantic call from the manager of the club. The missing chips had been traced to Casey and the manager was anxious to get them back. The club hoped to reopen, he said, and the chips represented a playing value of fifteen thousand dollars, so naturally he didn't want to be embarrassed in the event they got in the wrong hands and someone tried to cash them. If Casey returned them, the manager promised, he would receive a special initialed set for his personal use. Casey declined. The press-room boys, in their penny-ante game, had become accustomed to them and didn't want to go back to the cheap dime-store brand.

A motion-picture executive regularly visited the race track at Agua Caliente and invariably distinguished himself for malicious conduct. The business of squaring his beefs somehow landed in the lap of Al Sisto, a sports writer. One day, the owner of a large stable of horses asked Sisto to help him name a colt he was bringing out as a two-year-old. "How about calling him Running Heel," suggested Sisto, suddenly inspired. For years thereafter, each time the horse was entered in a race, Sisto telephoned the film man's secretary and left word that the horse named for her boss was running. To this day, when the horse is mentioned in the film man's presence, he goes into a war dance.

A malingering newsman, detailed on a special assignment for a few days, phoned his city editor from home, assuring him the story he was working on was coming along fine.

"Where are you now?" asked the city editor.

"I'm down here at the Hall of Records digging out some material," lied the reporter.

"Well, I'm glad it's coming along all right," said the boss. "By the way, where did you say you were?" The reporter gave a sordid picture of how he was working his fingers to the bone, painstakingly sifting through dusty tomes. "O.K.," said the city editor, "but will you tell that baby there in the Hall of Records to quit crying into the telephone."

For the last dozen years, Charles F. (Nick) Carter has been a publicity man at the R.K.O. studio. For some two decades before that he was one of the nation's topnotch newsmen, serving on papers in Texas, California, and Colorado and on the old *New*

York World. An incident that helped convince him that he should seek other work occurred during Aimee Semple McPherson's disappearance, reappearance, and subsequent embroilment with the law. At the time, Nick was a reporter for the *Herald-Express,* which was committed to the policy of sensationalizing Sister Aimee's every move; object: circulation. Nick's job was to keep the pot boiling, which meant hopping up at the most trifling details. When Aimee materialized out of the desert at Agua Prieta and returned to Los Angeles, she was summoned by the county grand jury to testify to charges that she had conspired to defeat justice, a loose accusation at best. There was some question that anyone in public office really wanted to prosecute her, for she held in the palm of her hand the twenty thousand votes of her devoted Four Square Gospel congregation, enough to swing most municipal elections.

One day, Nick was at his desk, beating out a story of Aimee's appearance before the grand jury. He had finished two pages of it, which had been rushed to the city desk to make an edition. All at once, in mid-sentence, Nick gagged. The hypocrisy of it all was too much for him. He got up from his chair, put on his hat and coat, shouted "I quit," and headed for the door.

Bill Levings, the city editor and a hard man, demanded where he was going without finishing the story. "You're liable to get fired," he said.

"You can't fire me, I quit," said Nick, and walked out.

Next day, Jack Campbell, the managing editor, summoned Nick and asked what the idea was. Nick explained he had become allergic to Aimee. He had written about her day after day and seemed to have acquired a nauseous condition at the mention of her name. Campbell persuaded him to return to work on Nick's own condition that he never write another story about her. Nick did, but he was never the same again.

There's a fantastic saga of stories about William Randolph Hearst and his whims. They're told, over a drink, with weary incredulity by ex-night city editors of the L.A. *Examiner*. They have to do with his unearthly requests, which are, of course, commands, at ungodly hours. Contrary to general belief, the publisher's castle at San Simeon, some three hundred miles north, is no ivory tower. He is always in close touch with his papers. The editions are flown up to him as they roll from the presses and he has been known to telephone, on receipt of an edition, and instruct an editor to fire the copy reader who wrote some tiny headline on page 26 which gave him offense. In some cases, the man has been summarily discharged, but rehired the next day.

Mostly, Hearst's requests are for certain midnight snacks not readily obtainable at San Simeon. One night, he telephoned a night city editor, much the same as a housewife telephones her grocer, and said: "I want six broilers. Got that?"

"Yes, Mr. Hearst."

"And I want twenty-four frankfurters."

"Yes, Mr. Hearst."

"And I want twenty-four rolls, not the round kind, understand, the long kind."

"Yes, Mr. Hearst."

"Then I want twenty-four ice creams. I want them done as Mickey Mouse and Donald Duck. Understand?"

"Yes, Mr. Hearst."

"And I want one bottle of rhubarb soda; not plain soda, rhubarb soda. Got it straight?"

"Yes, Mr. Hearst."

"Send them up on the plane with the twelve o'clock papers."

The staff was regimented into spirited action. They woke up merchants, bullied soft-drink entrepreneurs. Eventually, they rounded up everything except the rhubarb soda. To his surprise, the night city editor didn't get fired for the omission.

Bootjackers are free-lance newsboys, with foghorn voices, who invade residential districts at night. Sometimes they fudge a little in what they yell. One night a desk man received a number of indignant calls from subscribers and finally called the night city editor of a rival paper. "Will you kindly tell your boys not to shout fabricated headlines?" he pleaded wearily. "People keep calling in to find out if it's true the world is coming to an end."

Early in 1945, a crew of workmen moved into the little boys' room at the *Herald-Express* and set about painting, bracing, and replacing. The staff was delighted and one reporter, Frank Fisk, with the solemnity that at times distinguishes the profession, put a notice on the bulletin board announcing the unprecedented improvement. Soon, other staff members added their tributes and comments, some Rabelaisian. Telegrams from the governor, the mayor, and other public figures appeared, commending the paper for its progressive attitude toward the finer things in life, such as plumbing: telegrams, of course, these gentlemen never heard of. Cap Marek, assistant city editor and a man of many moods, became haunted with the thought that the new installations might be completed without a niche being carved for posterity. He conveyed his fear to a few sympathetic friends and they swore they'd die before they'd let the improvement go unheralded, to say nothing of unexpressed. All agreed, nothing less than the full Hollywood-première treatment would do. The staff swept into action. On the great day, cocktails were served, there were music and entertainment by Red Nichols' band; the Pied Pipers with Stan Kenton at the piano; Lee Tracy, who once got in trouble in Mexico while watching a parade; Doodles Weaver; Jack LaRue; Vince Barnett, and a few winos from a bar down at the corner who happened to wander in. At the witching hour, as photo flash bulbs sparkled and the band blew a hot fanfare, Noel O'Neill, beautiful Paramount starlet, stepped up and daintily snipped a huge ribbon placed across the door marked MEN, through which portal Jack LaRue walked a moment later: the first man to use the new facilities. Hits of the celebration, in addition to the photo of LaRue as trail blazer, were a cancan dancer and a new lyric written especially for the occasion by Bill Oliver, movie critic and composer, to the tune "Oh, Johnny!"

A newsman named Bill died and several of his comrades were at his funeral. During the service, the mourners seemed to hear a curious gurgling sound. They looked around, but couldn't place it, but as the minister finished committing the departed to the grave, the sound rose to an eerie holding and it was traced to Tom Higgs, a veteran police reporter. He was asked what the devil the idea was. Tom proudly exhibited his new hearing aid. "I got the preacher all right and the music came in swell," he explained exultantly, "so I turned it up to see if I could bring in old Bill!"

*Not responsible for headline readers who fall out of
their cars.*—NOTICE ON PAPER RACK AT BEVERLY
BOULEVARD AND VERMONT AVENUE

SOME of my colleagues in the observation business hold that
for awareness and understanding their preference is bartenders. I'll take newsboys. These wise and worldly gentlemen—
they're never boys—have always seemed to me the real critics of
the human race.

My favorite was one-legged Sammy Harwitz, who for years
before he died sold *Examiners* at Sixth and Main Streets and ran
the corner like a ward politician. Sam lost a leg in a railroad accident in Colorado and gained a philosophy: the philosophy of
complete, objective acceptance. The simple business of being
alive among people was to him a sheer joy. When he finished
peddling his papers, he hung around the block drinking in the
sights and the conversation.

Like all good newsboys, Sam made up his own ad libs. They
never necessarily reflected the headlines that happened to be on
the edition he was selling.

He had several standbys. One was: "Oh read about it—she
said she wouldn't, but she did!" Another: "He said she did! She
said she didn't! He's dead!"

Sam's corner was outside the busy Pacific Electric Station, in
his day a murky, barnlike maze containing the usual ticket windows, magazine and popcorn stands, restaurants, checkroom and
lost-article counters, and people rushing to and from interurban
cars and busses. It has been modernized in recent months and
now fluorescent lights and marble brighten the place.

Then as now the station was the hello-and-good-by terminal for servicemen and their girl friends, occasionally on the impromptu basis dictated by the fact that it is a step away from the honky-tonk atmosphere of Main Street and Skid Row. One time after midnight a coupé roared up to the curb and a sailor asked Sam if the last car had left for the harbor. Sam told him he could probably make it if he ran. The sailor, knowing failure meant missing inspection and possibly the brig, nevertheless gallantly bade the lady at the wheel a tender adieu and galloped off. In the flash of the coupé door opening and closing, Sam blushed all the way down to his crutch: the lady didn't have on a stitch of clothing.

One night a drunk weaved up to him, leaned on his crutch, and said: "Say, I'm going to give you a buck, see, and I don't know you from Adam."

"Well you ought to," said Sam. "I'm dressed differently."

Another time, a girl who had waited half an hour at the corner said to Sam: "I was supposed to meet a machinist's mate second class off the *Oklahoma* at nine-thirty. Did you see anyone like that?" Sam said he'd seen about twenty of them. "Doggone it, I got a flock of bills to pay and he said he'd be here," she mourned. "Seemed like a nice guy too. I got to know him because he's on the *Oklahoma* and I'm from Oklahoma; the state, you know." She was thoughtful a moment, then her manner changed for the worse. "You know, now that I think of it, I'll bet he wasn't on the *Oklahoma* at all. Probably on the *North Dakota* or some other boat. Darn it, you just can't trust these foreigners!"

Around 4 A.M. a sailor appeared in front of the P.E. Station to catch his car to the harbor. Sam told him he was too early so he sat on the curb to wait. Meanwhile he improvised new words to an old chantey. The sound of his voice intoxicated him anew and he extracted from a suitcase a bottle of champagne and smashed it over the entrance to the building. The clash of breaking glass was timed perfectly with the chorus of his song which had become, repetitiously, "Here's to you, good old P.E." Having launched his ship and finding it didn't slide down the ways as in the newsreels, the sailor suddenly sobered.

"Hey newsboy," he yelled, "where can I get a drink?"

"You can't," said Sam, "they don't start selling it until six."

The sailor was suddenly horrified. "I couldn't buy anything anyway—I'm broke!" His mood changed to deep sadness. "I must have been nuts," he said. "I bust a five-dollar bottle of wine and now I don't have a cent." Sam eventually saved his life. He gave him a dime for a beer.

Four blocks away, at Fifth and Hill Streets, another newsboy, known as Cutie, for years made local history with a single imperishable cry. He was a little fellow but such were the acoustics of the corner and the penetrating quality of his voice that it reverberated against buildings two blocks away. Day after day, hour after hour, despite what was in the news, he shouted: "It won't be long now!" Cutie, whose real name was Milton Spellman, died suddenly in 1945 after an operation. He never knew that the last time he called his trade-mark phrase it had an ironic personal twist.

Early in March 1946, three prisoners escaped from the county jail in a week. The newsboy outside the Hall of Justice, where the jail is located, shouted: "Get a program, folks! You can't identify the escapees without a program!"

Some hustlers in the outlying sections also come up with provocative headlines. The boy at Wilshire and LaBrea authentically called: "Bull-aw-dy murder! He stabbed her twenty-three times!" He liked it so well he repeated it for days. On occasion the same newsboy and the other boy on the corner, who sells a rival sheet, yelled: "Extra! Two newsboys starve on La Brea!"

A newsboy at Wilshire and Fairfax uses a confidential approach. He stands between the traffic lanes and as the cars stop for the signal he confides to the drivers: "Got a good story tonight, mister. Seventy-five-year-old school girl kidnaped." But one night business wasn't very good. "What's the matter?" he asked the motorists. "Don't you like these headlines?"

Hollywood newsboys lean toward the spectacular and occasionally toward fantasy. Newsboy Eddie, at Hollywood Boulevard and Highland, has a standard cry: "Extra! Charley McCarthy commits suicide." The boy at Hollywood Boulevard and Cahuenga shouts: "Movie blondes heartbroken! Peroxide factory blows up!" Another favorite is "Donald Duck murdered in Boyle Heights!"

The evening editions of two papers on one occasion had conflicting headlines on Stalin. One stated that because of his inflexible attitude, war was imminent; the other that the threat of war had abated. At a Beverly Boulevard corner, as a result, two newsboys seemed to be engaged in a debate.

"Extra!" yelled one. "Europe prepares for war!"

"Oh read about it!" shouted the other. "War called off!"

In a little while, they settled down to a new routine. "Extra," roared No. One. "Stalin wants war!"

"Shame on you!" retorted the other. "He does not!"

A Sunset Boulevard newsboy, not doing too well with his headlines, kept shouting: "Hey, there's going to be another war. Don't anybody care?"

• 14 •

Big money did not immediately soften Edgar Rice Burroughs' hatred of modern life. His great aim was to escape from civilization, and as soon as he had the money, he went to Southern California.—SATURDAY EVENING POST, JULY 26, 1939

E VER eager to celebrate something, Los Angeles, on August 13, 1946, brought out the bands and the bunting to salute the one-hundredth birthday of the raising of the American flag over the city. In late afternoon, several thousand citizens gathered for the ceremony in front of the city's outstanding landmark, the twenty-story City Hall.

Against a backdrop of banners and lithographs depicting a century of progress, with Frank Sinatra leading, they raised their voices in "The Star-Spangled Banner."

Edward Arnold came to bat, narrating in his stirring, thunderous voice a musical drama, "Ode to Los Angeles," written by Dave Rose and Edward James. A fifty-piece orchestra and a twenty-voice choir accompanied him, with Meredith Willson directing.

Little Margaret O'Brien then stepped to the microphone and led the adoring throng in the Pledge of Allegiance to the Flag. Jane Powell sang "Californi-ay" and they hummed along with her.

As the last note died, an ox-drawn carreta, a two-wheeled wagonlike carriage, hove into view. It had taken three days to travel from San Pedro, twenty miles, accompanied by impressive newspaper accounts of its progress. Four pretty girls, wearing poke bonnets, 1846 style, were aboard. A few cynics in the audience were willing to wager they hadn't made the entire three-day trip.

As the girls were officially welcomed, two dark shapes stabbed the twilight with a swift whoosh and disappeared. They were jet-propelled P-8os, which had taken off from San Pedro two minutes before. In this awed moment, George Jessel, master of ceremonies, played it straight. "Then it took three days," he said. "Now it takes two minutes."

The sun was dipping behind the Santa Monica Mountains as Rear Admiral Lloyd J. Wiltse, commandant of the United States Naval Base at Terminal Island, presented the battle colors of the cruiser *Los Angeles* to Mayor Fletcher Bowron. The mayor in turn gave the flag to a color guard which raised it impressively on the City Hall flagpole. A dozen men in buckskins, in miners' and ranchers' plaids, and in army and navy uniforms of a century before stood at attention.

"The American way of life is the best way in the world," said Mayor Bowron, congratulating the citizens of Los Angeles on their city's growth.

"You share the heritage of the finest possible tradition," said Governor Earl Warren. "But regardless of its past, regardless of its present, you can look forward to the future with full confidence that here we will always have a happy place to live."

Dusk blanketed the civic center as the last infinitive had been said, happily unsplit, and everyone went home presumably filled with nostalgia and visions of a wonderful future.

But just a moment: exactly what was being celebrated here? Why, the raising of the first American flag in Los Angeles Pueblo by Commodore Robert F. Stockton and Lieutenant Colonel John C. Frémont! Didn't the carreta travel the very route taken by the commodore on his way to town?

Well, the history books don't tell it quite that way, or at least they don't put it that simply. To be blunt about it, the flag which was raised over the city August 13, 1846 failed to stay put.

The Mexican population, for purely personal reasons, didn't like it there. In 1846, the conquest of California from the unappreciative Mexicans was virtually complete. On July 7, Old Glory was set flying at Monterey and within a few weeks a veritable rash of flag-raising broke out in Sonoma, Santa Barbara, San Francisco, San Diego, and Los Angeles. The coup has been described as dramatic, businesslike, and, if not exactly agreeable, satisfactory. Commodore Robert Field Stockton was appointed chief of all land forces in California and he acted immediately to secure the territory.

In Los Angeles, Captain A. H. Gillespie and seventeen men were detailed to make the coup stick. Gillespie was supposed to work things out with Mayor Don Juan Temple, who was left in office, the idea being that the city's twenty-five hundred inhabitants had full confidence in him.

No one was really angry at the Yankees. The Mexicans, or Californians as they were called, didn't care much. Gillespie, however, turned out to be a fourteen-carat heel. With fantastically bad psychology, he banned friendly social gatherings, a dastardly act to a warm, close-knit people, and tossed several leading citizens, for no apparent reason, into the guardhouse.

Hot Latin blood boiled and a band of Mexicans, without warning, chased Gillespie and his boys up Fort Hill, a knoll in back of the City Hall. After a siege of several days, Gillespie surrendered to General Flores on condition that he and his men be permitted to retire honorably to San Pedro.

They boarded the merchant ship *Vandalian* and were about to embark when the frigate *Savannah*, carrying 350 troops, sailed into the harbor, bent on rescue. Gillespie, still not clicking, seized the opportunity to wipe out his ignominy. Reinforced, he headed back toward Los Angeles. Halfway there, at Dominguez

Rancho, a unit of Californians met him, again turned him back to San Pedro. Six of his men killed in the action were buried on a hill near the harbor's mouth, known to this day as Deadman's Island.

When Don Juan Temple, whom Commodore Stockton had installed as mayor, heard of Gillespie's being chased up his own flagpole, so to speak, he retired wisely to his near-by rancho, taking with him two barrels of potent aguardiente and his family. To his surprise, Don Benito Wilson, an old friend, who had complicated the aspect of this comic-opera war by throwing his lot with the Yankees, was brought to him for safe-keeping; also a company of militia whom the Californians, in a burst of pique, had captured in a joust at Chino, some thirty miles away.

To Don Benito Wilson and his wife, living pleasantly as prisoners at Temple's bountiful ranch, further bloodshed was abhorrent. Under a flag of truce, Wilson approached Commodore Stockton and proposed that while Stockton held San Pedro, the port, the Californians should retire to their pueblo and remain peacefully until Mexico and the United States ended the war. The Californians, however, decided not to permit Stockton get the idea they were sissies. Troopers rounded up scores of wild horses and herded them back and forth across a gap in the hills, three miles inland. The dust they kicked up indicated a vast body of mounted troops and Stockton, who had no way of knowing they were riderless, pulled up anchor and sailed away to San Diego.

At approximately the same time, Frémont, in Monterey, sailed with a citizen army of 160 men to reinforce Gillespie. En route, he met the *Vandalian,* the vessel Gillespie had missed, and, learning that horses were unobtainable in Santa Barbara or San Pedro, returned to Monterey for reinforcements and animals. By this time it was October 28 and the Los Angeles flagpole was still bare.

It was the middle of November by the time Frémont finished

recruiting a mounted force of two hundred men, which included fifty Walla Walla Indians, and pushed south by land. Approximately the same time Stockton, with six hundred marines, marched toward Los Angeles from San Diego. With him was General Stephen W. Kearny and a company of dragoons.

They engaged the Californians in the narrow San Pasqual valley, between Warner's Ranch and San Diego, and were repulsed with heavy losses. The two forces fought a second battle at Montebello, ten miles east of Los Angeles, and a third at La Mesa, on the southeast outskirts of the city. The Americans won both and the Californians retreated to Verdugo Canyon.

All this time, Frémont was having trouble. Fearing ambush, he took a devious route. Ever since, the military historians have hinted he used poor judgment and, when the possibility of conflict appeared, showed downright timidity.

It was January 10, 1847, when he emerged from the hills into San Fernando Valley, there to learn of Stockton's cleanup. He muscled into the victory celebration, however, by arranging his own peace conference. The morning of January 13, 1847, Frémont, General Andres Pico, commandante of the Californian forces, and his cousin, José de Jesus Pico, signed a treaty of capitulation at an adobe house at the north end of Cahuenga Pass, now a beautiful concrete free-way. Two days later, Frémont lead his men through a heavy rain to the Plaza, near to the hill where Captain Gillespie, freed from Deadman's Island, had again raised the American flag.

Now what do we have here? It reads as if some people got together August 13, 1946 and solemnly celebrated the one-hundredth birthday of the raising of the American flag over Los Angeles whereas it wasn't raised so that it meant anything until January 10, 1847, one hundred and fifty days later. Another thing, the flag was hoisted up a City Hall flagpole, whereas in the original case Captain Gillespie, the villain, did the honors atop Fort Hill, a block away.

But Fort Hill is now a sad-looking mound, the top of which is used as auto-parking space, and under which there is a cavelike streetcar tunnel inscribed obscenely by mischievous Mexican boys, from whose ancestors the Yankees swiped the city.

No, it isn't at all the kind of place you'd ask the voters to come and watch history being re-enacted. The historians squirmed, of course, at this callous tampering with the facts. But a squirm, it must be kept in mind, is barely audible, at least not when Frankie Boy is singing the national anthem.

15

What America is, California is, with accents, in italics.
—CAREY McWILLIAMS, *Southern California Country*

BELVEDERE is an orphan community, five miles east of downtown Los Angeles. Somehow in the city's mad mushrooming it was overlooked. Perhaps it was unwanted. Belvedere is where the poor people live.

It remains an unincorporated area, outside the city limits yet surrounded by the city. As elsewhere, no line of demarkation is apparent except on the maps. It is "in the county," a local term describing dozens of such dislocated communities.

A frequently heard boast is that Los Angeles has no tenements. What is meant is that Los Angeles has no tall brick buildings in which people live on a cramped, degraded scale. In their place, Los Angeles has its shacktowns and one of them is in *La Barriada de Belvedere*, the District of Belvedere, as the preponderantly Mexican population call it.

Oddly enough, most residents of Belvedere live in one-story, single-family frame houses, old, but usually neat and well kept. Characteristically, every dwelling seems to have a potted geranium on the front porch.

The 1940 census gave Belvedere forty thousand persons but it now has well over fifty thousand. They are a drop in the bucket of Los Angeles County's estimated 250,000 residents of Mexican ancestry—largest concentration outside Mexico City— but in no other section are they so closely knit.

The older Mexicans were imported from below the border almost half a century ago as cheap railroad labor. They worked on the tracks and in the yards, doing the heavy lifting and the pick-and-shovel work. Some became migratory crop workers, traveling by jalopy in family groups to pick cotton in the San Joaquin and Imperial valleys, sugar beets at Lompoc, beans and peas at Nipomo and Guadalupe. Today they work for the suburban and street railways, for the gas and power companies, as auto mechanics, as cabinet makers.

Indeed, during the recent war a new bloc of *braceros* were brought in to work in the plane factories and shipyards when the nation's manpower became depleted. They brought with them the courtly manners of Old Mexico and the *señoritas* were charmed. The native Belvedere males, away at war at the time, have since reclaimed their girls but they still resent the presence of the new *braceros*. The Belvedere boys prefer the "Hi babe" school of romancing.

The *paisanos* of Belvedere vividly remember the depression of the thirties. All they ask, if things are tough, are *tortillas* and beans and chili. If things are good, they like meat and cheese and vegetables and beer. During the depression—they were the first to feel the pinch—they formed long lines in front of the relief warehouses, to receive their food dole. The Americanos insisted they have a rounded diet and supplied them with such things as sauerkraut and hominy. Without really knowing what they were, they traded them slyly for beans and chili.

Inevitably, life for the Mexicans and their Americanized families involves a clash of two cultures: the soft, patient resignation of the elders, the brash, uncompromising spirit of the youth. They have in common only their music and their food and their strong kinship.

By the time they are able to walk and talk, boys and girls of Mexican extraction, as those of colored or Japanese origin, are aware that they are the underprivileged. As they grow older, they attend the same schools as their fellow Americans and learn tragically of the economic ceiling, the limited opportunity placed upon them.

They react in different ways. The boys wear *pachuco* clothes and ducks-back haircuts. During the war, a high percentage joined the paratroops. It was the toughest branch of the service, they knew, and they wanted to demonstrate their fitness. On leave, they wore their high boots and tucked-in pants more proudly perhaps than anyone else. The girls wear their hair piled up on their foreheads and their bobby socks pulled up, lipstick generously applied, bold stares on their faces.

They are second- and third-generation Americans. They have electricity, radios, cars, charge accounts; yet they are pushed around.

One of the blots on the city's live-and-let-live reputation was the so-called "zoot suit" flare-up in 1943. For weeks, a reign of terror existed. Groups of servicemen hunted down and beat up boys of Mexican descent or ripped off their pants or clipped their hair, in many cases while policemen stood by. The incident which started the rioting was never acknowledged by the men in uniform or the newspapers. Several sailors in a bar in the Mexican section had attempted to entice two *señoritas* from their escorts and a fight started.

As a result of this and other incidents, mostly the jailing of youths on suspicion of robbery for the crime of standing on a street corner, some boys of Mexican descent have gone bad. They have formed gangs which have become a headache to police. They scribble their gang names—Puente, Clanton, Palo Verde, Dogtown—on buildings, fences, and billboards. Exhibitionists of a sort, they raid each other's dances, steal cars and accessories, commit assaults and robberies, sometimes murder. The boys who go bad unfortunately give a bad name to the entire Mexican population, which has no voice, no spokesman in city or county government.

But self-pity isn't in the Mexicans or their American children and grandchildren. They'd rather laugh, keeping in balance their high spirits and their gentle reserve.

There's Manuel Ochoa, one of the army of *paisano* shoe-shine boys. On good days he made fifty cents, on an average day thirty-five cents. You could tell when he was prosperous: he had ice cream and pop. At thirteen he was wise beyond his years. Half-way through a shine, he'd let you see the sweat pouring off his brow and remark: "This looks like a ten-cent shine." He would be testing; his price was a nickel. If your protest was good-natured, he knew he'd get the dime. Manuel didn't like school and he had an inner struggle carving out his future. He couldn't decide whether to stick to shoe-shining or switch to newsboying. If you turned him down bluntly with the explanation that you were too busy for a shine, he wanted to know what the idea was, trying to cut down on his revenue? If you got tough, he stuck his head in your office three more times, making faces, before he believed your "no." He had his economics worked out to the penny. He figured to get fifty shines from each can of goo. He had to take home at least thirty cents daily to his mother for *tortillas* and beans. Manuel became very proud of me when I went on the radio. He came in excitedly one day and wanted ten placards with my photo, the name of the station, and the time I broadcast, so he could have his friends display them. A few days later he came in very sad. In his Dead End accent he said: "I tried to listen to your program but my uncle turned it off. He say, 'Talk, talk, talk.'" Manuel came in to see me early in 1947, in uniform. He was one of the few of his platoon to survive the Battle of the Bulge. He was taller, huskier, twenty-one. As soon as his terminal leave was over, he said, he planned to give some attention to his future.

Juan, elevator boy in a downtown store, was in debt and his wife was going to have a baby. At his wit's end, he visited a finance company and asked if he could borrow a hundred dollars. What security did he have? Nothing except his job, he said. The man was very courteous but he had to refuse the loan; the security was insufficient. Next day Juan's fortunes changed abruptly. He won five hundred dollars in a cash-prize drawing. When his excitement cooled, he went to the loan office and sought out the man who had turned him down. *"Señor,"* he said, "I feel very bad that you did not have the hundred dollars to loan me. If you need it, I will be very happy to loan it to you."

Perhaps the great problem the *paisanos* present to police, courts, and probation officers is their indifference to the laws they didn't make and their submissive attitude when they violate them.

There was Pedro, twelve, pained intolerably when the dog catcher invaded his street and swooped up his pooch. It was true the dog had no license but it was also true the dog looked very unhappy inside the caged wagon. Pedro, realizing here was a situation requiring quick, resolute action, assembled his friends in a council of war. After a moment they deployed about the truck. Two of them asked the driver if he were looking for more of the bad dogs which were running loose, tearing up people's lawns and being a nuisance. He said he was. They drew a lurid picture of a section near by where additional hounds might be captured. Meanwhile Pedro unlatched the doors in the back of the truck, seeking his pet. To his consternation, the entire contents of the truck, twelve yipping dogs, knocked him down and scattered like smoke in the wind. By the time the driver caught on, the boys also had disappeared. The driver telephoned the police and three radio cars responded. In a little while Pedro and two companions were collared. They denied everything, claiming the truck doors had come open by accident. The officers knew they were licked. Helpless, they reproved the boys and sent them home.

When the misbehavior is of a higher order, the culprits meet their fate in Belvedere Justice Court, a small, homelike building at 201 North Gage Street, just off East First Street. Order is kept and prisoners are guarded by a unit of deputy sheriffs under authority of Sheriff Eugene Biscailuz, headquartered downtown in the Hall of Justice.

The courtroom is boxlike, a small replica of all courts. A rail fence divides a few rows of hard, curved folding seats from the counsel tables and bench. Much of the business is handled through an interpreter, a kindly lady adept at rephrasing instantly.

The court is presided over by Judge M. B. Marion, the only elected official in Belvedere. Being a township, it has no local government.

Short, husky, owlish-appearing behind his spectacles, Judge Marion is seemingly tough but actually kindly. He is more father confessor than judge and by informal, direct questioning of defendants gets quickly to the core of the cases before him. Sometimes his questions are personal or irrelevant but he can tell how far to go, knowing the character of the people.

Occasionally there is a wife-beating case or a homicide or a back-fence brawl, but mostly the court has to deal with men who drank too much at the wrong time: *los borachos*. The case of Alberto, charged with intoxication, was unique because the complaint was filed by a mortician. It seemed that each time Alberto drank he was seized with the urge to see dead people. His arrest resulted from the dead people and, more particularly, the undertaker, becoming tired of seeing him. In court, Alberto could give no reasonable explanation for his strange behavior. On such occasions, he said shyly, he was simply at the mercy of his whims. The judge pried a little and came up with the answer. Alberto confessed he was henpecked at home by a garrulous wife. Corpses, as every mystery-story writer knows, don't talk back.

Miguel was a grizzled old fellow of sixty-five. He was charged with drunkenness and his breath proved it. When he quickly pleaded guilty, the judge asked, suspiciously: "Have you ever been in here before?"

"*Sí, señor*," said Miguel. "Don't you remember, it was about two years ago? You asked me in what year Columbus discovered America."

"I remember," said the judge. "You were *boracho* then too, weren't you? And, as I recall, you couldn't answer the question."

"No, I could not answer then, but—" with the pride that knowledge brings—"today I know, 1492!"

The sobriety test was good enough for the judge, who recommended leniency inasmuch as Miguel already had spent several days in jail.

Inadvertently, the newspaper column in which we report some of the doings at Belvedere Justice Court figured in one case. Skimming through a batch of arrest reports before hearing the cases scheduled for the day, Judge Marion was attracted to one bearing the name Juan Fernandez. Opposite OCCUPATION was written *Poet*.

When Fernandez' case was called, the judge asked: "What is your occupation?"

"I am a janitor," said Fernandez.

"Any other occupation?"

"No, your honor."

"I don't understand. This report states you said you were a poet, when you were arrested."

"I theenk, Judge, maybe I was pretty dronk."

I printed the item, using the fictitious name José Rodriguez. But the matter didn't end there. Six days later the judge recognized the "poet" in court again, on the same charge. You could have knocked him over with a tortilla. He called him to the bench and asked if he hadn't been in court a few days ago.

"Remember," said the judge, "I asked you about being a poet?"

"Oh no, your honor," said the defendant, "that wasn't me, that was Juan Fernandez. I am José Rodriguez."

Aware that we had used a *nom de Bastille*, the judge said: "So you read Señor Weinstock's column too."

"Well," explained the prisoner, "there's nothing much else to do in jail."

Alfredo was born in Chihuahua, Mexico. When less than a year old he was brought to the United States by his parents. He had worked as a golf caddy, an orange picker, a truck driver. One day during the war he became moody. His two younger brothers were in the army, helping the government, but he, Alfredo, twenty-five, was not. He stopped at a bar and had some beer. If only he could help his country! When he signed up for the alien registration he thought automatically he would become a citizen but he had not, he had merely been placed in the fourth class of the draft. He had more beer. The laws of the Americans, he thought, were very confusing. Suddenly the beers added up inside him and he saw things clearly for the first time. He WAS a soldier, helping Uncle Sam. He decided to go home and tell the glad news to his mother; but he found her unsympathetic, very unsympathetic. He was surprised at her attitude. Had she no patriotism? When the police came he was astounded. Later, in court, charged with intoxication, he felt crushed by his old confusion. The judge asked whether he remembered staggering around the living room, abusing his mother, and running, half-clothed, into the street. Staggering? He had been marching, he told the judge. He had focussed his eyes straight ahead, looking neither to the left nor to the right, army regulations! Imagine! The police officers, the judge, even his mother, thinking he had been merely drunk! Clearly they didn't understand how it was in the army.

Into Belvedere Court one day came a sheepish but twinkling-eyed *paisano* named Epifanio. He was instructed to tell what had happened. Well, he wasn't certain. He knew only that the customs in the great city of Los Angeles were much different than in his little city of Santa Ana. On this sad day, in any event, he rode in on a truck to see his good friend Tellez. The truck driver dropped him off on a strange street. Having only a vague notion where Tellez lived, Epifanio stopped at a store, as he would have done in Santa Ana. By a rare circumstance it was a wine store. Neither the wine merchant nor a well-dressed customer knew Tellez' address but the latter, obviously the *bon vivant* of Belvedere, offered him a drink. Epifanio was honored and when they drained the bottle, Epifanio, alert to the demands of hospitality in a strange city, bought another bottle. The honor of Santa Ana was at stake. The next thing he remembered was sitting on a curb a mile from the store, painstakingly trying to piece together the contents of a lost three hours. The gendarmes who appeared were no help. They didn't know Tellez' address either. But they were very kind; they gave him a ride in their fine automobile. Unfortunately the ride ended in jail. He would be very happy, he told the judge, to return permanently to his own small world, and not bother anyone further.

The charge against Carlos was disturbing the peace. His story was so confusing, witness after witness was summoned to make sense of it. The facts seemed to be that Carlos went on a binge with his friend Lopez. They ran out of wine and while this was to be deplored, a more critical problem was that they ran out of money too. Then confusion; how to explain police finding Lopez, very drunk, propped up against a fence? Gone were his jacket, his pants, his shoes, and Carlos. It remained for a Señor Garcia, a liquor dealer, to put together the jigsaw puzzle. He testified that Carlos had come into his store and tried to barter a jacket, a pair of pants, and a pair of shoes for a bottle of vino. As for Carlos, he simply couldn't remember. He was ordered to take a memory course, the one with bars on the windows.

Though overshadowed in this alcoholic saga, the battle of the sexes comes in for considerable attention also at Belvedere Justice Court. There was the case of the man charged with battery. He had viciously beaten his lady friend. She was in court and bruises were visible on her face and arms. They sat silently glaring at each other as the judge read the arrest report.

At length he looked up and said: "Say, why don't you two get married?" The man grumbled something unintelligible. The judge turned to the woman and asked: "Would you marry him?"

"Yes," she said eagerly.

The judge turned to the man. He explained that the maximum sentence for his offense was six months in jail. Did he think he wanted to marry her?

The man, still sullen, said he guessed he did.

"All right," said the judge, "you two go downtown and get a marriage license and come back here."

"But I have a marriage license," the woman broke in, reaching into her purse. "We got it four years ago, but we never used it."

A recess was taken and the judge performed the ceremony in his chambers. The woman was bright-eyed, the man doggedly reluctant. As they walked out, she smiled defiantly: "I don't care if he leaves me now."

A policeman was investigating a traffic accident when a *paisano* came up to him and said anxiously: "*Señor*, please, come with me to my home." The officer asked what the trouble was. "My wife, she is bad since she is with this other woman," said the Mexican. "I cannot go home." The officer tried to explain he could do nothing, there was no law violation. "Ah, but *señor*," pleaded the *paisano*, "I love my wife." How long since he had seen her? "About four months. But this other woman has been married seven times and she tells my wife bad things about me." The officer went on writing notes about the two damaged cars in the street, trying to ignore the unfortunate husband. "*Señor*," said the *paisano* dramatically, "if you will come home with me I will give you a dollar." The officer said he didn't want the dollar and that, though he was paid to take care of trouble, he could not interfere in a domestic dispute. The *paisano* made a gesture of resignation—it could have meant desperation, even violence—and turned away.

"Hey," said the policeman, "where are you going?"

"Oh, I think I go down to a show and go to sleep."

In the last week of July 1940, Jorge and Manuel sat listening to the broadcast of the Democratic National Convention. Between them was a radio. Next to it was a bottle of *quimica*, a blend of claret and muscatel, twenty cents. Roosevelt had just been nominated for a third term.

"Are you not glad, my friend," asked Manuel, "that *El Señor* Roosevelt will run for *Presidente* another time?"

Jorge was thoughtful a moment, then said: *"El Señor* Roosevelt is a good man, but remember when *El Señor* Hoover was *Presidente?* Those were the good days!" Manuel said nothing so Jorge continued: "Do you not remember that in those days no one had the work? All day long we had the repose. In the afternoon, we visited the mission for the vegetables, perhaps a little *frijoles* and a piece of carne. *Sí*, those were the good days."

Manuel, as if he suddenly remembered something, protested: "How can you say that? Look what Roosevelt did when he became *el jefe*. He brought us the beer and the wine, and one thing more!"

Jorge caught the dramatic ring to Manuel's voice and he asked: "What do you mean?"

"You do not know?" said Manuel. "You are very ignorant, Jorge. It was *El Señor* Roosevelt who started the Uapa [WPA, pronounced as a word]. He gave us shovels to rest on instead of just lying around waiting to go to the mission. Now we get a check twice a month to buy the food and the clothing and the wine."

Jorge snorted. "Checks! What we want with checks? No, I like best the good old days!"

Enrique, charged with being drunk, was asked, when he appeared in court, what had happened. Well, it was a long story, he told the judge. With a friend he had visited the home of another friend. There half a dozen other *paisanos* were assembled. The wine was fine and in the course of the evening the conversation turned to the European crisis, this being before the United States got into the war. Enrique and his friend promptly allied themselves on the side of democracy. The others championed fascism. The debate was at first merely spirited but quickly became furious. In the heat of it, Enrique's supporter disappeared, leaving him to hold the fort single-handed for democracy. Enrique and the vino, however, were equal to the task. In time the battle narrowed to himself and a businessman.

"The angrier I became, the more I drank," said the defendant. "And the more *boracho* you became," added the judge.

Enrique shrugged. Imagine his discomfiture then, after saving the world for democracy single-handed, to wake up in jail, wondering how he arrived there. His manner indicated he considered this epilogue an outrage.

"Now just a minute," said the judge. "Look at you. Look at the mess you got yourself into. And this man you were arguing with—he's free."

Again Enrique shrugged, indicating he would accept martyrdom if necessary.

"Do you want to go to the county jail for a while?" asked the judge severely.

"Oh no, your honor," said Enrique, suddenly a mere *paisano* charged with intoxication, "they all believe in democracy there already!"

Speaking of the war—and the Los Angeles County casualty lists were heavily studded with names like Garcia and Gonzales—the *paisano* population seemed at times confused by the complex nature of our world-wide operations. A young messenger boy delivering a piece of copy to a newspaper office was asked, apropos of nothing, "George, what do you think of the war?"

"Ees a good war, I guess," he said. "I don' read moch about it but everybody seems to be weening."

Then there was the young Belvedere boy who enlisted in the army, one jump ahead of his draft board. He made one provision, though. He insisted on being sent to Fort Lewis, Washington. "I wish to see *El Presidente*, Panchito." The recruiting officer shook his head. Oddly enough, he was sent to Fort Lewis, where he soon became disgusted. They wouldn't let him see the President. Not only that, they acted very strangely when he asked.

The incident concerning Perfecto came to the attention of authorities but he got off with a warning. Perfecto was devoted to his prize rooster. He watched adoringly as it strutted and arched its plumage. But during a rainy spell the rooster developed a cold; its feathers drooped and it sat disconsolately, making wheezing noises. Perfecto worried for several days, then thought: "What would I do if I had a cold?" Aha, he had it. He tied a scarf about the rooster's neck and administered wine. Soon the alcohol took hold and the rooster went leaping and screaming through the neighborhood, stumbling and falling occasionally. Elated at his success, Perfecto repeated the treatment. The rooster began crowing at night and chasing dogs in the daytime. At first amused, neighbors became alarmed. They called on Perfecto. He was ready for them. With great ceremony, he removed the scarf and called their attention to how proudly his rooster once more held himself. "See," he said, "the cold is gone."

Each Easter Eve the residents of Belvedere observe El Sabado de Gloria. It is a festive occasion. They gather at Brooklyn Avenue and Ford Boulevard and, through the co-operation of the neighborhood merchants, there are music, street dancing, and entertainment. The high point in the observance, of course, is the burning in effigy of Judas (pronounced Hoodas) Iscariot. Several thousand of the faithful were on hand one Sabado a few years ago and, looking at the villainous dummy, they could scarcely contain themselves. They anticipated the moment when flame would be touched to the hated image and they could howl with satisfaction, having insured their enthusiasm with some alcoholic fire, but in the midst of the preparation for the ceremony Judas burst into flames. Someone had set him off prematurely. The crowd gasped. Meanwhile cold justice swiftly pre-empted the high place of El Sabado de Gloria. A young man was collared and according to a complaint filed later he "did willfully, unlawfully and maliciously destroy and injure personal property not his own, to wit, a straw figure in effigy known as Judas." The accused effigy burner pleaded not guilty and demanded a jury trial. His sacrilegious boldness, however, got him nowhere. For his high crime the culprit, found to have been drunk, was ordered to pay the cost of Hoodas, twenty-five dollars.

The next year, as Easter rolled around, the incident was more or less forgotten. The Belvedere merchants made plans for a bigger and better Sabado. Judas, they promised excitedly, would be designed to resemble Hitler; but three days before the scheduled event, the sacrilege of the year before was revived. The offender, by pure chance, appeared in court and the judge recognized him as the premature effigy burner. He lectured to him on his callousness, for he had thrown the observance out of kilter. A Judas, he made plain, could not be whipped up on short notice. "You better watch yourself Saturday night," he admonished. "Hoodas cost thirty-five dollars this year!"

It's high time!—Toast given derisively at the
cocktail hour by the Regulars in a Skid Row
Muscatel Mosque

16

THE per-capita consumption of alcoholic beverages in Los
Angeles is something between a teaspoonful and a barrel-
ful—I never was good at statistics. It's safe to state, however,
that many thousands of persons, not necessarily members of the
W.C.T.U., don't drink any, and many other thousands drink
too much.

The caste system in drinking runs the full gamut. In the
plush red-leather and chromium spots of Hollywood, Beverly
Hills, and the Sunset Strip, thousand-dollar-a-week writers
touch nothing but imported twenty-year-old brandy. At the other
end of the alcoholic scale are the Skid Row derelicts who, in the
good old days, procured a quart of fourth-grade wine for fifteen
cents. Many of these zombies have been carted off to Lincoln
Heights Jail, which has possibly the busiest drunk tank in the
world, more than a hundred times.

But they're brothers under the skinful and chances are they'll
wind up side by side in the same alcoholism-cure spa or the same
chapter of Alcoholics Anonymous, institutions which both flour-
ish in Los Angeles. They're pathetic figures, but they get off
some good lines.

Los Angeles originally had but one Skid Row: East Fifth
Street. Now they've burgeoned everywhere—at Second and
Figueroa, Pico and Georgia, Third and Hill. Every bar in town
is potentially another Wino Junction.

A highly regarded branch is in the vicinity of Echo Park.

Here the winos have imagination, verve, and moods. On occasion these gentlemen, after polishing off a jug, experience a deep urge for roast duck. Now even a wino's foggy logic will tell him that to get roast duck he must first have unroasted duck, and where do you get unroasted duck? Well, there are some in Echo Park Lake and sometimes they come ashore.

Ducks, as everyone knows, are wary. They'll take your food but they'll stay suspicious. But the Echo Park winos are more than a match for them. They feed them bread day after day, building up their confidence. The day a duck comes too close he's dead.

One night a wino stricken with duck fever, after days of taming the object of his affections, grabbed it and put it under his coat. As he emerged from the park, the two officers in a cruising radio car saw him.

"Stealing a duck, eh?" said one, stepping from the car.

"What do you mean?" said the outraged wino. "This is my pet duck, Wellington."

"Pet duck!" laughed the law. "That's a good one!"

"Well, it is. I work all day and poor Wellington gets lonesome. So at night I bring him over to the park for exercise. I let him swim and have fun with the other ducks."

The officers were unconvinced, but reminded themselves that this was Los Angeles, where daffy things happen.

"Here, I'll show you," said the wino. He put down the duck and took some bread from his pocket. "Here Wellington, here Wellington!" he called.

The duck followed him hungrily and snapped the bread from his hand. "Good boy, Wellington," said the wino.

The gendarmes guessed it was all right and, shaking their heads, drove off.

Two drunks began talking harmlessly to a girl on a Hollywood streetcar. One offered her a piece of candy. Not wanting to be antisocial, she ate it. Then the other offered a chunk. She declined. He insisted.

"No really," she said, "I have to think of my figure."

He studied her a moment, up and down, then said: "Better take it, your figure ain't so hot."

An inebriate weaved to the counter of a café in the southwest part of town and borrowed a nickel from the waitress, whom he knew. He went to the phone booth but fumbled the dial, losing his nickel without getting his party. He borrowed another nickel from her and as he disappeared into the booth again he shouted recklessly to everyone: "Boy, when I phone, I phone!"

A good-looking blonde, a little tight, came into a Sixth Street bar and sat moodily drinking. Half a dozen men sat about, thoughtfully and quietly converting beer bubbles into daydreams. With sudden decision, the girl asked the man nearest her: "I wonder if you'd marry me, tonight. Just marry me and that's all. I'll pay you for your trouble and I'll pay for the Nevada divorce. You won't have anything to worry about." The man said he was sorry, he had a wife. She put the same proposition to the others and they all declined, too. Without further explanation, she resumed her seat and began drinking again.

Pershing Square, a block-long patch of green, is Los Angeles' Union Square. It is inhabited by uninhibited, garrulous, arguing men for the most part, but others sit quietly on benches drinking in the sunshine. A member of an evangelical sect handed a bench sitter a pamphlet and said: "If you'll only listen to me, I'll show you the way to heaven."

"Listen, sister," retorted the sitter, "if you'll give me a dime I'll find a saloon and show you how to go to hell on a handcar!"

A man drunk as seven hundred dollars but very cagy demanded a sobriety test as he was taken in hand by an officer. At the jail hospital he gave the correct answer to eight times nine he walked backward twenty feet without faltering, and he untied and tied his shoelaces. The officer, a little desperately, reached far down for his clincher. Fixing the accused man with a mackerel eye, he said, "Repeat after me the word trinitrotoluol."

Without batting an eye the drunk said: "How do you spell it?"

Everything was quiet and orderly in a Westside saloon, with a dozen persons chatting pleasantly, when a boisterous fellow weaved in and demanded nine beers.

"Bill," said the tiny girl behind the bar, "you can't drink nine beers."

"No," replied Bill, "but these eight friends of mine need a drink." With a sweep of his hand he indicated eight little men who weren't there.

The girl appealed to the invisible eight. "Boys, you don't want any more beer, do you?" She turned to Bill and said, "See, they shook their heads."

Bill staggered out, disappointed, and a customer complimented the girl. "Oh that's nothing," she said, "this place caters to a family trade and I don't want him wasting his money, he's had enough. A few minutes ago I took fifteen dollars away from him and gave him an I O U, so when he comes in tomorrow morning he'll have something to help relieve his headache."

After the eighth drink, a *boracho* expressed great affection for the bartender. "I'm gonna bring you a preshent," he said. The bartender didn't press the point. A few days later the customer, drunk as usual, came in with a package and elaborately presented it.

"There's them socks," he said.

"What socks?" asked the bartender.

"Them socks I told you I was gonna bring. All you gotta do is rinse them out."

A drunk loaded with packages boarded a crowded streetcar during the rush hour. He was too far gone to grab a strap and he swayed with each lurch of the car. For blocks, while passengers smiled, he maintained a bleary-eyed, stupefied silence. Finally he roared: "Say, don't nobody live nowhere?"

Two men overindulged at a party and when time came to go one offered to drive the other home. As they started, the car owner said: "I think I'll get a little sleep. You drive." The second man took the wheel. In about fifteen minutes he became drowsy, awakened the car owner, and said he'd better drive. Some twenty minutes later they changed again. Two hours later they realized they weren't getting anywhere except soberer, and reality hit them. One lived in Eagle Rock, the other in Huntington Park, ten miles apart. Each time one took the wheel he headed for his own home.

Two winos were arguing heatedly. Suddenly one sent the other sprawling with a vicious right to the jaw. The victim staggered to his feet, stood thoughtfully for a moment, then said, emphatically: "No!" Down he went again from a left hook. He got up slowly and said: "Awright then, if you inshist I'll shake hands." He did and they walked off into the night, arm in arm.

Bunker Hill, atop Angel's Flight, is packed with drama. Unlike Skid Row, where the dregs of humanity parade, Bunker Hill has an aura of respectability, a feeling that the rent is paid. The hill is an orderly pattern of old houses and apartments. Old men sit on the porches, gossiping or watching neighbors labor up the hill. Inside, the houses are full of alcoholics and their secret sorrows, pulp writers, men on parole, pensioners, and some bad girls. One pensioner, on receiving his monthly check, always paid his rent, bought enough groceries to last—mostly dried and canned stuff that would keep—then got drunk and remained numb as long as his money permitted. On a particularly sad occasion, he muffed the sequence: he got drunk first. As he stumbled home, the landlady scolded him bitterly. When he started to explain he had met a friend, his teeth dropped out. "You ought to be ashamed of yourself," the landlady stormed. "Now go to your room and stay there. And to make sure you do

I'll keep these teeth." This was the supreme humiliation to a proud gentleman. The next day, however, the landlady softened. She didn't relinquish his teeth; she fixed him some oatmeal so he wouldn't starve.

A noisy drunk in a downtown bar sounded off with "The United States Navy is no good, it can't fight, it can't do anything." Three sailors, seated in the shadows, were reaching the boiling point. As one started to get up, a tall Texan restrained him. "Leave him to me," he said. He sat down beside the offensive guy and ordered drink after drink. When the fellow was at the falling-down stage, the Texan escorted him out, whispering to the sailors to stick around. He returned in half an hour and reported his mission accomplished. "I took him over to a tattoo place on Main street," he said. "When he wakes up tomorrow he will find a large American flag on his chest and under it GOD BLESS AMERICA."

A drunk on an S car singled out a man with a discharge button, tapped him on the arm, and said: "Old pal, old pal, were you a Seabee too?" The man said no. Ignoring it, the drunk hauled out a bottle of whisky and waved his arm in a mighty circle to invite everyone to have a drink. To pacify him, his new-found friend took a short gulp. Delighted, the ex-Seabee jerked a bottle of wine from another pocket and said: "Here, old pal old pal, have a chaser!"

During the Shrine convention in 1938, a noble said to an elevator boy: "I'm sure having a swell time but I hope you never see anything like I just saw." The elevator boy asked what it was. "I was sitting in my room," he said, "and all of a sudden a great big cheese sandwich came out from under the bed on roller skates."

A woman in a bar got very drunk, then nasty, then loud. When the management tried to shush her she said she was going out and commit suicide. She argued with herself as to the best method, then called a cab. When the driver arrived she said:

"How about a drink?" She explained she wanted to be driven to the Colorado Street bridge in Pasadena so she could jump off. The driver declined, got tired of her heckling, and left. Four times more she summoned cabs and went through the same routine.

The fifth driver ingeniously asked, "How much money do you have?"

She inspected her purse and said: "Six dollars."

"Sorry lady," said the cabby, "the trip would be seven dollars."

The woman became more maudlin than ever. The suffering headwaiter, who had been standing by unhappily, unfolded his wallet—and said: "Here, lady, is that extra dollar you need."

Radio police answering a disturbance call came upon a drunk and disorderly citizen. When they tried to quiet him he said huffily: "Gentlemen, I don't like your language. When you address me, say please."

The officers bowed in unison and one said: "Sir, please consider yourself under arrest," and waved him to their car.

A stranger, unbelievably intoxicated, sat next to a woman on a streetcar and asked: "Where did you get those beautiful violets?"

She wasn't wearing any flowers but smiled: "Oh, someone gave them to me."

The drunk pondered heavily a moment, then said: "They're pretty, but if it had been me I would have bought you gardenias."

A drunken woman, singing and talking to herself and waving aloft a half-filled bottle of whisky, was accosted by a policeman near Pershing Square. He chided her for her unseemly conduct but because it was New Year's Eve, merely took away the bottle. She gave it up with an air of having wondered all along why she had been carrying it. Just then two sailors came by and complimented the officer for his fine work in behalf of law, order, and public decency. One took off his cap and brushed the officer's sleeve. The other dusted imaginary specks from his shirt. "How about the bottle?" they asked. At first he shook his head. Then he held up the bottle to the light and, maintaining a severe countenance, poured all but the last inch into the gutter and gave it to them.

A short, fat, red-faced man was nodding over his beer in a saloon when a gospel worker came by and shook her tambourine under his nose. He blinked, looked up, and said: "I'm sorry, lady, I just barely got enough to get drunk on."

By now it can be stipulated that winos are eccentric characters, a necessary introduction to an incident that happened to an ex-marine. He parked his car on Maple Avenue, to avoid bucking the midtown traffic whirlwind, and walked to his destination. He returned an hour later. As he got in his car, a woman—he called her a "rundown babe"—rose up from the back seat and whispered hoarsely: "Be a little quiet, will you?" He thought it was a new type of touch and prepared to defend himself. Then he saw a huge gentleman cuddled up on the floor. The large reclining invader assured him everything was all right; they were merely playing hide and seek. The car owner said that was fine but he had to mush on. "O.K.," said the rundown babe. She cautiously opened the rear and ran hell-bent into an alley. When she reached a post she yelled "Free!" The man monster next sneaked pantherlike out of the car. He was ambling across the sidewalk when another fugitive from the drunk tank streaked past him, latched onto the pole, and hollered "One two three for Joe."

Enraged, Joe bellowed, "You lousy baboon, you peeked when you was counting!" A hot argument ensued and a crowd began gathering. The car owner sprinted to the corner and ducked into a tavern. Over a beer he pinched himself and wondered whether he should go out to the veterans' hospital for a checkup. "Did you see the crowd up the street?" asked the bartender. Yes, he said. The bartender mumbled awhile, then shouted:

"Dammit, now they'll run through here all afternoon, playing that silly game!"

A stranger in town asked a drunk how to get to the post office. The drunk pulled himself together, pointed north, and said: "You go that way." He caught himself. "No, hold it," he said, pointing south, "it's that way." Again he caught himself. "Wait a minute now." He shook his head sadly. "I'm sorry, but you can't get to the post office from here."

A woman drunkenly attempted to light a cigarette as she staggered along Fifth Street. She paused in front of the Public Library, threw the cigarette away unlighted, then looked about her absently. From a parked car, fifty feet away, a man called to her plaintively: "Mary, don't be quite so contrary, please."

Wes, a bartender in a Sunset Strip restaurant, is proud of the fact that he pours the stiffest jigger on the boulevard. A regular customer came in and found Wes strangely tense and anticipatory. "Keep your eye on that guy over there," he whispered. "He's had nine of my martinis and he's still sitting up." Just then the nine-martini man got up to make a telephone call or something and collapsed like a sack of meal. "That's better," smiled Wes, his professional standing vindicated.

A screwball had Hollywood bartenders terrorized for a while. He went into bars, ordered a drink, and stared fixedly at the bartender. He ordered a second, then a third drink, continuing his gimlet-eye treatment. When the mixologist was busy at the other end of the counter, he replaced his glass eye with a spare. The next time the bartender came by he found himself looking incredulously at a man with an American flag in one eye.

A gray-haired, distinguished-looking waiter in a Hollywood bar fascinates the customers with his routine. As he whisks trayfuls of drinks, he calls out, to no one in particular, "Temperance! Temperance!" One time, threading his way through a crowd, he shouted: "Gangway! There's fourteen dollars on this tray!"

Perhaps the answer to Los Angeles drinkers' overindulgence

is more bartenders like Pete, who handles the bottles in an expensive Hollywood Boulevard bar. Not long ago, he got religion and his attitude on drinking underwent a deep psychological change. He doesn't waste any time on old timers who, as he sees them, are beyond redemption, but he is likely as not to attach himself to a less "reprobate" customer as he serves him a drink and lecture him on the wayward path he is taking. How does he stay on the job? Some customers insist that in his program to discourage people from alcohol, Pete pours his jiggers short. Naturally the management would like that.

17

Good-bye California and your damn geraniums!
—SIGN ON EASTBOUND JALOPY, LOADED WITH BED-
DING, FRYING PANS, AND SUITCASES, ON HIGHWAY 66

FOR a place where the sun shines three hundred days a year, Los Angeles can be awfully cold. Lack of neighborliness seems, at times, almost the rule.

It may be that this unfriendliness is some kind of disease, like hay fever or sinus trouble, carried in the warm or moist air, settling on those who are most susceptible. Personally, I attribute it to "The Apathy."

Six months' residence is sufficient to give a person the Apathy. He feels all right; he is keen, alert, and civil to his mother-in-law. Suddenly he just doesn't give a damn. He doesn't care particularly whether he ever votes or whether he ever washes his car or what time it is.

This indifference grows and in about a year, unless he takes cold showers or something, he sinks from the Apathy to the Anonymity. He is swallowed up in the expanse of the city and becomes part of its aimlessness.

He carries on in his immediate circle of friends, of course, but not beyond that. Strangers, big and little shots alike, mean nothing to him. They're just more of the faceless, nameless people the town is full of and which, without realizing it, he has become one of.

As a consequence, Los Angeles is an anonymous city. Under the spell of the Apathy, a man knows who Bing Crosby and Ingrid Bergman are but he doesn't know the name of his councilman or his next-door neighbor. Moreover, he doesn't care. All he wants is for people not to bother him. For his part, he remains aloof; asking nothing, giving nothing; not even common courtesy.

An old lady was assisted by the conductor from a Venice Boulevard streetcar to the curb. When she arrived there safely, she thanked him and said: "I'll bet you're not a Californian!"

The technique of the brushoff has been developed into a fine art. Easterners who arrive with a letter from a mutual friend are held at telephone wire's length for days, trying to say hello. One time a businessman with a reputation for viciousness received a phone call from a man just arrived from the main office in New York. Could he drop up and see him, the New Yorker asked. The head man, either to impress the visitor or because he was that kind of a person, barked: "I'm too busy; I can't see you today." Awed, the New Yorker begged meekly for just a few minutes. The local yokel relented brusquely. "All right," he said, "I can give you fifteen minutes tomorrow at ten sharp." The visitor was there on the dot, then waited a full hour. When he got in, the executive asked savagely what he wanted.

"My business is very simple, you rude baboon," said the man from New York. "You're fired!"

A bank called a newspaper advertising department to send a man over to pick up an ad. The paper sent a new salesman. He scrutinized the copy, then said dubiously: "I guess it'll be all right." The bank man asked what he meant.

"How long have you been in business?" persisted the salesman.

"About fifty years," said the bank man. Finally he exploded: "Listen, you seem worried about whether we can pay for a one-inch ad! Take this to your boss." He tore a page from a booklet. It was the bank's statement listing assets of six hundred million dollars.

A fire started on the back porch of a house on the Eastside. The woman there, having no phone, grabbed her child and ran next door. When the neighbor came to the door, after frantic pounding, the mother said: "Please call the fire department; my house is on fire!"

The lady was reluctant. "You'll have to give me a nickel first," she said. "My calls are limited."

The excited mother promised a nickel as soon as she could go back into the house for her purse.

A noted writer, lecturing before the Ebell Club, urged the audience to get closer to the common people. Only by this direct contact, he said, might real understanding be achieved. As he concluded, the stony faces of the richly dressed, well-upholstered clubwomen made him realize he had been too daring, his appeal hadn't clicked. Relating the incident to a friend as he left town he said sadly: "I should have remembered the old adage: see no Ebell, hear no Ebell, speak no Ebell."

Another thing, the town seems always full of strangers. Visitors ask bus drivers how to get places and bus drivers say they never heard of the places, they're newly arrived. The champion was a man who wearily asked a newsboy: "Do you hold an opinion on how the hell I can get to Union Station?"

During the war, even during the streetcar strike of 1946, motorists maintained their reserve. Every morning, thousands of workers lined the curbs, waiting for any transportation that might come along, and looking hopefully at men driving solo in their sedans. Some motorists looked back at the pedestrians but nothing happened. With the exception of brash high-school boys, neither would make the first move to break the ice.

Politeness does prevail, of course, in elevators and theaters. Elevator operators in most buildings say, annoyingly: "Seven, please?" Classic instance of excessive politeness occurred when a beautifully uniformed theater usher, attempting to awaken a snoring patron, nudged him unmercifully, meanwhile repeating: "Thank you, sir!"

When I printed in my column the quotation about the geraniums that heads this chapter I added: "Yes, the people from

Texas, Oklahoma, and Arkansas are returning there, in bitterness. They have found us unneighborly and smug."

Affirmation came in the next mail. Mrs. J. M. B. wrote:

You know, you California people are not very good hosts. I cannot remember an Oklahoma state fair but that Oklahomans were invited to the land of super fruit and vegetables, sunny beaches and mountain playgrounds. But when we accepted your invitation we were treated like poor relatives. We came to California, for the simple reason that jobs were scarce at home and California was a utopia extending a welcoming hand. We are leaving California because we do not like the people here. We prefer a place where kindness and hospitality are the rule, not the exception. We like to live where people with children may rent a house with no questions asked; where men and teen age boys would never sit in a bus while elderly people stood. We also prefer our nine months of sunshine and three of rain and snow to your three of rain and nine of fog and clouds. We are going back to the land of sunshine as soon as we may.

Another correspondent signing "Okie" wrote:

Most of us came here because of the war effort. We're here because you Californians cried for manpower and womanpower. We're here because we are patriotic, because you couldn't handle the job. We're here because this is still a free country. As for sky-high salaries, may I mention the sky-high cost of living? No, that was no incentive for us coming here. We came because we felt it our duty. But as soon as this mess is over with, you can have your goldanged, over-soaked, unsunnied California with its "pumpkin size oranges," "five pound lemons," your dirty fog, reckless drivers, gestapo attitude—and the geraniums, too!

The native sons aren't happy either. Frank W. Gibson wrote:

I was born and raised in L.A. But surely this town is becoming a terrible place to live. Everyone seems cold and rude. I never noticed it as much as this week when I had to resort to the street car while my car was being repaired. During the war people seemed a little friendly, but now they are like a bunch of wildcats thrown together. It seems the dollar has replaced all the early teachings. I would call it treason to our fellow man.

From the island of Shimya in the Aleutians, Sergeant Gary Sherman wrote:

The city always possessed a hard and selfish core, now it has become intensified a hundredfold. On my return from Europe, where I spent three years, I was so shocked by the turn for the worse that had overtaken L.A. I signed for an additional year, to ride over the rough spots. On this three by four rock, with nothing but fog, wind and rain, I'm wondering whether I'm not perhaps better off. On Shimya at least there is peace and quiet. No wonder so many combat vets are staying in. The dream country that we all longed to see again is a nightmare, a very rude awakening to too many. There was a day when California hospitality, warmth and friendliness was a reality. But people came, bringing with them their twisted, narrow, frustrated points of view, their culture, or lack of it.

A municipal employe who has lived in Los Angeles for nearly half a century became acquainted with a new neighbor, a woman, and one day, over the back fence, she said: "People are different here; they aren't friendly like folks back East."

"Wait a minute," he said. "Your neighbor on the other side

came from the same state you did. The one next to us came from Pennsylvania. The one directly behind you came from New York. The one next to him came from Illinois. They all came from back East. You're kicking about your own kind of people!"

The lady hadn't thought of that. She guessed he was right.

· 18 ·

The climate is nice, but the people are cold.—Un-
IDENTIFIED WOMAN FROM KANSAS, QUOTED BY DALE
CARNEGIE, OCTOBER 15, 1943

THERE'S no average resident, any more than there's an average New Yorker or Chicagoan or San Franciscoan. But
there's a man you should know about. Sooner or later, in Los
Angeles, a person is bound to meet him.

It may be that he is, in some obscure way, a product of the
actinic rays of the sun beating down on his skull, the thing mad
dogs and Englishmen stay away from. He has no particular vo-
cation. He may have been, at one time or another, a grocery
clerk, insurance man, hotel clerk, ad salesman, newspaperman,
bookmaker, or actor.

He simply would rather not work. It isn't that he doesn't have
responsibilities. He has: usually a wife, two kids, overdue rent,
unpaid gas bills, a telephone shut-off notice, a threat from the
finance company that this time it's "or else."

His life, as a result, is very exciting. It is a constant race
against time: not Mr. Luce's time, but the stopwatch time of the
landlord, the sheriff, and the loan company, or all three.

He may lose one of these sprints but he is never daunted, even
when a truck backs up the driveway. Life merely becomes more
complex. He now has one more man to outwit, the driver of the
truck.

No matter how low his fortunes, he maintains his standards.
There may be no food in the house but you can bet there is beer
in the icebox. The children may look in vain for milk but there'll
be a carton of cigarettes. As a matter of fact, our man isn't

sure but that cigarettes and beer will sustain life indefinitely.

He lives by the telephone and the only real calamity is a shut-off because the bill is delinquent. That licks him a little and he's liable to forget his good intentions and go on relief, which wouldn't be for the first time.

He is not, as all this might indicate, a sad, hopeless, or moody individual. On the contrary, he considers himself only a step away from fame and fortune. He has written a play or an outline for a radio program or somehow he has gathered sordid but documentary information about persons in high public office which he is certain he can sell to the opposition when the next political campaign comes along. Or perhaps he has a foolproof system to beat the horses, requiring only the backing to get it printed in booklet form. While one or another of these projects is jelling, he stays home and listens to the radio. He is a great student of radio trends. He never misses the Pot of Gold programs and he is always submitting batches of material to quiz programs.

Getting a job never occurs to him. As he sees it, only chumps tie themselves down to a desk eight hours a day, thereby forfeiting all opportunity to test wits on a free-lance basis with the great big economic world. No, he carries on, with ruthless determination.

His friends, incidentally, think none the less of him, though he shamelessly cuffs them for any extra Hamburger or pie or hotcake flour or money they happen to have around the house. As a matter of fact, some friends admire him for his fortitude.

He has no conscience. He will unhesitatingly hock a chair or a clock or a radio from the furnished apartment he calls home if his beer or cigarette ration is threatened.

If things really get desperate, he may get a little money by refinancing his fifteen-year-old automobile, neglecting to inform the bank, naturally, that he still owes eight payments on it. With his resourcefulness and resilience, he can last a long time before breaking down and going to work, as other people do, but seemingly he fights a losing battle, and inevitably will have to move in with his brother-in-law.

Wrong; he sells the play or the radio program or the blackmail material or gets a sucker to print his horse-race booklet or hits the Pot of Gold.

• 19 •

*Hollywood is wonderful. Anyone who doesn't like it
is either crazy or sober.*—RAYMOND CHANDLER

Los ANGELES, or rather Los Angeles plus Hollywood, is second
only to Washington as a news source. If Lana Turner sits
down too hard, the wire services have her in the hospital with
contusions, abrasions, and complications, thus presenting each
client paper a fine opportunity to print a new photo of her ex-
pressive but saddened derrière.

The wire services aren't so eager to spread across the nation
the strictly Los Angeles stories, unless they're crackpot enough.
As a matter of fact, a wire-service bureau chief will tell you if it
weren't for the stuff pouring out of the motion-picture publicity
factories, Los Angeles would be as dull as Chicago.

Nevertheless many eerie outcroppings take place in Los
Angeles, with or without benefit of national attention. They
constitute a news phenomena that could hardly happen anywhere else.

The view from the Colorado Street bridge in Pasadena isn't
as good as it used to be. A seven-and-a-half-foot chain-mesh fence
along the sides gives motorists the sensation that they're in a
kind of cage. Well, they are.

In the twenties, particularly toward the latter part, the bridge
became *the* place to jump off. By the time the depression came
around, no self-respecting suicide would be caught dead anywhere else.

The city of Pasadena, naturally, became very unhappy about

the bridge and the jumpers. They were giving the town bad publicity.

Nothing was done, however, until October 1933, when in one week three persons thudded one hundred and fifty feet into the dusty Arroyo Seco below. Aroused city authorities ordered the police department to keep a man on duty at all times.

Despondent folk were not deterred. They came to the bridge for a long, last look at life and the Rose Bowl, which is off to the north, then to leap into infinity, and no cop was going to stop them. Suicide No. 48, a man named Pederson, made this quite clear the next month, November, when he shot himself through the head as he jumped.

All sorts of suggestions were frantically considered. In April 1935, some attention was paid to a recommendation by the state highway engineers that the bridge be torn down and another one, suicide-proofed, be built in its place. The cost, $450,000.

Nothing happened except more leaping and more brooding by Pasadenans until June 1937 when the suicide count was eighty-nine. By this time enough was enough. The Pasadena board of directors voted seven thousand dollars to erect a barricade on the sides.

There is reason to believe the decision was spurred by a reckless splash of newspaper headlines. In February, the body of a man was found under the bridge under conditions that meant at least suicide, but possibly murder. A Los Angeles paper which had campaigned to abate Pasadena's so-called death span gave the case tremendous notoriety. In May a mother first threw her baby over the side, then climbed over herself: a double-header that left the family circulation gasping.

So the fence was erected and the L.A. paper crowed that through its efforts the public had been protected against its impulse toward self-destruction. It didn't come in time, however, for a man named Alfieri, who on June 29 made the score an even ninety. A Pasadena paper, resenting the L.A. sheet's meddling so far out of its bailiwick, derisively started counting over again, labeling the dead man Colorado Street Bridge Suicide No. 1 A.F., (After Fence).

The wire screening slowed the jumpers but it didn't stop them. In January 1938 a man named Menafee became No. 91 and in March 1939 a man named Campbell made the grade as No. 92, but they must have had acrobatic training: they edged around the fence.

Almost every night the Los Angeles sky is sliced apart by arc lights, symbols of a mad addiction to "premières."

Only a few are motion-picture premières, a publicity device designed to attract attention to a film that may or may not need it. For these, grandstands are set up, bands play, and movie celebrities arrive in a swirl of mink, ermine, and tuxedos to be introduced over a microphone to awed thousands.

The rest serve to notify the public of the launching of super-markets, gas stations, auto display rooms, malt shops, theater bank nights, and hot-dog stands. They are a subject for anguish to the most hardened resident.

The technique has been developed to its present acme, or nadir, by R. N. (Nep) Hovey, who in the last fifteen years has "opened" five hundred markets. He considers it nice work if he can get it.

Once he is engaged and the date set, he supervises erection of a platform in front of the market, arranges for searchlights, decorations, talent, gags. Usually he officiates as announcer over the public-address system, sandwiching commercials between musical numbers. Sometimes he fills in as drummer in the band, members of which wear cowboy costumes and feature hillbilly music.

The primary factors are lights, flags, sound, and entertainment. No holds are barred to capture the audience. Common attractors are cake cuttings, men walking on stilts, prize drawings, and the taking of motion pictures, to be shown at the neighborhood theater. Nep also introduced balloon-blowing contests, jitterbug contests, and his triumph: a man hanged alive.

In this piece of pantomime, a posse runs down a horse thief and strings him up to a gallows. He really hangs from it, but doesn't mind: he has a steel brace concealed down his back.

Super-markets are most frequently glorified but occasionally Nep is summoned for special jobs such as searchlighting an offshore gambling boat or a legal draw-poker house in Gardena or Hawthorne. These, of course, call for much more conservative treatment.

Earl William Muntz, thirty-two, used to be a midget autorace driver in Elgin, Illinois. Neither this fact nor any other phase of his rather humdrum career contributed to his having become overnight the most vivid personality in Los Angeles.

He was sprung full blown upon the community in 1943, as Madman Muntz, a used-car screwball. "We buy 'em high, sell 'em low," he said in horrible singing commercials and in the craziest billboard campaign ever seen. Anyone knows this statement is economic fakery but the town quickly became Muntz-conscious.

Schoolboys mimicked his lines. Radio comedians made him the butt of jokes. He became a byword, like Kilroy. More important, he sold thousands of cars, stealing the thunder from scores of other long-established dealers who also advertised heavily. He audaciously moved into the center of Auto Row, at Eleventh and Figueroa Streets, announcing the fact with a billboard of a street marker changing the name of Figueroa to Muntz Boulevard.

In 1942, Muntz operated a used-car lot at Los Feliz and Brand Boulevards in Glendale. He was about broke. He made a deal with a Hollywood exploitation man, Michael Shore, to handle his advertising. Shore went into the silences where publicity men track down their inspirations. He came out with a new idea: selling used cars through a dealer's daffy personality.

He made Muntz a benevolent screwball. Needing a trade-mark, he put commercial artists to work creating a figure. After eight tries, one evolved the tiny, long-nosed, pinch-faced Napoleonesque character which appears on billboards.

Other used-car dealers have resented Muntz. They complained he was ruining the racket by spending money like a drunken sailor, but at no time did his budget exceed nine thousand dollars a month.

The impact came from Shore's copy which Muntz, by the way, never sees in advance. One billboard showed the little Napoleon in cocked hat and high boots, selling hot dogs. The caption: "The automobile business is fun—but a man's gotta make a living!"

Another, showing him with one hand outstretched, the other tucked inside the flap of his red underwear, was titled: "I wanna give 'em away—but Mrs. Muntz won't let me. She's crazy."

Others: "I buy 'em retail—sell 'em wholesale. More fun that way!" "Medical authorities agree—walking is good for you." "You too can be a wealthy pedestrian!" "Just sound your horn (We pay by ear!)" "Even Santa Claus believes in Muntz!" "She'll look good in mink!" "Remember . . . money isn't everything! (You fool)." "West coast distributor: U.S. Mint." "And you thought they had it buried at Fort Knox!" "A million dollars for your car . . . or would you rather be a pig?" "You look terrible behind that wheel!"

Many of these, of course, are predicated on the fierce competition among dealers to persuade car owners to sell them.

The campaign made merchandising history and Muntz today is a fair-haired boy with Henry J. Kaiser, who has named him Kaiser-Frazer distributor in Los Angeles, Chicago, and New York. To commemorate the New York appointment, Muntz quickly purchased the house on Ninety-Second street, glamorized by Twentieth Century Fox, from which the FBI spied on the Nazi spies during the war. It won't hurt a bit.

When he isn't busy running his expanding empire, Madman Muntz usually may be found in night clubs with movie people, whom he likes very much. A fellow in his position, you know, has to live up to his personality

Each Christmas season, Hollywood Boulevard becomes Santa Claus Lane; Wilshire Boulevard's Miracle Mile, Beverly Hills, and the downtown section become what is sometimes called "a riot of color."

Generally the decorators are content with papier-maché candles, Christmas-tree effects, or whatever strikes them as appropriate and significant to remind the shoppers that their duty is to blow their dough like little ladies and gentlemen.

In 1940, however, someone dreamed up Christmas decorations with a motif for the downtown section. The first inkling I received that something new had been added was a telephone call from a harassed reader demanding desperately: "Who is Nicky Foodle?" I gave him Brushoff No. 27, reserved for escaped lunatics, but he was insistent. "It's your duty to find out, I'm going nuts," he pleaded. "Listen, I've read all the nursery-rhyme books. I've turned Mother Goose over in her grave. I've called the Public Library. No one knows who Nicky Foodle is, but there he is, on all the Christmas banners on Broadway."

Still disbelieving, I went to Seventh and Broadway and sure enough, swinging overhead on a banner was a pert little guy in green tights labeled Nicky Foodle. Surrounding him, on other banners, were other little characters, obviously his playmates, named Jimmie, Judy, Slim Pickens, Captain Tintop, and the Cinnamon Bear.

After some fast sleuthing, I learned they were characters in a radio serial, "The Cinnamon Bear." The way the story went, Judy and Jimmie, while decorating a Christmas tree, discovered the top ornament, the silver star, was missing. They asked their mother to let them search an old trunk in the attic for it. She did, but she shouldn't have.

In the trunk they found a tiny teddy bear and a strange type of telescope. They fumbled around with them awhile but suddenly caught on to the miracle: when viewed through the telescope, Teddy came alive. Not only that, he told them the silver star had been stolen by the Crazy Quilt Dragon and taken to Maybe Land. Judy and Jimmie promptly "degrew" themselves and took an airplane for Maybe Land, where they encountered all sorts of adventures and improbable persons, even for a radio serial.

Twenty-one programs later they came upon the missing star but alas, it was broken. But in Program Twenty-one, they met a pert little guy in green tights named Nicky Foodle who offered to take them to someone who could fix it.

And who do you suppose that was? None other than Santa Claus himself!

Since 1940, the Christmas decorations downtown have been singularly free of any motif.

Muscles Beach is a nickname the high-school set has given a stretch of beach front just south of the Santa Monica Pier. It isn't listed on any map. The youngsters thought up the name themselves, in healthy self-derision.

They play volley ball as if their lives depended on it. They flex their biceps on the parallel bars and the rings. They strut; they preen; they comb their hair. Some even go in the water.

The males are daring young men on flying trapezes. The girls are daring young ladies in what look like chemises, some strapless. Nowhere will anyone see more handsome, fit kids wear less more becomingly. They may not know the multiplication table but they are certainly pretty.

The whole philosophy of Muscles Beach was summed up by

a brash, tanned eight-year-old. Carelessly kicking sand on my magazine as he plodded by, he announced with awe and reverence to four fellow eight-year-olds: "Gee, all the good-looking girls are down this way!"

Ellsworth (Sonny) Wisecarver is no different from other growing boys with one exception, he likes his women grown up.

In the lush spring month of April 1944, when he was fourteen, he eloped to Yuma with Mrs. Elaine Monfredi, twenty-one, and they were married. The law caught up with them in Denver. Extradited to Los Angeles and charged with child stealing, Mrs. Monfredi was indignant. She told reporters she didn't know there was a law prohibiting a girl from falling in love and getting married. True, she'd had some previous dealing with the little guy with the bow and arrow before she met Wisecarver. She had, in fact, two children to show for it, and there was a certain vagueness as to whether she had married Mr. Monfredi. Some talk was to the effect that they had been wed in Nevada, but someone stole the marriage license or something.

When the case got to court in March 1945 there was considerable judicial hemming and hawing. The evidence indicated that Sonny had more or less swept Elaine off her feet instead of vice versa. The child-stealing charge, a felony, was dropped on condition that she plead guilty to a lesser offense, contributing to her husband's delinquency. She was sentenced to a year in jail but the sentence was suspended on condition that she remain on probation for three years. Wisecarver was made a ward of Juvenile court.

Eight months later, in November 1945, Sonny was at it again. He met pretty Mrs. Eleanor Deveny 25, at a party and they decided to go out and get a Hamburger. One thing must have led to another, or perhaps it was late and they had trouble finding a Hamburger stand. At any rate, the posse began organizing again. This time they were located love-nesting in Oroville, a small town several hundred miles north of Los Angeles.

Like her predecessor, Mrs. Deveny had two children and was indignant. "Sonny boy is the kind of guy every girl dreams about but very seldom finds," she said. "He is more of a man at sixteen than a lot of men are at thirty-five. I love him more than I do my own husband."

Sonny said, "I don't care a hoot if I ever see her again."

When Mrs. Deveny had her day in court, her husband, Corporal John Deveny, recently returned from duty in Japan, was a spectator. She pleaded not guilty to the delinquency charge.

Sonny was committed to the California Youth Authority for an indefinite period as an incorrigible and a potential sex delinquent. He stayed put until July 1946, when he escaped from a correction camp, and sought refuge in Nevada. He was apprehended three months later in Ely, Nevada and held for a month, but when California authorities, whose No. 1 problem child he had become, failed to request his extradition, he was released. He went to Las Vegas where he worked as a window trimmer, a grocery clerk, and a bus boy in a hotel. There he met Betty Zoe Reber, also seventeen, a theater usher who one night escorted him to a seat. Last March they were married quietly in Saint George, Utah by an elder in the Mormon church. They've settled down in a forty-dollar-a-month house trailer in Las Vegas, to prove, as Sonny told reporters at his wedding, "that my kid mistakes are behind me."

The public keeps asking plaintively: "Don't you think it's about time they stop calling him Sonny?"

Among the seven wonders of the so-called Plaster Athens of the Golden West is an impossible phenomenon called "The Farmers' Market." It is a spread of some hundred shops and booths contained in a series of white, shedlike structures at Third and Fairfax. Raw and prepared foods of every conceivable sort are vended and specialty shops sell hardware, furniture, talking birds, Indian craftware, pottery, antiques, patent medicines, books, and art objects. A button shop sells only buttons. A goggle shop sells only goggles.

But food's the thing: chefs working in glass-enclosed kitchens prepare and sell fresh-ground sausage, almond duck-and-egg foo young, enchiladas, corned beef, fish, fudge, and frijoles.

The Market is the product of a meeting of the minds of cadaverous Roger Dahlhjelm, ex-land promoter and Stanley-steamer salesman, and Fred Beck, an advertising writer. They were broke when they met in 1933 but had a basically simple idea: borrow a vacant field and invite farmers to sell absolutely fresh vegetables and fruit from trucks direct to housewives.

When the market opened in July 1934, a dozen farmers were on hand, paying fifty-cents-a-day parking charge. Today, according to the national business weeklies, it does an annual gross business of something like eight million dollars. The shopkeepers are now on a rental basis. Several have become independently rich.

Dahlhjelm's management has been astute and forthright. There are no leases and he unhesitatingly ejects tenants he finds selling bum tomatoes.

Beck's ballyhoo is primarily responsible for the project's fantastic success. In the early days, he whooped up interest with milking contests, square dances, corn-husking tournaments, circuses, and old fiddlers' bees. His biggest contribution is a daily column in the *Times*, financed by the farmers and shopkeepers passing the hat. Beck set himself up as a Keats of the Beets and a Milton of the Melons and in a short time had a greater readership than the syndicated maunderers.

During the wartime food shortages the merchants decided to stop advertising. They had little or nothing to sell. Beck announced his daily reports on love and intrigue among the rutabagas would cease. His readers shouted no, he couldn't do that to them. The clamor was such that the *Times* hired him as a staff columnist. In thirty days Beck realized he wasn't happy and returned to his bananas and beans.

Today people gladly stand in line to get waited on at the Market. It is the town's biggest independent food-retailing operation. Dahlhjelm and Beck are local celebrities with the incomes of chairmen of the board and a vacant weed lot on good days is the mecca of thirty thousand people who sit in sunny patios eating fried fish and cup cakes at Vine Street prices. In a sane city it couldn't happen.

Elysian Park is a large, quiet, brush and tree-covered hill off North Broadway, offering from its crest an unobstructed view of the Southern Pacific, Union Pacific, and Santa Fe railroad tracks, the trickle known as the Los Angeles River, and the haze-covered industrial section. Though only five minutes from the civic center, the park is somehow remote. It has become cut off, paradoxically, by recently constructed free-ways which slash through it.

Early in November 1937, a three-inch crack appeared in the earth near the crest. Five days later the crack measured three feet.

Reporters, photographers, radio announcers, geologists, and engineers swarmed to the widening crevice. Policemen kept sight-seers out of the park. A fire siren was kept handy.

Two hundred feet below, several thousand persons stood by day and night, waiting for doom to strike. Shortly after 10 P.M. November 26, a million tons of earth and rock, approximately one hundred yards of hillside, slid away.

Geologists made clear that the slide was simply a matter of the law of gravity catching up with a batch of loose, rain-soaked earth that happened to be on the side of a cliff. The public would have no such nonsense. Mysterious forces having to do with earthquakes, witch doctors, sin, or radio static clearly were at work.

Eastern papers headlined LOS ANGELES SLIDING INTO OCEAN. Relatives in Nebraska and New Hampshire wired, as they had done after the 1933 quake: ARE YOU ALL RIGHT?

During the excitement, one paper printed a piece of folklore to the effect that a spell was cast over the area seventy-five years before. Antonio Feliz, who died in 1863, willed his land to his niece, Petronella, went the story, but when she tried to take it over she found a new occupant there. Petronella, according to the paper, turned her face toward the Verdugo Hills and called down a curse on the old homestead. She invoked the wrath of heaven and hell to kill those who had cheated her and asked that fire and water destroy the rancho. So saying, went the story, she fell dead. All in all, it was a pretty good tale, but the Federal Writers' Project, checking history, found it didn't apply to Elysian Park but to Griffith Park, which was doing fine.

Reporters prodding about for news leads came upon a closed-up tunnel in the face of the sliding cliff and the more daring of them removed the barriers and went in. They were able to continue into the cliff some thousand feet, plodding through a muddy six-foot cavern. They found many subsidiary caves and what seemed walled-up rooms. They also found fragmentary evidence that the system of underground passages might have dated centuries back, to the days of the padres. The reporters formed a club, the Trogodolytes, and planned further safaris inside the magic mountain. But suddenly their bubble burst. Kids in the neighborhood, it was disclosed, had been using the cave as a playhouse for years. In more recent years hoboes had used it for their private depression.

Now Elysian Park is very quiet. From a nine-day wonder, the landslide is just something geology professors tell their classes about.

Nightly, at nine o'clock, Eastsiders with keen ears may hear three long, mournful, train-whistlelike blasts.

It is the curfew, a curiously preserved anachronism. It first sounded in 1900, when the city enacted a curfew ordinance to curb youthful after-dark exuberance. The Southern California Gas Company was appointed official curfew blower because it had the only plant in town that could get up enough steam at that hour to make enough noise.

For years, old residents, on hearing it, set their clocks, locked their doors, and prepared for bed. Policemen who found youngsters wandering the streets admonished them severely and sent them trotting home. The term juvenile delinquency, now very important in Los Angeles, had not yet been discovered.

One night the whistle failed to blow—it was being cleaned—and residents complained mightily. Without it, they wrote the gas company, their lives were dislocated. They didn't know what time it was, therefore were liable to stay up beyond their usual bedtime.

For the last fifteen years the whistle has been more or less meaningless. Traffic noises and the spread of the city have limited its range and therefore its effectiveness. It has become particularly useless in reaching the jive generation for whom it was intended. Things don't get started for them until around 9 P.M.

But the curfew ordinance is still on the books and the night crew at the Aliso Street compression plant, whence it emanates, still blow it; no one has told them not to.

Whether the Beebe family's personal cosmic rays are a boon to mankind, or merely a nuisance to the neighbors, remains, as we go to press, a matter for the courts to determine.

The uproar started early in 1945 when stories of marvelous curative powers came from the Cosmic Research Laboratories,

2109 Fashion Avenue, Long Beach. By August the lame and the halt were thronging by the thousand to the place and the neighbors were incensed.

In time the matter was brought to the attention of the Long Beach city council and public hearings were scheduled. The neighbors demanded abatement of what they termed a nuisance. Roy Beebe, in his own defense, said he was working for humanity. He said he gathered cosmic rays in his back-yard laboratory and treated patients with ray baths, ray-vitalized water, and ray-impregnated wheat.

Someone thought to ask Dr. Robert Millikan, Cal Tech's cosmic-ray researcher, his opinion and he said that cosmic-ray treatment was bunk. Captain W. B. Wolcott of World War I, on the other hand, said the treatment had cured him of paralysis he had suffered from for seventeen years. Others said their nervous disorders were relieved by Beebe's ray treatment.

Nevertheless the city council voted five to three that the cosmic-ray plant was a nuisance and told Beebe to take his rays somewhere else. Beebe told them he had intended doing so anyway but had been stalemated by the housing and building tieup. He was given a deferral until he could find new quarters.

The subject flamed anew in April 1946, when skeptical deputy sheriffs raided a sprawling alfresco establishment in a field at 123rd Street and Santa Fe Avenue and arrested Charles and Paul Beebe, sons of the discoverer of the ray treatment. The brothers had advertised that their stratospheric radiation method relieved everything from psychoneurosis to arthritis, the officers said. This, they said, was naughty, and required the posting of one thousand dollars' bail.

But when they came into court the brothers, through their attorneys, filed demurrers to the sixteen counts against them on the grounds that they didn't constitute a public offense. Judge Stanley Moffatt agreed and ordered the prosecution to amend its complaints. Whatever the outcome, scores of Beebe's patients will always be grateful for the relief he gave them and certain that he is a great humanitarian, persecuted by unbelievers.

Jim Moran, who looks like a tired fullback, has made a career of screwballism. He sold an icebox to an Eskimo. He found a needle in a haystack. He changed horses in the middle of a stream.

Perhaps his most sensational stunt was hatching an ostrich egg. On Father's Day 1946, he appeared at the Los Angeles Ostrich Farm in a sweat shirt and a pair of "hatching pants"— shorts with an impressive bustle of ostrich feathers, fashioned by a Hollywood dress designer. He announced that out of his deep love for the animal kingdom, he was taking over the hatching of an egg abandoned by an ostrich couple, Joe and Eve.

He spent his days squatting in a specially constructed wheelchair, with a basket slung underneath to hold the egg, and by the merest coincidence reading Betty MacDonald's *The Egg and I.* To newsmen he made no secret of the fact that International Studio, which was filming the book, was paying him two thousand dollars.

After nineteen days, four hours, and thirty-two minutes of Moran's tender, motherly care, the egg hatched. He didn't mention that, warmed by the sun in normal birth, the egg probably would have hatched in about forty-two days.

On Monday, September 16, 1945, the Reverend Charles G. Long, a retired missionary, warned the world from his Pasadena home that the world would end the following Friday.

The prophetic date, he said, came to him in a vision seven years before. He backed up his belief with the quotation from the II Peter, iii: "But the day of the Lord will come as a thief in the night; in which the heavens shall pass away with a great noise, and the elements shall melt with fervent heat; the earth also, and the works that are therein, shall be burned up."

On Tuesday, Reverend Long and his son Richard, founder of the Remnant Church of God, reiterated their gloomy forecast and entered upon a day of atonement. Swami Paramhausa Yogananda, from atop Mount Washington, disagreed. Destruction, he said, was thousands of years away.

Nevertheless, on Thursday, father and son, and their followers, prepared for doomsday. The end would come, they said, at 7:33 A.M.

A swarm of reporters and photographers appeared at the Longs' home early Friday, figuring it was as good a place as any to get atomized. They were not received too hospitably but Reverend Long held out a faint hope. "If people repent their wrongs," he said, "this will not come to pass."

When Friday came and went, Reverend Long prayed with his congregation and handed out rain checks on the end of the world. The most mundane note of the whole incident was sounded by the Pasadena Board of Education. Lifting an eyebrow at the publicity the story was getting, the board announced Thursday that, end of the world or no, the kids better attend school Friday or they'd be sorry.

Page 377 of the Los Angeles telephone directory has five listings for a woman named Dolores at 634 South Serrano Avenue —the Dolores Auto Driving School, the Dolores Personal Service, the Dolores Realty Co., the Dolores 24-Hour Chauffeur Service, and the Dolores 24-Hour Courier Service.

Page 381 of the yellow classified directory lists the Dolores Courier Service at the same address, with the subtitle: LET DOLORES SHOW CITY IN A PACKARD SUPER 8.

Between the lines there is the story of a defiant woman—Mrs. Dolores Gunn, a blond divorcée in her middle forties. The story started in 1939 when she was convicted of procuring two girls for immoral purposes and sentenced to pay a twenty-five-dollar fine or serve five days in jail. The two girls testified that the gentlemen who made dates with them through Mrs. Gunn's escort service gave them drugged liquor and turned out to be policemen.

In April 1941, she was back in the toils. She paid a twenty-five-dollars fine after pleading guilty to violating a city zoning ordinance.

In September 1942 she was arrested for operating an escort bureau without a license. A plain-clothes detective had dated a thirty-year-old woman through the bureau and he said they violated the law. At her trial, Dolores said she was conducting a lonely-hearts exchange as a patriotic duty: servicemen could obtain dates without charge. Furthermore, she felt the besmirch on her character could not go unanswered. She sued the city, the mayor, the chief of police, and several vice-squad officers for seventy thousand dollars' damages. Despite her unique defense, she was convicted and sentenced to thirty days in jail. An additional 150 days was suspended on condition that she refrain from operating the escort bureau. She filed notice of appeal. The Superior Court, however, denied her appeal in March 1943, contending her motive was not patriotism but money. She surrendered and served thirty days in Lincoln Heights Jail. On her release she blasted jail conditions, charging prisoners were treated inhumanly.

She was back in the news in June 1943 with a fiery letter to the City Council. Identifying herself as founder of the Dolores Escort Bureau for the prevention of prostitution, she questioned the authority of a police officer who gave her a traffic citation for ignoring a stop signal. She charged she was being persecuted but the traffic judge didn't see it her way. He found her guilty and fined her eight dollars.

In February 1945 she filed a petition and qualified as a candidate for mayor in the municipal election. Her goal was to unseat Mayor Bowron, who she charged was behind her so-called persecution. During the campaign, she drove through the city in a

1939 Packard limousine with critical remarks about the administration and nostalgic references to her stay in jail. Beneath a drawing of a crude bunk was the caption: ELECT DOLORES MAYOR AND TAKE THE STEEL OUT OF THE STEEL BUNKS IN THE L.A. CITY JAIL. She received only a few hundred votes. Bowron was easily re-elected.

In October 1945 she was arrested again for operating an escort bureau without a license. Two patrons who called on her paid ten dollars for the names and phone numbers of pleasant female companions. They were police sergeants. But when they called to arrest Dolores they were unable to find the ten-dollar bill they had given her. It was, of course, marked. This time Dolores was fined $150.

Anyone else probably would by this time have seen the handwriting on the wall and taken up a new career; not the resourceful Dolores.

By eliminating the word "escort" and substituting "courier" and "chauffeur," Dolores today operates a thriving business. And business is good. She has six Packards and three Cadillacs in use.

Her girls are now "couriers" or "chauffeurs." In response to a telephone call, a girl driver will pick up any gentleman interested in the many points of scenic interest in and near Los Angeles. He hires the girl driver as he would a taxicab driver. He is expected to tip her as he would a cabby. He can have the girl drive him around for an hour, for twenty-four hours, or for three months, just so Dolores receives her fee: $3.75 an hour. The fare can direct the female courier to dinner, to a night club, to New York, or to a daisy-picking safari in the moonlight.

Vice-squad officers occasionally try to break into the act, but Dolores, who says she can smell them over the telephone, handles them herself. When they hand her a down payment on her services she quickly remembers she needs gas and pulls into a service station. The gasoline man thus gets the marked bill.

"Aren't politicians stupid?" she says.

* * *

An East Fifth Street saloon was padlocked by the law but passersby noticed a black cat sleeping in the window. Someone must have complained for shortly thereafter a sign appeared in the window: NOTICE. THIS CAT IS BEING TAKEN CARE OF. DON'T WORRY. A week later the sign was penciled over to read: NOTICE. *These cats* IS BEING TAKEN CARE OF. DON'T WORRY.

20

If you just keep on writing long enough you'll say something.—MORTON THOMPSON, *Joe, the Wounded Tennis Player*

FOR more than eleven years now, I have been writing a daily column about ordinary people and the extraordinary things that happen to them. It isn't a name column. I dissent from the opinion that names make news. This is heresy, of course, seven miles from Hollywood and I'm sure it puzzles some of my friends in the motion-picture publicity business who have been known to transport movie gossipers into an ecstatic drool by merely murmuring: "Here's one that happened to Olivia on the set today."

I look for human interest and try to stay even with current trivia, effluvia, flotsam and jetsam. I think I have the sharpest bunch of postcard contributors in the country although I wish some of them wouldn't drink so much and decide to call me at 3 A.M. with something they just thought of.

I am addicted to lost causes, Mexican food, rhyming twoliners, objective writing, unaccompanied piano playing, understatement, and people. I am fortunate in being able to write anything that comes into my head, although when my head hurts the subscribers suffer too.

The only advice I ever got came from Manchester Boddy, the publisher, who said: "Just keep it in good taste." There have been times when I imagined he was looking over my shoulder and frowning at what I was writing but I quickly assured myself this was impossible—he was out on his wonderful ranch in La Cañada, tending his camellias and writing a book of his own.

People have been tricked into believing that writing a daily column is a wonderful, exhilirating experience. They sidle up and ask how things are behind the scenes. I don't know. The people behind the scenes always look like the people out in the audience.

As for the glamour of it all, writing a column isn't dull, but it isn't wonderful. You get to go a great many places and talk to many nice people but you always have to sit down and write what you decide you will permit them to say, and if your type-writer is in an ugly mood and fights back you've got trouble.

To put it bluntly, being vital in print once a day is a neat trick if you can do it. No one can. The trick is to make the stuff seem vital. A columnist has two choices. He can be a reporter or he can throw the words. I try both. Life is easier that way.

I attribute my longevity as a columnist to my early training as a working newsman, during which period I cultivated a host of friends in the business whose brains I now pick, and to a recurrent nightmare in which I visualize a horrible empty space with eyes. It is the space in the paper for which I must write a column tomorrow.

The nearest I ever came to literary immortality was *L'Affaire Girdle*. On February 18, 1941, in a paragraph captioned STREET SCENE, I printed this item: "Not so soon will the gents forget an episode at Sixth and Hill. As a blond young lady stepped from a streetcar, her girdle fell off."

That was all—two short sentences—but they changed my life. The repercussions were tremendous and to this day I receive sly references to my experience as a girdle expert.

Girls by the score said I was naive and had been taken in. Removing a girdle, they said, was an engineering feat. Not even a contortionist could lose one. Even the wife of a university psychology professor said it couldn't happen, at Sixth and Hill Streets or anywhere else.

I was forced to admit in print a few days later "The rumor that I have the girdle situation in hand is without foundation."

Diagrams poured in, showing the differences between a full girdle, a panty girdle, a garter belt, and other intimate foolers.

The item simmered along for a few days and would have died the death of all such trivia, but Charles R. Moore of United Press got the idea it might entertain U.P.'s 1740 clients. He put the film-studio publicity men to work and they came up with sparkling quotes from their lady actresses.

The story hit the front page of the *New York World-Telegram* and others along the way. My own paper printed it, with my photo alongside Dorothy Lamour's *en sarong*.

Wherever I went, I was backed into corners and subjected to belittling conversation to the effect that girls couldn't lose girdles. I stood foursquare on my original reportorial premise: they could and did.

A patient I knew polled the fifty-two nurses at San Fernando Veterans' Hospital. Of these, forty-four said "Impossible," two said "It never happened to me," two said "Pretty fresh, ain't you?" and four became sick from laughing.

Constant Reader demanded that the blonde who lost the girdle be subpoenaed and made to testify yes or no under oath. A bellhop in a downtown hotel wrote: "I am an authority on the subject. Girdles can and do come off and without undue urging. It's been going on for years."

A girl named Josephine wrote: "Girdles can come off if they have a zipper moving upward with the raising of the arm upward. Just a few deep breaths of fresh air and does the zipper give! I know. I don't wear a girdle but I do wear shorts with a zipper and each time I have to be double sure the lock is locked, or else."

A police sergeant, who insisted he be nameless, said he wouldn't be knowing about girdles but one time in 1926 he lost his shorts. He removed them simultaneously with his trousers before bathing and changed to clean ones. Somehow the soiled ones stayed in his right pants leg. They emerged in the middle of a big crowd at the Pacific Electric Station.

One man suggested: "Maybe the gal grabbed her mother's girdle in her rush to get to work. Or maybe she'd been reducing. Find out. People want to know."

I was especially grateful to a lady in Whittier who special-deliveried as follows: "I blush, for I am a girdle loser. It was in a theater lobby at a matinee in New York. I dropped my bag. As I stooped quickly to recover it—tragedy. My girdle fell off, completely dragging my hose downward with it. It was a rubber reducing corset. The top edge had split and run like a stocking."

Average Citizen was of the opinion that I underestimated the importance of the phenomenon. He wanted a demonstration arranged. He thought the 103,000-seat Memorial Coliseum would accommodate those interested, with movie stars and girdle tycoons co-operating.

Leo Baron, an old newspaper friend, air-mailed the U.P. story as it appeared in the *Kansas City Journal* and included his own diagnosis:

> The thing that dropped off that pretty young thing probably was a goongiddy. A one-armed paperhanger who read the story over my shoulder at lunch today explained about a goongiddy. In his mother's day, it was a contraption worn around the waist and came equipped with pocket compartments to store snuff, wig oil and oil of wintergreen to ward off the pip. It also had an anti-crawling device. Some goongiddies, he said, were used as gun holsters, while others were used by the more sentimental as a vault for love letters.

Two girls wrote in claiming to be the one who lost the girdle. One wrote: "That goongiddy item really did it. I positively did not lose a goongiddy. I could have come to your rescue long ago but I was curious to see how you would handle the girdle situation. You know, I'm afraid it will be a good many years before I can look at a girdle and not think of you."

Another girl was inspired to verse:

> You're girdle conscious now, I see.
> To be dropped off or not to be.
> You've missed the gist of the thing, I fear,
> You've failed to make the matter clear.
> So much depends on the build of the lassie,
> Is she skinny or has she bumps on her chassis?
> A curve, you know, loses half of its oomph
> If it doesn't precede or follow a boomp.
> Does she hook up or zip up or wiggle in?
> Does she wear the darn thing next to her skin?
> Believe me, boy, you've a hard row to hoe,
> There are so many things you just got to know.

Vindication was belated, but nevertheless sweet. In January 1944 an elevator operator in a Spring Street office building told a passenger: "I didn't believe Matt Weinstock a few years ago when he told of a lady losing a certain undergarment getting off a streetcar but I do now. I lost mine running from the streetcar to the building this morning."

A former Los Angeles man simultaneously wrote, from Chicago, that he saw the same thing happen to a dignified lady at Fifty-Third and Hyde Park there.

In both cases the ladies stepped clear, stuffed the things in their purses, and blushed their way out of the vicinity. All in all, the notoriety was a very sobering thing and I found myself becoming increasingly compassionate with the girls who wear body shapers. Naturally, I am the first to concede that rubber isn't what it used to be.

Early in 1934, when I was a city editor, a husky fellow came into the editorial room and asked if we could go somewhere and talk. He was very profane and very tough-looking.

When we adjourned to a private office he said: "I've been told I could talk to you without you hollering copper. I want to make a deal for a friend of mine."

His friend was Pretty Boy Floyd, sought by three states for murder, bank robbery, and whatnot. Floyd, he said, was in hiding, an hour from the office.

"I didn't expect you to believe me," he said, "so I'll tell you what you do. Go down to the police station and get a copy of Floyd's fingerprints. When we get to the hideout you can get a set off Floyd and match them."

I mentioned that Floyd was hot as a stove and that the police might get wise. "Ah they're dumb," he said. "He was dancing the other night at the Coconut Grove."

The deal he wanted to make was unbelievably naive. Floyd was running low on money. He wanted five thousand dollars for his own signed story of his career. He also wanted the paper to go to bat in correcting a great injustice. Pretty Boy hadn't meant to kill those deputy sheriffs and bank cashiers. What could he do when they came after him with tommy guns? If Floyd were given an opportunity to tell his own story, sympathetically, of course, the emissary felt certain the governors of the various states that wanted him dead or alive would relent. Pretty Boy, he said, would surrender if assured of life imprisonment. He didn't like the idea of the electric chair.

I explained that five thousand dollars was the same as moving out the printing press and that I didn't think he appreciated to what extent public sentiment was against Pretty Boy. At length, after I explained that no paper could press buttons and cause assorted sheriffs, governors, and FBI men to change their plans, he realized his cause was lost. Disappointed, he thanked me for my honesty and reminded me, as he left: "You're not talking about this, you know." It was with some relief that I read of

Pretty Boy's demise at the hands of FBI man Melvin Purvis and others on a farm near East Liverpool, Ohio, in October 1934, after a frantic two-year chase through Oklahoma, Iowa, and Kansas.

I always wondered whether the burly visitor was really Floyd's emissary. Later disclosures proved he was. Official records show that Floyd's pal, Ed Davis, convicted murderer, was captured in a Los Angeles apartment March 1, 1934, and at the time authorities trailed Floyd to a hideout near Lancaster. When they arrived he had departed.

After the emissary's visit, I was slightly uncomfortable. A killer on the loose isn't my idea of pleasant company.

In some quarters, I'm known as "The Chain Breaker." This is because of the sadistic manner in which I toss Good Luck of London chain letters in my wastebasket, a hell of a way to get famous.

People who say they aren't superstitious but still don't want to take any chances send them in for me to destroy. They haven't the nerve.

Everyone, certainly, has seen these letters. They state: "The Luck of London was sent me today and I am sending it to you. This chain was started by an American officer. It has been around the world four times. The one who breaks the chain will have bad luck. Gracie Fields won ten thousand dollars after sending it. P. M. Ambrose won five thousand dollars but lost it when he broke the chain."

Recipients are instructed to make four copies within twenty-four hours and send them to persons they wish to receive fame and fortune.

The letters vary a little. In some Gracie Fields is stated to have won seventy thousand dollars and the unfortunate Mr. Ambrose to have lost fifty thousand, but what are a few zeros among superstitious people?

One day I had a few moments with Gracie Fields in her

dressing room at N.B.C. before she went on the air and asked about her connection with the chain-letter madness. It had plagued her, she said, for years. She had no idea how the letters got started or how her name came to be used. Wherever she went though, people asked about them. Most persons, she said, took the attitude of an elevator operator in the Waldorf-Astoria, who told her: "I don't believe the stuff but you're doing all right so I don't suppose it'll do any harm to keep the chain going."

One time, however, she encountered a woman who had broken the chain and had bad luck. Her husband had died and she blamed Miss Fields for being associated with an ill-omened venture.

The interview solved one thing: except on the radio, Gracie doesn't talk in Lancashire dialect.

A publicity man for an airline telephoned and insisted he buy a lunch. I hadn't seen him for months and was glad of the opportunity to talk with him. Instead of a fast blue-plate special, the lunch was a gourmet's dream. Afterwards he explained. His budget for entertainment had split its seams and to repair the deficit he had used my name heavily on his expense account. "I really owe you this one," he concluded. "In New York they think you're the heaviest eater and drinker in Los Angeles."

One of the pleasures of writing a column is the mad irrelevance that goes with it. One day I received this letter:

Dear Mr. W. I am the tall, thin, dark-haired woman everyone in the know in Southern California is talking about. The grapevine began about a year and a half ago. A silly story of me trying to get masculine glad-eye by artificial bust buildup. There are perhaps several versions to this. Every car, bus and train I ride, every downtown café, bank and department store seethes with conjecture and speculation when I appear. My husband attributes such interest to the incongruity of the story with my ladylike appearance and good looks. Could be? Since I am a constant reader of your column, perhaps you will do me the kindness of informing my public (1) I am a normal, happily married woman with two children, (2) never had any idea of trying to be a sweater girl, (3) definitely am not a poor little thing and need no sympathy. Amusing in the beginning, the scope of the thing is disgusting. Please omit my name for obvious reasons.

* * *

Once upon a time, I was a managing editor. As such, I hired and fired a number of men. One day at a bar I met a reporter I had fired months before. I told him I regretted having done so as he was an able newsman.

"The reason I let you go," I said, "was that I could never tell whether you were drunk or sober."

"You know," he said thoughtfully, "I could never tell either."

A junior-high-school friend notified me that the Good Humor man in a Westside beat, when asked "What have you got?" replied "Kidney trouble." The kid admitted that naming fifteen flavors all day long would get monotonous but thought he overdid it. I printed the item and the Good Humor man promptly reformed. He changed his reply to "A headache."

One day I received a flurry of calls from readers reporting mystic symbols all over the sky. Over Laurel Canyon one spelled *Boo*. Over South Gate another spelled *Sock*. Over Montebello, *Bad Boy*. Over West Los Angeles, *Love*.

The explanation came from a pilot. Seemed a few flyers were

testing new P-38s and discovered they exuded in their wakes beautiful white plumes of vapor, caused by some unusual atmospheric condition.

"When you're up twenty-five thousand feet and find you have turned into a comet," he said, "you think perhaps the folks down below would like a spelling lesson."

I have to tell how I became part of the Independence Day celebration in 1939. A reader shot off some firecrackers and after they blew apart he noticed the powder was wadded in old newspapers. One particular cracker, sent me as a souvenir, contained my column for one day in October 1936. The firecrackers were made by the Kwong Hang Sing in Canton, China. Inscrutable, those paper salvagers.

The nearest a columnist gets to a rebel war cry is founding a fictitious organization. I've launched dozens of them. The most successful was the You Can't Do That to Me Society. I also tried to bring the light to the peasants on matters difficult for them to understand, fillers for instance.

Fillers are the irrelevant two- or three-line items in newspapers which always seem transplanted from somewhere else. At the end of a story about Russia, or the island of Palmyra, or Katharine Hepburn, you'll run into a paragraph stating: "The whiffinpoof is considered a very sacred bird in a remote province of Turkestan." It's a filler. It's there because the make-up man in the composing room needed something just that size to fill an awkward space in a type form.

Readers, of course, naively assume they should make sense. One woman made a *cause célèbre* of them, bringing it to us in the form of indignation over the telephone. She accepted readily enough the one that stated "The leather in a pair of men's oxfords would make an officer's pistol holster." She snickered but held her peace on reading "Wild tribesmen of Ceylon shoot from a sitting position and hold the bow with their toes and feet." But when she read "Paleodictyoptera, one of the first creatures to fly, had six wings," she became excited.

The one that got her though was "Moose will dive in deep water after food and their tracks have been found on the bottoms of lakes 12 feet below the surface." She refused to accept the statement without proof, and unable to locate any underwater moose tracks, she demanded I do something about fillers. I quieted her by telling her my classic filler story.

In April 1945, Raul Chavez came upon a filler stating that an egg with three yolks, the first such discovered in the area in twenty-five years, had turned up on a farm in Missouri. To Raul, who worked in the Canoga Egg Store on Robertson Boulevard, the filler was a challenge. He cut it out and went to work matching it.

It was real work, too. Raul's egg emporium handles an average of two hundred cases of eggs daily. There are thirty dozen to a case, which adds up to seventy-two thousand eggs a day. Holding each one up to the light can get tiresome.

Early in March 1946, Raul triumphantly sent to my office two eggs with the ragged clipping. They were three-yolkers, he was certain. When I opened them they were only two-yolkers.

On March 20, 1946, another egg carton appeared on my desk. It contained one egg and a note: "This egg has either three or four yolks."

An impromptu première was arranged and amid cries of "That's a yolk, son!" the egg was banged open. You could have knocked everyone over with a white leghorn's tailfeather when two pairs of ochre eyes stared back at them from the saucer. Yes, the egg had four yolks, a one-in-a-million longshot. I had a nice breakfast and Raul got a nice clipping.

Along with 162,000 others, I was caught short after the war when it was discovered there weren't enough places of shelter to go around. I received a fast thirty-day OPA eviction notice and faced a bleak future in the gutter when a benevolent brother, Charles, took us in. A tiny upstairs bedroom on busy Beverly Boulevard became home.

A look out the bedroom window was always a shock. A huge billboard, a two-sheet, nothing else, filled the landscape.

When I moved in, I found myself blinking at a king-size bottle of cleaning fluid for sinks and bathrooms. Overnight it became a whisky ad. A few weeks later, as though by magic— we never saw the workmen change it—another brand of whisky appeared. Next, a huge box of macaroni.

Then the macaroni was replaced by a poster urging votes for a man who wished to become lieutenant governor of California (and did). His large photo made him out to be a very stern fellow with an accusing glint in his eyes. Even when my back was turned I felt his steely eyes gimleting through me. I thought I was alone in my uneasiness until a lady named Hilda who shares my fortunes confided that he embarrassed the hell out of her when she faced him while brushing her teeth in the bathroom next door, which also fronted on the billboard.

I wrote about all this in the column, concluding on the note that it was no use his glaring at us, we weren't going to vote for him. Moreover, we appealed to the billboard gremlin to bring back the whisky ad or even the cleaning fluid for sinks and bathrooms.

The next morning around 7 A.M. I glanced sleepily out of the window to see whether old Gimlet Eye was still prying. To my relief he was gone. In his place was an ad for a candidate for the United States Senate (he didn't win). Just the name and an X—no photo.

And then I practically jumped out of my pajamas. In a lower corner of the billboard was a printed sign: SORRY MATT WEIN-STOCK.

Now this is one of the things that doesn't happen. Fighting

bill boards had always been considered safe, like fighting wind-mills. Now one was fighting back, or at least talking back, add-ing to the world's heavy burden of chaos.

A little telephoning turned up a fey fellow named Hal Brown, president of Pacific Outdoor Advertising, who had decided to top my playful, mild item. Sometime around dawn, a crew had removed old Gimlet Eye and softened my personal scenery. Anonymously, Hal Brown wanted us to know he was sorry we had been terrorized.

Election Day came and in due time the photoless candidate's poster was replaced by an ad for my own paper, the *Daily News*. In the same lower left corner a printed footnote inquired OKAY MATT? It was O.K. but by now the neighbors were aware some kind of game was going on.

The big coup came on Independence Day, 1946. A few min-utes before 7 A.M. I saw two hardy fellows in overalls on a scaf-fold, feverishly pasting up a new poster. They had been told doubtless that columnists never wake until noon. Little did they know that a blond, blue-eyed young lady of three months named Jane determined who woke up when.

I dressed quickly and went out for a look just as the workmen finished the job. I fell back staggered. The new poster was just for me—and maybe twenty thousand passersby on Beverly Bou-levard. Specially drawn, it had a five-foot firecracker exploding with a sunburst effect, under which heavy two-foot letters greeted HAPPY FOURTH, MATT. Like a poke in the eye.

Someone had gone to a great deal of trouble, I said to the workmen, hoping to get them talking, as they removed the scaf-folding. They played dumb. "All we do is put them up," said one. "And double time today too," said the other.

During the day, a few cars stopped and people in them glanced accusingly at the sign, the house, and behind the shrub-bery, ostensibly wondering what sort of deviltry was afoot. I huddled inside the house. One anonymous guy telephoned to wish me a Happy Fourth, like it said on the billboard, heh, heh, heh.

The exploding firecracker lasted for three days, then the men with buckets of paste and brushes got busy again. Their next effort was an ad for something called Gallo Glacier, a hot-weather drink achieved by mixing port wine with soda water in a glass of ice. The billboard portrayed this setup against a cool green-and-white snowy background. The inevitable footnote stated MATT, IT's IN YOUR ICEBOX, COLD! With frost on the word COLD.

Sure enough, a mysterious gentleman had come to the door with some samples of the wine, with instructions to the lady to put one of them—it had a red ribbon around the neck—in the refrigerator.

Suddenly I realized the implications, the possibilities. What I had here clearly was a magic wand, an Aladdin's Lamp. Did I want steak, beer, mayonnaise, a bathing girl? All I had to do was say so; no box tops, no coupons.

I said so in the column. I wrote that I didn't want to push my luck but perhaps the billboard pixie who was making my life so interesting had among his clients, say, a real-estate agent with a house to rent. I would be delighted to meet him halfway, or even nine tenths of the way.

While the pixie was handling this matter in his own mysterious manner, his career came to an end. Someone discovered that the billboard was not quite far enough away from a high voltage line to meet the exacting demands of a municipal ordinance. One day, men with hammers and nail pullers came and removed it. We're still living in the bedroom.

One day a kindly lady telephoned and said she detected some astrological bond with me from reading the whimseys I occasionally put into the column and asked: "Did you get them?"

"No," I said guardedly, not knowing what she was talking about and wishing I hadn't picked up the receiver.

She was surprised; she had sent them and had every reason to believe they had come through as conditions had been perfect.

Finally I summoned courage to ask, "Sent what?"

"Thought waves," she said.

She sent them, she said, to all her friends.

21

California! Land of the lemon grove and the nut!
                                        —VACHEL LINDSAY

L OS ANGELES abounds with what have come to be known as
    "characters." They are the innocents and the eccentrics,
daft or uninhibited folk, who do what they do because they feel
like it.

There is no pattern to their conduct, only a sense of utter freedom. Some are fugitives from the bemuscled men in white coats
who carry strait jackets; some are ordinary citizens in protest
against what is normal; others are simply part elf. They belong
in no particular economic stratum, though most of them are
more familiar with the Midnight Mission than the Biltmore
Hotel.

On the gutter level, two downtown characters are standouts.
They belong to the restless tribe of transients who roam the
streets and sit in railway waiting rooms and on Pershing Square
benches. If they don't have flophouse money, they sleep in all-
night movies on Main Street. When they are rousted out at
8:30 A.M. they head for the washrooms at the railway and bus
terminals or those in public buildings. One of these two, a
ragged drifter approximately eighty, used to go through setting-up
exercises near the men's room at the Subway Terminal Building. The trainmen on duty called him Bernarr Macfadden and,
when his quivering knees bent during his floor-touching exer-
tions, they called out: "Hey, Bernarr, you're cheating." The second oldster wore a red bandana around his neck and his hat
and lapels were covered with campaign buttons. Some went back
to Presidential elections of twenty years ago, Liberty Bond issues

of World War I, and 23 skidoo. Usually a hunk of French bread stuck out of his coat pocket. One day Buttons saw Bernarr exercising and remarked: "Boy, you certainly get some screwballs around here!"

There's John the Baptist, as he is called. Huge and sturdy, with long white hair and beard and pink cheeks and wearing a rough shirt and white overalls, he tramps barefooted through downtown streets. Though the living image of a biblical prophet, he is to passersby a nut, a religious fanatic. To John the Baptist, passersby are lost souls, caught in the false values of a degenerate civilization. He stares at them pushing and fighting in the shopping or traffic rush. His eyes twinkle; a smile plays around his mouth. Suddenly he throws back his magnificent head and roars with laughter. He enjoys his joke sometimes for fully two minutes, then shoulders his bundle and disappears in the crowd.

Occasionally a hoaxer disturbs the natural charm of Los Angeles' host of innocents, such as the amateur naturalist who attracted some attention a few years ago with the claim that Silver Lake, a municipal reservoir, contained a monster which he had named *Reptilensis Silverlakus*. On foggy nights, from his hillside porch overlooking the lake, he said, he regularly watched the huge reptile rise out of the water. His theory was that the lake snake was nothing but a common old sea serpent, left high and dry when earth movements raised the hills out of the Pacific. Surprised to find himself landlocked, the monster decided to make the best of things. The phony naturalist's story broke down in the early days of the war when he claimed to have seen the lake snake, in an impatient mood, turn on the lights around the lake so it could frighten the dogs which broke the stillness of the night and disturbed it. The hoaxer at length admitted that three quick snorts of bourbon gave a better outline of *Reptilensis Silverlakus* in the mist.

Motion-picture bit players include in their ranks a number of "characters." Recognition is slow for these troupers, though some of them are former stars. The trouble is that they become typed in one role and nothing else is expected of them. Some of them lose ambition and become discouraged. Not so Max Wagner. For years Max played Gangster Number Three in one of the great clichés of the movies and he played it well. The scene is familiar to everyone: The squealer cowers in a corner of a room. The door opens and Gangster Number One, a very sinister fellow, takes four steps toward him. Behind him is Gangster Number Two, who takes three steps, folds his arms, and glowers at the stoolie. Next comes Gangster Number Three, who takes one step in, then leans menacingly against the wall. Gangster Number Four closes the door, locks it, removes the key significantly, and leans against the door, smirking nastily. At this point, Gangster Number One barks "Now you rat, talk fast!"

Sometimes, of course, the four furtive gentlemen are G-men and the stoolie is the hero in a tough jam, but the routine is the same: four steps, three steps, one step, and lock the door. The menace is always effective, even though the menace boys know how grooved their roles are. Well, the big moment in Max Wagner's life will always be the day the director, as a tribute to his sinister interpretation, promoted him from Gangster Number Three to Gangster Number Two.

Another time, Eddie Hart and Frank Marlow had parts in a crime picture, playing gangsters. They were two of six gunmen trapped in a room by G-men. The director lined them up in advance for instruction.

"Now when the G-men crash in and start shooting," he said, pointing to each of them. "you're dead, you're dead, you run for the door, you're dead, you keep shooting, you hide behind the sofa."

"Hey," whispered Marlow, "what's the difference if you're dead or not?"

"If you're dead you don't work tomorrow, that's the difference," said Hart, the veteran.

The cameras started rolling and the G-men rushed in shooting. Things went fine for a moment, then the director yelled "Cut" and tore out a handful of hair.

"Hey Marlow," he screamed, "you're dead."

"Oh no I'm not," said he more aware than anyone of this uncertain future, "I'm just wounded."

A customer went into a West Los Angeles store and said: "I want a package of cigarettes, some chewing gum, and my money back on this can of soup." The clerk asked what the trouble was with the soup. "Nothing," said the customer, "only it isn't the best I ever tasted and I want double my money back." The clerk wanted to know what he was talking about. The sharpie took him outside and showed him a soup ad on the side of the building stating DOUBLE YOUR MONEY BACK IF IT ISN'T THE BEST YOU EVER TASTED. Subdued, the clerk handed over the cigarettes, gum, and a few pennies and made him sign a receipt.

A man was brought to Georgia Street Receiving Hospital with 125 penknife wounds in his body. While working on him, attendants asked what had happened. He and an old friend had been playing pitch with an old deck of cards, the perforated fellow said, and, in dealing, he had given himself an extra card. Blotterlike, two had stuck together. His friend, already embittered by bad luck, simply went to work with the only weapon handy, his penknife.

"You're going to prosecute him, aren't you?" one attendant asked.

"Oh no. The first thing I do when I get out of here is buy a new deck of cards!"

A man who owns three motor-fuel stations had a customer who made a habit of driving into one or another of them around closing time and presenting a hundred-dollar bill as payment for his purchases. The attendant never had change and had to say "That's all right; I'll get it next time." The customer always paid, but until he did the books were thrown out of kilter. About this time the gas-station man came into some loose money. At each of his stations he placed a hundred dollars in one dollar bills in envelopes on which were written *Waiting for the hundred-dollar guy*. Several days later he received a phone call from one of his attendants. "We got him chief," he said, elated, and went on to explain the look on the hundred-dollar man's face as he, the attendant, nonchalantly loaded him down with the only change he had, a hatful of "ones."

A sight-seer loafing in front of a peep show on the pike at Ocean Park was joined by a man who emerged from the place and who began chatting casually about the weather. Suddenly he said, "Got to go now," and rushed up to the box office, eagerly purchased a ticket, and went inside. In a few moments he returned. He made no explanation of his conduct and the bystander didn't inquire. Without warning, he repeated the routine, threading through the crowd, buying a ticket, ducking inside. When he came out again, he noticed his new-found friend's puzzled expresion. "The regular shill's out to lunch," he explained.

A well-dressed, scholarly gentleman wandered into a news-paper office, accosted a photographer, and asked irrelevantly how he could get into the M.G.M. Studio. The photog joked that he didn't know; he'd tried to get in there himself.

The stranger explained, "You see, I'm dead. Feel my arm; see if I don't feel dead."

The photog complied and agreed solemnly that he did indeed feel dead. "That's why I want to get into the studio; I'm going to haunt Mr. Blank." He whispered the name of a prominent M.G.M.-er.

"Why?"

"Because I don't like him. I haunt people I don't like."

Impressed, the cameraman agreed to help. He told the haunter the way to get in the studio without difficulty was to have a police escort, which, with a telephone call, he arranged. The caller, as his uniformed convoy arrived, thanked him profusely.

Seven years ago, a woman died in Room 310 of the Edgerly Apartments on Hope Street. Since, her husband has continued paying the rent, fifteen dollars a month, with orders that nothing in the room be disturbed. He never sleeps in the room, using it only as a storeroom for personal belongings. The manager has repeatedly asked him to give up the room, or at least permit removal of his belongings to the basement storeroom, but the tenant, who lives elsewhere, has refused. The matter has been in court, before the OPA, and before the health and fire departments, and no action has been taken. The absent tenant, a man around sixty, explains simply: "I am going to haunt the place."

A boy in a dramatics class at Hollywood High was called upon to give an original pantomime. He stalked to the stage, then stood motionless for three minutes. "What were you portraying?" asked the instructor. "Man going down in an elevator," said the boy. The class howled but the teacher suggested he transfer his talents to some other class. "How do you like that?" said the youngster tragically. "Any producer would pay a lot of dough for that belly laugh."

A woman came into the main post office to cash a money order. The clerk gave it a quick, routine glance and asked her to endorse it. She returned in a moment and handed it to him. On the back she had written *I heartily endorse this money order*. MARY JONES. The clerk explained he didn't mean it that way. "Just sign it like you would a letter," he said. When she returned the next time she had written *Yours very truly*, MARY JONES.

A crochety oldster came to the ticket booth in the Pacific Electric Railway Station and asked for a round-trip ticket to Pasadena.

"Forty-four cents," said the clerk.

"It didn't used to be that much," snapped the customer.

The clerk said it had been that much for the last seven months.

"How far is it to Pasadena?" the customer wanted to know.

"Thirteen miles," said the clerk.

"Didn't used to be that far," muttered the fellow, walking away.

A polite Hollywood Boulevard panhandler unsuccessfully begged a girl for a quarter. She went into a store and some time later, retracing her steps along the boulevard, was accosted by the same fellow. "Oh, pardon me," he said, recognizing her and tipping his hat, "I asked you before."

Don Roberts and George Glass, two newsmen turned publicists, got themselves some space in the papers as founders of a new organization, "Society against the Steamed Frankfurter." Glass was president or Big Mustard; Roberts was vice president or Little Mustard. Their brochure stated: "We who remember the hot dog in its day of golden brown glory, when it was fried instead of steamed, are campaigning against the stuff now served at football games, racetracks, and baseball parks. Let us return to the real McCoy, the fried frankfurter, bursting with hot juice, begging to be bitten. Meanwhile, let us present a united front against the steamie wienie." The society's crest: crossed frankfurters on a field of long buns with the motto TO A DOG IT SHOULDN'T HAPPEN.

A small, wizened man about fifty, the extrovert type, sat in front of a woman about thirty-five, the housewife type, on a Pico Street trolley. At Georgia Street he shouted at something out the window "They got you that time! Thought you could get away, eh?" The other passengers couldn't see a thing. A few blocks farther, he turned around and told the lady "I'm going out to see about a job. I put an ad in a paper. I'll take a job as a dishwasher, but not dishwasher and busboy. No sir! You got to watch these places. They hire you as a dishwasher and make you work as a busboy too. Not me!" The woman mumbled something. Obviously, she wished he would go away, somewhere far. At Alvarado, she got up to get off. As she passed by his seat, he shouted: "Migawd, she's got pants on!" They were slacks. The other passengers virtually died.

This story goes into this chapter, instead of the wino chapter, because it involves champagne. A very forceful citizen attended a champagne breakfast and by late afternoon was working on his fifth magnum in a café with some newspaper friends. Suddenly he said, "Ah, this reminds me of my beautiful Ingeborg. What a dollie!" He explained she was an Olympic Games swimmer and diver from Norway who had once visited Hollywood and he had toasted her in champagne. On an impulse, he said: "I must call Ingeborg." He changed a handful of bills into quarters and put in a person-to-person call to Trondheim. "Poor Ingeborg, probably all alone, with no champagne," he mourned, standing at the phone. "I shall adopt her." He had a drink on it. In a while he cleared New York, then London, then, after handfuls of quarters, Trondheim. "Put Ingeborg, the diver, on the line," he commanded. Trondheim didn't get it. "She's a beautiful dollie," he explained. "Used to swim a lot." Nothing happened and he became suspicious. "Say, who runs things there?" The operator said the civil authorities did. "Well gimme the mayor," said the champagne drinker. "I want to adopt Ingeborg, the diver. I'll get the State Department O.K. in the morning." The mayor was not available. "Nuts to this," he said, "get me Berlin, get me Hitler!" He actually got Berlin and when it seemed to him the co-operation lacked the proper enthusiasm, he threatened to join the R.A.F. and bomb the place.

At this point, the operator cut in with "I'm sorry, I cannot make the connection."

The newspaper friends who heard all this will always believe the call was the root of the State Department's trouble in Europe.

A few reporters were sitting in a small café, watching a cockroach track up a lemon meringue pie, speculating whether it would spell out Pepsi-Cola, as the skywriter does. A stranger sitting three stools away broke into their research. "Hey Al, there he is again," he called to the proprietor. "Is it all right if I take a try at him?" Al said it was O.K., he'd been trying to trap the so-and-so all day. The stranger pulled out a .25 automatic, took aim, and blasted at a large rat visible in the doorway to the kitchen. He missed, swore, replaced the gat, and resumed sipping his coffee. The newsmen almost fell off their stools.

Occasionally, the exquisite joy of living in Los Angeles is too much for someone. There was the man of about forty who suddenly, in the downtown section, began screaming "Everybody's crazy, everybody's crazy." A policeman came over to investigate. The screamer pointed at him and yelled: "You've got Chinese blood! That's what's wrong, people don't know where they stand any more. Everybody's fighting everyone else. They're all crazy."

"How about *you*," asked the officer. "Are you crazy?"

"No, not me," said the fellow.

But without warning, he got down on his hands and knees and barked like a dog and crawled through the officer's legs. At length, he cooled off long enough to answer questions and said he was from Death Valley. The officer asked whether he had a wife. He said yes and gave a telephone number. The officer called the number and asked for her. He got a landlady who said he had no wife.

"I can't understand it," said she, "he always seemed all right."

"What books do you read?" the officer asked, taking a new tack.

"I don't read books," said the screamer. "I only read the constitution of the United States. And my country's wasting away."

His case, a psychopathic officer said, is fairly typical.

A middle-aged woman came into the law office of Robert A. Neeb Jr. and asked quietly: "How much will you charge to defend me in a murder trial?"

"That all depends," answered Neeb, wondering if she'd already done the job, and, if so, why she wasn't in custody.

"I'm thinking of *killing my husband*," she said.

Neeb realized he had something different on his hands and decided to discourage her, whatever her intentions, the realistic way. He quoted a large fee. The woman was dismayed.

"That's a little more than I can pay right now," she said, "but I may be back."

Neeb asked her why she wanted to kill her husband. She said because he beat her. Why didn't she move, he asked, so he couldn't find her. He always found her, she said, and beat her some more. He tried to reason with her on the basis that her chances of beating a murder charge were slim and she was throwing away her life. She said she knew all that.

"I've made up my mind," she concluded, "and as soon as I can afford it I'm going to kill him."

Things became too hot in Alaska for two men about town named Al and Oscar and they left hurriedly and separately. Al arrived in California broke, and was forced to resort to his ace in the hole, a human-automaton act. He persuaded a clothing merchant to let him sit motionless in the display window staring at passersby, with the provision that anyone who made him laugh, or change expression, would receive a new suit or overcoat. Occasionally, he jerked to make the act look good. He attracted a great deal of attention. Business was good. Al ate regularly. One day Oscar, just arrived in town, saw his friend in the window. He pointed to his frayed lapels and fringed pants. Al didn't tumble. After all, eating was more important than friendship. Soon, Oscar was back, wearing a different, unbelievably tattered coat and pants. He leaned over and exhibited two patches on the seat of his pants. Al laughed all over the window and the grumbling merchant kicked through with a new layout for Oscar.

When Oscar had gone, the merchant stormed: "What's

the idea? I thought you said you never changed expression."

"I never saw him before in my life," lied Al, hoping to get by.

"Well, if you laughed once, you're liable to laugh again," said the merchant. "You're fired."

A fair share of the nation's magazine-and-book output comes from Los Angeles; but for every successful writer there are a thousand hopeless amateurs. They read *Liberty's* short short stories and say to themselves "If I couldn't do better than that I'll eat my typewriter." After a few rejections, they are certain the editors don't read their submissions but merely send them back in the return envelope with printed refusals. One unsuccessful plugger decided to test this rumor. With his manuscript, he sent this letter:

An ugly rumor is going around, Mr. Editor, that your short stories are read by a robot. It's being bandied about that thousands of them roll by him on a moving belt and his radio controlled arm is so timed that he reaches out and clutches each 500th manuscript. This would explain some of the stories you print. But please tell me it isn't true. Make some mark on the rejection slip to indicate my story *is* touched by human hands.

Someone on *Liberty*, recognizing the subtle approach, accommodatingly red-penciled the outline of his hand on the rejection slip.

A radio man—let's call him Harry—forgot about a few traffic citations and one night a policeman rang his doorbell and escorted him to Lincoln Heights Jail. As he walked along a corridor, a voice called out "Hello, Harry, what're you doing here?" It belonged to a fellow—let's call him Larry—who was a hot spieler of commercials, known in the trade as a "dynamiter." Harry explained he was in on a traffic rap.

"And you?" he asked.

"Drunk," said Larry.

He'd just finished a series of spot announcements for an alcoholic cure, he said. That should have been an omen, but oh, no. Then he'd made a batch for a wine company. That really should have put him on guard, but with the money he received for them, he went on a lost weekend and was captured by the police department. As he was being booked, he heard himself, transcribed, coming over the sergeant's radio, plugging the wine.

A process server was assigned to hand a legal, blue-covered document to an actor notorious for getting in jams. He was warned to be careful, the guy was a bad actor, he had broken the last fellow's arm. The process server, however, caught him in an affable mood and the actor, accepting the summons with resignation, invited him in for a Scotch-and-soda. Over a period of years, the process server has been back a number of times, on business. Invariably, a party was in progress and he was welcomed as an old friend. In recent years, the actor took a new tack. After snatching the summons, he introduced his friend as his "personal process server." Striking a pose, shaking hands with him, he shouts: "Hey look everybody, this is a take." The process server has gotten so he can hardly wait to go out and see his pal again.

A radio man, afflicted with horrible hang-overs, has discovered that for him the only way to prevent utter disintegration is to talk incessantly, about anything. On these occasions, his friends stay away from him, to protect their eardrums, but one time a friend was trapped and after half an hour of steady oratory he said: "Hey, why do you keep up that jabbering?"

"Why?" said the hang-over man in horror, "if I don't keep talking, I'll have to listen."

Some years ago, Charles Carson, the writer, founded the Kit Carson Society, the aim of which is to perpetuate the memory of the famous scout. Himself a distant relative, he made known that all descendants were eligible. One day an old, whiskered desert rat invaded his office and asked whether he could join. He was from Arizona, he said, and came over as soon as he heard of the society. He hoped it wouldn't cost too much as he was nearly broke. Charles Carson told him no fees were required and that he could have been spared the long trek. All he had to do was present proof of his relationship, which he could have done by mail.

"Related, hell!" said the old man. "I *am* Kit Carson."

Charles Carson was bewildered and mumbled Kit's 130th birthday was December 24, 1939.

"Oh that guy!" said the desert rat. "You mean that fellow born in 1809 who claimed he was Carson? I've had trouble with him. He's an impostor; I'm the real Carson."

Faced with a tough situation, Charles Carson came through nicely. "Obviously, you're right, but, you see, the society is only for relatives of Kit Carson; there's no provision for Carson himself."

The old fellow winced and trembled as the logic penetrated. "My boy, you're right," he said. "It would violate the rules if you took me in, and no Carson should stoop to dishonor." Straightening his shoulders, he walked from the office, a broken, disappointed hero.

Popeye is a "pearl diver." He works all day in a cheap restaurant, washing dishes and mopping floors. Each night he has a few drinks in a Skid Row bar. Technically he's a wino and a screwball, but with variations. Inveterate winos buy it by the bottle, it's cheaper. Offer to buy Popeye a bottle and he's insulted. "Don't be silly," he says. He buys it by the glass. Furthermore, he will permit a stranger to buy him a drink only if he approves of the stranger. Thus, he remains a man of character. Popeye's name comes from his perfect imitation of the comic-strip spinach eater. He has no teeth and the crunched expression he gives his face, with a corncob pipe in his mouth, is authentic Popeye. After a few glasses of wine, he goes into his strange, trancelike spiel. He gets off his stool and simply talks a blue streak. Quotations from Plato, Voltaire, and Shakespeare; the written wisdom of the ages and the gutter philosophy he lives by, tumble from his mouth. Suddenly he interrupts himself with something that happened that day. "So I told the boss," he will say pointlessly, "that he'd have to get a new mop." Just as suddenly he returns to his trance. "You know Judge Landis?" he asks the air. "You know how he became a judge? Well, one time he sentenced a man to life. The crook said, 'I'm sick, I'll die. I can't serve life; I'll never make it.' So the judge says, 'Well, do the best you can.' "

One time a reporter playfully placed a police badge in Popeye's pocket. When he found it, the reporters chided: "Oh, playing cop, eh?"

"Honest fellows," he said, "I'm not really a cop. I couldn't make civil service; I'm too short."

He usually has an amused audience, but if people walk away from him he doesn't care; he keeps on talking. His audience is imaginary anyway.

Daily at 5:55 P.M., for two years, a small, thin, wizened man with his coat collar turned up appeared like a wraith in a café on Sixth Street near Main. He never bought anything or said hello. He merely stepped inside the door and glanced furtively at the clock. The time always changed him to a tense, frightened gazelle. He sniffed the air, darted out, and ran like hell. When he stopped coming, the regular eaters speculated. They had a pretty good mystery built up around him. When the big changeover to busses took place, they learned the truth: he was only a man running for a streetcar.

In the mountains above Altadena lives a man known to hikers as Horace the Hermit. His home is a ramshackle affair he built himself of packing cases, signs, galvanized iron, and cardboard cartons. One Sunday, the big day for mountain marchers, a party of climbers who lived at the foot of the canyon wondered why he was never at home when they came by his house, so they could show him off as the local screwball. After some weeks of checking they learned the truth. To escape the Sunday hikers, Horace spends the day in Los Angeles.

An apartment house near Hope and Venice caught fire and as the firemen rushed inside with ladders and hose, the landlady gasped: "Old Mr. Smith in the back, on the third floor—he must be asleep."

The firemen plunged through the smoke, beat on Mr. Smith's door. They got no response, so pushed it in. "Get up," a fireman shouted, "the place's on fire!"

"Oh no you don't," said Mr. Smith. "You fellows get the hell out of here. My rent's paid up!"

They finally convinced him.

22

It isn't the heat, it's the humanity.—STAN ADLER

ONE of the first things a columnist must learn is never to shake his head and say: "Now I've seen [or heard] everything." Los Angeles is a never-ending phantasmagoria, in Technicolor, with polka dots.

After a while, the columnist learns to accept things as they are. If he manages to hang on to his sanity, so much the better. What I'm leading up to is that this is another chapter on "characters."

As passengers boarded a P.E. Santa Monica Boulevard bus they were attracted to a weatherbeaten old guy of about seventy, wearing a ten-gallon hat. A noise like a baby crying seemed to emanate from him. When the old guy was certain he had the newcomers' attention, he pulled out a baby's bottle half full of milk and took a pull at it. Now and then he'd furtively pull the zipper on a blue-canvas beach bag in his lap and hold the bottle to it. When he got off in Beverly Hills, passengers saw he had a doll in the bag. As he stepped down, a girl behind him exclaimed: "I go all around the world and I come back to Hollywood and see this!"

A man who looked as if he'd slept in his clothes drove into a gas station near the Lockheed aircraft plant in Burbank and asked where the lavatory was. The attendant, busy with a lube job, motioned to the back. When the fellow didn't reappear, the attendant went looking. He discovered the stranger had gone into the place marked LADIES. He called through the door and only after considerable persuasion enticed the fellow out. The odd one said he was merely resting, then added: "That's a nice place you have in there. Put a telephone in and I'll rent it!"

Two old codgers stood in the forecourt of the Public Library, surrounded by a flock of pigeons which they were ostensibly feeding. Closer observance, however, revealed that while one was feeding them, the other was reluctantly holding his bag of corn close to his chest and that they were exchanging harsh words. At length, the one who was doing the feeding blew up and shouted: "Aw, go find your own pigeons!"

Two lobby loungers in a Hollywood hotel were discussing a broken-down actor who lived there.

"He has a good character face," said one. "Why doesn't he get a job as Santa Claus?"

"Naw, he tried that last year," said the other, "and every time he'd get a kid on his knee he couldn't resist telling him about the time he made twelve hundred a week."

A one-armed veteran, who is proud of his self-sufficiency, steers first-time visitors toward a closet and says: "Open that door and take a look." From the dark recesses of the closet, a dozen human arms seem to reach out for the umpchay. If he doesn't run shrieking, the vet explains the government buys him a new artificial arm every two years but that the first one fitted so well, he hasn't needed any of the others.

A fey Hollywoodian celebrated his discharge from the navy by going on a rip-roaring binge. He cashed some war bonds; then some more; hardly missing a drink between trips to the bank. The third time he visited the bank to see if his hoard was bare—it was—the manager told him that through a clerk's error he had been overpaid fifty dollars. The exuberant civilian said he wouldn't know as he had encountered a low fog. Would he pay it back? asked the manager. Otherwise the clerk would be stuck for the money. He said he would but at the moment he was broke. Would he sign a note or take out a loan? Of course. Suddenly it occurred to the fun-loving sailor that for the first time in his life he had a bank over a barrel. On the loan application, opposite the question "What do you intend using this money for?" he wrote "Have new system to beat the horses at Santa Anita."

Two pals had been out late and one said: "Why don't you spend the night over at my place?" The second saw no reason why not. In the middle of the night they were awakened by a loud buzzing. It was a huge dragon fly. The host got up, folded some newspapers, and after frantic wall slapping seemed to have slain the insect. At least the buzzing subsided.

"Hey, come on back to bed," said the guest sleepily. "He's done for."

"Well, I want to be sure," said the host. "The so-and-so is liable to put in some long-distance phone calls."

A woman who likes all animals was in her apartment when she heard a cat meowing. She playfully meowed back. She couldn't see the cat because an abutment of the building cut off her view of the ground. The cat meowed back and she repeated the call, this time putting plenty of oomph in it. The call went back and forth a dozen times, loaded with quavers, innuendo, and passion. The lady was exultant. "I can speak cat language," she told her husband at breakfast next morning. "I've got him in my power."

Just then the man a few doors down the hall, who drove to town with her husband, dropped in. "The funniest thing happened to me last night," he said. "I meowed at a cat and he meowed back and we kept it up for twenty minutes."

A man walking along Santa Monica Boulevard saw flames billowing from a fourth-story window. He raced up the stairs and knocked on the door he thought was the one where the fire was. It wasn't and the people inside were nettled at being disturbed. He tried two more doors with the same result. Finally he came to one with smoke oozing out from under. He pounded on it. A man opened the door as far as two chain locks permitted and asked drunkenly: "What do you want?" The knocker told him his apartment was on fire. "O.K., let it burn," said the fellow, slamming the door. The Good Samaritan got to a phone and called the fire department. Then he rushed back to the burning apartment and broke down the door, falling flat on the burning carpet. In due time, the man inside and a lady were rescued and the blaze was extinguished. As the good Samaritan stood ruefully studying his soiled clothes, the apartment manager appeared and said: "Oh, so you're the guy! Well, don't think you're going to get away without paying for breaking down that door!"

A Pasadena girl, daughter of wealth and position, decided one day she could no longer live a life of parasitic ease but must up and do. She got a job as a forelady in a shop employing a number of Mexican women, a position which gave her a wonderful opportunity to test her social theories. The first morning she addressed each of them cordially in her high-school Spanish with "Good morning!" The women shrank from her in terror. The next day the same thing happened and the girl, in her ninety-dollar dress and her twenty-dollar shoes, was mystified. When she told the boss he asked what she had said to them.

"I merely said good morning," she replied.

"But how did you say it?"

"I said 'Buenos Dios, Buenos Dios!'"

The boss howled. "If you wanted to say good morning you should have said 'Buenas dias.' You have looked at each of these women the first thing in the morning and said 'Good God, Good God!'"

A woman found a key on the sidewalk with a tag instructing the finder to return it to a certain address. The address was only a block away so she walked there and rang the bell.

"Well, what do you want?" a man growled.

She explained she had found the key and was returning it.

"Migod, another one," he moaned.

"You don't have to swear at me, mister," she snapped. "I'm just returning your key. You could at least be polite."

"Look sister," he said wearily, "see that house next door? Well the guy there and I had a fight. So he's trying to get even. All hours of the day and night I get lost keys, like this one. I've gotten about seventy of them already. Now will you please go away and leave me alone!"

A woman fainted on the sidewalk at Seventh and Grand and was carried into a drugstore. The inevitable crowd formed and latecomers asked others standing by "What happened?" In some mysterious manner, word got started through the throng that the bank across the street was being robbed. In a few minutes, an ambulance, summoned for the lady who had swooned, came up, siren screaming, and officers shouldered their way through the mob into the bank. Eventually people began wondering why they were standing there. No one knew. By this time the lady who had fainted walked out of the drugstore under her own power. Seeing the crowd, she asked what was going on. "Something going on over at the bank," a bystander said vaguely.

A few movie writers were huddling around a bottle when one had a brilliant idea. Arthur Caesar, he said, always ribbed them with his gags; why not get back at him? "It's 5 A.M.," he said. "Let's wake him up and tell him to come over." He dialed Caesar's number. After a first ring, without a "hello" or "Who's this?" Caesar's voice came through clearly. "I can't sleep either; where's the party?"

Along Main Street near the civic center, where a large portion of the Mexican population buys clothing and supplies, the stores have signs in their windows: SE HABLA ESPANOL AQUÍ (Spanish is spoken here). A Midwesterner sank his savings in a shop on Hollywood Boulevard and almost immediately realized he could not compete with the larger stores. Day after day he sat in his place, watching the crowds go by ignoring his bargains. Finally, in a gesture of desperation he put a sign in the window ENGLISH IS SPOKEN HERE. Business was so bad he was lonesome.

Every year or so, the Ham and Egg Pension movement comes before the voters and the pre-election controversy is usually very bitter. During one campaign a prominent attorney blasted the movement over a local radio station. After each broadcast the telephone switchboard went white with calls from adherents of Thirty Dollars Every Thursday. "You keep that dirty dog off the air or we'll do thus and so!" they shrieked. The calls became a serious problem but at length the studio manager, who had a sense of humor, solved it. Each time the board overflowed with protests, the key was opened and a male oriental voice said politely "Me no understand. Me Japanese janitor. Trank you."

A movie comedian went broke and lived furtively, for behind every telephone pole lurked a creditor. Among them was a friend who operated a noted Hollywood café. The actor had borrowed five hundred dollars from him. One day the actor's agent unexpectedly got him a ten-thousand-dollar role. The actor hammishly accepted on condition that a thousand dollars of it be paid in advance. When he received the check he promptly paid his five-hundred-dollar café tab. Never again, he resolved, would he be taken broke. He celebrated his decision alcoholically and wound up hiring two taxis and loading them with groceries from the café.

A friend, seeing the loaded cabs, asked: "What you got there?"

The comedian dug deeply for a tag line, then whispered: "Sh-h-h, wolf powder!"

A termite inspector, working off a sucker list, called a lady named Mary Frances and asked if she wanted her home inspected and treated if it had any borers from within. "Listen, you stay away from here," she said in alarm. "This house is eaten through. The termites are all that's holding it up!"

A woman went into a dime store to buy a mousetrap. They

were two for a nickel, the clerk told her. "But we only have one mouse!" she protested, with irrefutable logic.

Gary Breckner, the radio announcer, handled the remote-control dance-band broadcasts from Catalina Island Casino one summer. On one occasion, he announced that the next tune would be "Do You Care?" A little while later he was summoned to the phone.

"Mr. Breckner?" asked a strange woman.

"Yes," he said.

"I care," she said, and hung up. He traced the call. It came from Cleveland, Ohio.

A teacher in the personality class at a downtown business college was instructing her classroom of girls in the poise that comes with correct posture. To illustrate, she pulled up her skirt slightly and paced off a few steps. The room exploded with laughter. "What's the matter?" she demanded. "My legs aren't so bad." Students pointed across the street. There a man hanging out of an office building was peering into binoculars, studying the teacher's not so bad legs.

An elderly woman who looked as if she had stepped out of a *New Yorker* cartoon made some purchases at a Sunset Boulevard grocery, then asked for five pounds of sugar. The clerk asked for her ration book.

"What's that?" she asked.

"You mean you never signed up?" he asked, incredulous.

"Why no," she said. "I did see something in the papers about it but I thought that was all over."

The clerk tried to explain what she had to do to get sugar. She told him she'd have none of such silliness. Gripping the counter to keep from blowing his top, he said: "Lady, it's this way. You used to need only money to buy sugar but now you need money and a ration book." When the woman became convinced the stubborn fellow wouldn't sell her any sugar, she extracted a bundle of ten-dollar bills, easily two hundred dollars' worth, paid for what she had bought, and huffily scurried toward the Silver Lake hill country.

One reason for Los Angeles' desperate postwar housing shortage was the inadequacy of the hired help. Despite this, a contractor noted for his fault finding demanded the best. One day he visited the site of a large housing project and promptly went berserk. The men were loafing, he said; the job was behind schedule; the ditch was a terribly sloppy job. The foreman stood by silently but at a lull in the tirade asked softly: "How is she for length?"

To keep a column breathing day after day, you need dozens of vice presidents in charge of overheard conversations. One veepee was in a downtown restaurant when two chatty girls about twenty came in for coffee. One got to talking with the waitress and in a moment held out her hand and exhibited a ring. "That married guy gave it to me," she said. Then she continued, "What do you think? His wife was in to see me today and asked me what it was worth to take her husband off her hands. I thought I'd kid her and I said a thousand dollars. She came back this afternoon with a purse full of bonds and a fifty-dollar bill. I asked her if she was kidding and told her to put her money back in her purse. I don't want any money with him." My eavesdropper sat stunned for a while, then went out to catch a streetcar. He had to wait a long time and pretty soon the two girls came out and chalked a series of squares on the sidewalk and were boisterously jumping hopscotch.

A restaurant in the 2000 block on West Seventh Street went out of business. This notice was posted on the door:

To whom it may concern, an explanation of things as they are. Our failure to succeed can be attributed to several causes. One is that certain laws of this state deprive a man of the liberty to freely deceive and defraud his fellow man. In good old Constantinople a man enjoyed liberties in these respects. But the chief cause of our failure can be attributed to the incredulity and stupidity of the people from whom we took our supplies. Their simple minds could not be convinced that they would be paid some day next week or so. Due to this faithlessness on their part and their refusal to co-operate with us in our underhanded undertaking here, we now await further developments. MRS. ALEXIS, late of Constantinople.

At the City Hall there's a Baby Board, where prospective mothers receive charitable assistance. One day, a woman telephoned asking for someone to come out immediately to visit her neighbor who expected a bundle from heaven. The Baby Board girl asked a few questions, including the name of the prospective mother's husband. "She don' have to have no husband jus' 'cause she's gonna have a baby!" she was told indignantly. "Yo-all knows that!"

A quiet, orderly sub-executive of a business house astonished his colleagues by collecting, in advance, a sum of money due him and skipping town, with another man's wife. A week later, the staff received a second jolt. A stranger came in to see the boss, identified himself as the cuckold husband, and applied for the departed employe's job. "He took my wife," he said, "I ought to at least get his job."

A customer in a Wilshire Boulevard restaurant reached for the sugar container and tried to pour some in his coffee without result; the spout was clogged. He tried again and again and the inner conflict between exasperation and coolheadedness was horrible to behold. At length he rose, master of himself and situation. Making certain no one was near, he heaved the container against a wall, where it splattered like a bomb. With a calm smile, he stepped to the cashier and asked: "How much?"

A big department store is noted for the politeness of its clerks. They rush up zealously each time a shopper pauses momentarily and ask: May I help you?" A sadist, posing as a shopper, irked by this procedure, made a point of visiting the store daily and replying: "Certainly. We're doing a little shoplifting; come right along."

A few days before the last presidential election, a young English teacher walked into his classroom at Los Angeles High School and noticed written on the blackboard *Ann Sheridan for President*.

"Who's responsible for that?" he demanded sternly of his class. A shy youngster in the back of the room confessed. "I will thank you to erase it!" said the prof. Shamefaced, the youngster obeyed. When he returned to his seat, the teacher picked up a piece of chalk and in identically sized letters wrote *Lana Turner for President*. Then he smiled diabolically, and started the regular lesson for the day.

A young man out of a job deluged downtown business firms with the following tongue-in-cheek letter: "To all prospective employers. I am out of a job, therefore available for an executive position with your firm. Please let me know the hours, salary, special inducements in the way of working conditions you offer. Also, why did the last man leave!"

A customer in a crowded Spring Street restaurant ordered a cup of coffee and the waitress in serving it placed it to the right of his apple pie. "My, my," he said, "of all the times I've had my arms around you and still you don't know I'm left-handed!" She never had seen him before.

A man getting a shoeshine downtown noticed the rag-snapping youth department glancing admiringly at his pants.

"You like this suit?" he asked. It was an expensive pinstripe.

"Well, I was just thinking," said the boy. "My, my, those pants would make a good shine rag."

A girl who works at a film studio went to a concert with her boy friend and they found themselves seated next to a particularly obnoxious child star. To the girl's amazement, her escort, who had always seemed civilized, asked the child star to autograph his program. During intermission, she brought up the matter in a very chilly manner. "Oh, I did it for my pal, Joe," he laughed. "Boy, will he burn when he gets it! We hate each other."

A radio writer who has experienced the full cycle of the Hollywood brushoff developed a technique in telephoning. He'll play along when a secretary asks "Who's calling please" although he's very coy about revealing his identity, but when telephoning a friend, he simply will not go for the piece of secretarial barbed wire "What did you wish to speak to him about?" In a very nasty tone he replies: "I want to know what he's going to do about my wife!" He gets through immediately.

A Western Union boy rang the doorbell at a Beverly Hills home and said curtly: "Telegram for Miss B." After handing it to her, he said: "Didn't you used to live in the 1600 block on South Orange Drive?" She said she did. "Well," said he, looking about him, "I like this place much better."

A classic item in fire-department rescue-squad circles has to do with a call from a lady in the south part of the city. A neighbor lady seemed to be dead, she said. Would they rush right over? On arrival, the rescuers found the patient indeed limp and pulseless. Nevertheless, they applied their artificial respirator. After a few minutes it was apparent they were too late.

"Did you call a doctor?" the woman was asked.

"Oh yes," she said, "I called him last night but he said she was dead. Then the coroner came and he said she was dead. That's why I called you: to get her alive again."

A young man about town telephoned his girl friend and dipped low in profanity. Every other word was a bad one.

"Joe, I wish you wouldn't use that kind of language," she said.

"Oh I don't give a this or that," he said. "No one will hear me."

Just then a strange, solemn voice broke in. "The Lord will hear you, young man!"

The young man cleaned it up, remembering he was on a party line.

F.D.R. enumerated the four freedoms and Norman Rockwell did a masterful job of painting them. Advertising men and others, of course, have been kicking around No. 5. With some it's freedom of the skies, freedom of enterprise, even freedom of freedom. It remained for a Los Angeles medicine firm to touch bottom. No. 5, according to its ad, was freedom from gallstones.

A girl with an escort on each arm stopped suddenly on Main Street, braced herself on one fellow's shoulder, and took off a shoe. Then, displaying an expanse of thigh, she rolled off her stocking, threw it in the gutter, and replaced her shoe. She repeated the performance, removing the other stocking. By this time the inhabitants of a saloon were streaming to the door, pushing each other and yelling: "Get out of my way, I can't see."

The girl waved an acknowledgment to the appreciative audience and explained: "They had runs in them."

A passer-by shook his head and said: "I never saw anything like that in Chicago."

A middle-aged woman boarded a streetcar on Broadway and held passengers spellbound as she paused at the coin box to remove her right shoe. She held it under the motorman's nose so he could see the weekly pass which lay flat in it; then put it back on and sat down. The motorman, bug-eyed, turned around to the passengers. Reassured he was still in the world of reality, he started the car.

Among jazz addicts, Los Angeles is down in history as the turning point in the career of Benny Goodman. His hot music had been received indifferently elsewhere and he came to the Palomar in 1937 very discouraged and at the point of breaking up his band. He was an instant success and went up into the big money. So impressed were the youngsters with the band's wild beat and maddening din on his first appearance, they merely stood ecstatically and stamped their feet, cheering at the conclusion of each number. All except one liquored spectator: as each tune was finished, he shouted over all the rest: "Hurray, they scored another touchdown!"

• 23 •

Californians are a race of people; they are not merely inhabitants of a state.—O. HENRY, *A Municipal Report*

A ND then there are the unprecedented, unaccountable, spontaneous things that happen:

A man around fifty, the Casper Milquetoast type, came into a recording studio on Hollywood Boulevard with his attorney and said he wanted a record made: a last will. The microphone was set up and Mr. Milquetoast, given the go-ahead, suddenly became a roaring, snarling tiger. For eight minutes, he told off his relatives in exclamation points. One member of his family was getting a pittance because he was such a heel. A sister was being cut off because the guy she married wasn't trustworthy; he'd have the money away from her the moment she cashed the check. When he finished, the two sound engineers, at the attorney's cue, were cut in and identified themselves as witnesses to the testament. As he departed, a quiet, mischievous smile played over Milquetoast's face. Clearly he had never had the courage or inclination to tell his relatives what he thought of them.

Pale and beaten after the double feature, a woman lit a cigarette in the lobby of a downtown theater as she stopped at the checkroom for her bundles. A uniformed usher dashed over, clicked his heels, and said severely: "No smoking here, ma'am!"

"I'm very sorry," said the woman, "I didn't realize—"

The usher looked over his shoulder, relaxed from his rigid posture, and smiled. "Aw, that's all right, I'm just being officious!"

A car drove into a service station at Washington and LaBrea in midmorning for some gas. The attendant noticed the driver was nude—at least from the waist up, which was as far as he could see—and figured he was heading for the beach. While airing the tires he looked up in amazement to see the driver, his companion in the front seat, and three women from the back seat walking to the rest rooms some seventy-five feet away, all naked. Passing traffic was demoralized momentarily, but when the driver returned, noting the attendant's consternation, he said: "Don't worry about it, buddy, we're nudists," and they drove away.

The Pueblo takes a back seat from no one in the matter of divorces, which run a dead heat with marriages. A young couple was married by a judge, after which they just stood there. "What, no wedding kiss?" laughed the judge. The groom made a halfhearted pass at the girl and she listlessly turned her cheek. "Hey, what's this," asked the judge, "no enthusiasm?"

"Aw, don't you remember us, Judge?" said the girl wearily. "You married us a couple of years ago. Well, my divorce wasn't final so we had to go through it again."

A stranger finished a big meal in an East Fifth Street restaurant, then drew himself up to his full height and said dramatically: "All right, I haven't got a cent; call a cop." His daydreaming interrupted, the owner replied: "Oh, I wouldn't do that, but hereafter just don't give *me* all your business."

One of the questions on the application form given persons wishing to be certified for relief was: "What is your favorite recreation?" One family wrote, "Swinging through the air on a trapeze." The relief worker thought she detected a note of derision and asked what the idea was. "We meant it," said the applicant. "My husband and I are acrobats. If it wasn't raining, I'd take you out in the yard and show you."

Artists, amateur and professional, fill a large part of the landscape they don't paint. One old gentleman came into Mc-

Logan's artist-supply store and asked to see a brand of paint that would last five hundred years. He was doing a little something for posterity, he explained, and naturally wanted the best. Mr. McLogan, used to artists' idiosyncrasies, produced his regular brand. Not wishing to let a fine gag die, he said, as he wrapped it: "If this doesn't last, come in and we'll refund your money." The old gent gave no sign he caught the gag.

A vacationer found a mountain retreat that fishermen dream about. It was off the beaten path, in a valley surrounded by towering mountains and shaded by patriarchial pines, with a stream threading through. Our man and his wife went into a log building with a sign FRESH TROUT DINNERS.

A woman took the order, stepped to the back door, and called: "Jack, I want trout for five dinners."

"O.K., Mom," answered a voice, "but it may take five or ten minutes. They aren't biting very good today."

An itinerant bakery man, who announces his approach by whistling madly, informed one of his customers he expected to start his vacation the following Monday. "That is," he qualified, "if they find a substitute. Gosh, I hope they don't get the same fellow they had last year. He was a pianist and every place he made a sale he stopped to play the piano, if they had one. Practically ruined my route."

A streetcar bumped the rear of a truck, causing negligible damage except to passengers' nerves. As required, the conductor passed out forms for passengers to fill out. One woman was so upset she couldn't for the life of her remember her name. She finally did, and her companion explained to a fellow passenger: "She's been married three times and she gets mixed up."

The head of an industrial firm detected a slowdown in production, and one day, without warning, he decided on a flash inspection. Strolling through the plant, he came upon a workman sleeping in a chair. Another workman, trying to save the situation, stepped to the sleeper to rouse him. The boss stayed him. "Let him sleep," he said. "As long as he sleeps he has a job. When he wakes up, he's a fired son of a gun."

A young man at his wit's end trying to find a job finally sought out an employment agency. A few days later he received a call. "Do you drive a car?" asked the agency man. He did. "Have you a chauffeur's license?" He had.

Just then a fussy old gentleman walked over. "Oh, no, no," he said, "he won't do, he's too tall, I want a man who's short and stocky. You don't think I'm going to buy another uniform, do you?"

A fashionably dressed woman, shopping in a big department store, fell in love with a street dress with jacket, had it fitted, and paid for it, $125. She told the saleslady she would return in a few days for the final fitting. That was twenty-five years ago. The store heard no more from her until four years later when she appeared for her final fitting. This time, she asked that the dress be held at the store until she called the next time. Once a year since that time, twenty-one years ago, she has revisited the store to try on the dress. The clerks indulge her whim as if it were not unusual. They know now she's a mental case.

Telephones are put in daily in Southern California, but it will be a long time before the supply catches up with the demand, so great has been the influx of new residents. Meanwhile subscribers must sweat out party lines. In some instances, the feuding is very bitter.

One woman picked up the receiver to call a number, and Party No. 2 on the line snarled: "We're using the line—if you don't mind."

"O.K.," said Party No. 1, "but you always listen in."

"I do not," said the second party. "Not since I heard you swearing that time."

A distraught gentleman appeared at the lost-and-found counter of the Pacific Electric Station, Sixth and Main, and reported that he had mislaid his trained-flea act, the famous one which has fascinated the folks at Long Beach. Fay Phillips, the attendant, told him it hadn't been turned in and asked: "Where were they?"

They were in a Gruen watch case, the owner said. "Awfully smart they were, too," he said sadly.

How could they be identified, asked the attendant.

Oh, that was easy, each had a wire around its neck. "What worries me," he said, "is that they'll only live three hours without food."

As she dusted, washed, and ironed, a slavey in a Westside home told her mistress she had problems. A very jealous and insistent guy was pestering her. Next day the girl didn't appear for work. The mistress, grown fond of the tidy helper, telephoned her home. There she learned the girl was in the hospital with assorted hurts. That guy had done it. When contact was established, the slavey identified the fearsome assailant. "He was my boy friend before I got married to the fellow I'm divorced from."

Harry Smith, Vermont Avenue *restaurateur*, is a man of stern justice. One day he surprised a customer carving his initials on the side of the bar and told him to stop. The customer put his knife away. A few minutes later, the fellow again was slashing at the woodwork. On an impulse, Smith seized a huge bread knife, rushed outside, and streaked a yard-long scar on the customer's new black coupé.

During a poorly attended football game at Gilmore Stadium, a frankfurter vendor sounded a new low in professional disgust with "Awright, folks, get a hot dog and spoil your supper!"

As a buildup for a picture of the same name, billboards appeared around town asking cryptically WHO IS KING OF THE UNDERWORLD? On one, a childish scrawl replied *Boris Karloff No. 1, My Teacher No. 2.*

The driver of a garbage wagon, after making a collection out in front, rang the doorbell of a house and said plaintively: "Pardon me, sir, but could you let me have a couple of aspirin tablets?" The householder was glad to be of service, but, mildly curious, asked about the odd request. "Mister," said the chauffeur sadly, "you never drove a garbage wagon on a hot day with a hang-over."

A customer in a shoe store noticed that every few minutes the clerk chuckled. "A little while ago," he explained, "a woman came in with a contrary little boy. She kept saying 'Come on now, kiss me.' He kept saying no. Finally she asked why. 'Because you won't ride my tricycle!' he said."

During the war, a stage was erected in downtown Pershing Square and programs were given daily to sell bonds. One day, as the band was playing "The Star-Spangled Banner," two women walking through the park threaded their way through the crowd standing at attention. As the women neared the platform, an old man, hat in hand, whispered: "Don't you know you're supposed to stand when the national anthem is played?"

"Oh, we're awfully sorry," said one woman, jolted out of her conversation, "we're from out of town."

Don Blanding, the poet, has autographed thousands of his books of verse. Big, handsome, and forceful, he gets the ladies dreamy-eyed, but not always. A woman buying a book he had autographed in a Hollywood store noticed the signature. "Hey," she complained, "this one's been writ in." The clerk explained it was the author's autograph. "Well, I dunno," she said. "I was going to get the book for my sister and I don't think she'd like one that was writ in."

A man ordered a bottle of homogenized milk in a restaurant operated by foreigners.

"How do you say again, please?" asked the waiter, who was also the owner.

"Homogenized," repeated the customer.

The waiter smiled happily. "Wait," he said, "you don't go away please." He disappeared and returned with another man. "Now please," he smiled, "you say for him."

"Homogenized."

The newcomer was equally delighted. There's that beautiful word again, his face seemed to say.

Now also delighted at spreading so much happiness with so little effort, but a little baffled, the customer said: "Better let me have coffee instead."

A zombie-appearing woman came into a Hollywood pet shop, looked about furtively, then asked the proprietor: "Got any snakes?"

"What kind of snakes?" he asked. "What did you want them for?"

"I want to see what they'll do if I look at them," she whispered huskily.

A salesman in a big downtown clothing store was normal in all respects except one. He had a phobia for customers who, when he asked "May I help you?" replied: "I just want to look around." One day, a customer said it and something snapped inside the salesman. "Of course," he said politely. "Come with me." He escorted the man to the elevator. They went to the roof of the building and to the edge. "Now," snarled the salesman, "you can see the whole damn city!" He left the customer standing there, getting his wish. As for himself, he went downstairs, got his hat, and never came back.

A man of unflinching convictions discovered that a dog in the neighborhood was using his front lawn for calls of nature, senior grade. He put up with the nuisance until his lawn mower developed the glanders. Then he called on the neighbor lady who owned the pooch. "I'm a reasonable man," he said. "Now, Mrs. Bonbon, you have a front lawn. I'll meet you halfway. Why don't we make a deal? Let Rover do his dirty work one day on your lawn and one day on mine." She hit the ceiling and, land-ing on her feet, chased him out of the house, screaming "Dog hater!"

A truck drew up for a stop signal. Lashed securely was an airplane; a real one, not a prop. A nameplate on the truck proclaimed it the property of Twentieth Century Fox Studio. Inevitably, on the side was a banner advertising the film "Ramona." During a fleeting five seconds, which seemed to have a hazy disassociation from the world, an elderly lady at the curb remarked sharply to her companion: "There you are. See how they change things in the movies! There wasn't any airplane in 'Ramona.'"

Tom C. Harrison, the artist, drove past Saint Augustine's Church, the first house of worship in Culver City, and saw in the façade of the old-fashioned, harshly simple, belfried frame building an ideal subject. He talked it over with the caretaker, an aged fellow, who became excited that the place he watched over would be immortalized on canvas, but he was also puzzled that anyone wanted to paint such a weatherbeaten, ramshackle building. "If you'll wait just a little while, this is going to be torn down and our new church built. Then you'll really have something to paint!"

A credit store in this city finds it has a customer who has, as they say, reached a point. He sent them this letter: "Every month I take all my unpaid bills and put them in a hat. I pick out one and pay that for the month. If you don't stop sending me threatening letters, I won't put your bill in the hat."

Hoping to capture some vagrant sun rays, a lady dragged an army cot onto the back-yard lawn. Settled for a luxurious sunbath, she looked up to see her neighbor making similar preparations. At the moment, prospects seemed ideal. As they talked, the inevitable fog swept in. "I was telling my husband," the neighbor lady said, "it's got to quit fooling around. Either the sun shines tomorrow or I stay in bed."

It had been a busy day for doorbell ringers: first an old-gold solicitor, then a magazine salesman. But the old lady was still polite, as a vegetable peddler came to the door, though she declined his wares; but he wouldn't take no for an answer and kept up a barrage. As she shut the door in his face, the old lady heard the closing volley. "My cousin was apeddlin' house to house. Last week he went home and hung hisself!"

Two wives gossiping over the back fence became loud and eloquent.

"I tell you, I don't trust any man," said one. "They're all fickle."

"You're telling me," said the second. "Do you know what I caught my own husband doing? He went out and bought a cemetery lot for his mother, but do you think he got one for me? I should say not!"

A quiet, cultured man appeared in court one day, charged with malicious mischief. Systematically, with cold, dispassionate technique, stated the complaint, he had taken a club and broken every window in his mother-in-law's home. His attorney, making a point of his clear record, expressed a desire to plead him guilty and apply for probation. But the judge caught an undercurrent of something and prodded for details. Yes, the defendant admitted, he felt some justification for what he had done. His mother-in-law, he said, had estranged his wife from him. When he had come home on this particular occasion, she wasn't there; she was at her mother's. The same thing had happened many times, but suddenly the torment of weeks welled up. When police arrived at his mother-in-law's house, the defendant himself was surprised to find a club in his hand and broken glass all over the place. He was not a violent man. The jury was only out a few minutes. The verdict, not guilty. The judge was about to call the next case when the jury foreman called: "Your honor, please look at the back of the verdict slip." There the jurors had written *We recommend that the court reprimand the mother-in-law.*

A stranger in town arranged to meet a friend at Third and

Figueroa Streets. He waited a long time, then on impulse went into a tavern near the corner, and saw his friend. Before he could get to him, he was intercepted by a girl he described as a "cute little chick." Her antics from this point he described in a tidy little essay titled "Why I Like L.A." which he sent to me. He wrote:

> She looks at me and I look at her. Without a word she points a finger at me and goes into a terrific "grind," ending in a tremendous "bump." I have been a connoisseur of burlesque technique for 27 years but never have I witnessed a more artistic if impromptu performance. When this artiste did her final "bump" for me, she punctuated it so positively I knew instinctively I had just witnessed something magnificent and esthetic. At the same time it was so absurd and insane that I burst out laughing.

• 24 •

*Oh, I don't know, the public is no worse than any-
body else!*—Girl on Wilshire bus

For trivia in quick flashes, journalism's three dots are still the
greatest invention of the twentieth century:

A Melrose avenue druggist, weary of insults, posted a sign
Coffee 5 Cents. with criticism 15 cents . . . Two sailors
and two girls strolling past Sixth and Main Streets stopped in
front of a display window. One girl stared at the sign Atchison,
Topeka and Santa Fe. "Well for gosh sakes!" she shrieked.
"There really is such a thing! I thought it was just a song!" . . .
A police reporter, each time he leaves the press room, calls to
his comrades: "If anyone wants me, I'm out having a hot muscatel sandwich."

The dead silence in elevators has always annoyed a fun-loving
ad man. When he has a co-conspirator along, he always draws
a gasp from passengers by remarking casually: "But when did
you first find out your wife was tattooed?" . . . If a customer
seems about to be stricken with intoxication, Goldie, bartender
at Cardo's on Spring Street, whips a sign out from behind the
counter and flashes it under the customer's nose. It reads "Danger. Hang-over Under Construction" . . . An Eastside motel's
printed list of regulations, posted in each cabin, has the warning "We will not tolerate acts of God."

A picket outside a Wilshire Boulevard theater remarked to
himself, loud enough for a patron at the box office to hear: "Tch,

tch! For eighty cents you can buy a tip on a horse!" . . . A minor attraction at the Southern California Industrial Exposition at Pan Pacific Auditorium was a middle-aged woman, whose job was lifting a toilet lid . . . An insurance agent's billboard at Firestone Boulevard and Manchester Avenue states DRIVE CAREFULLY. YOU MIGHT HIT ONE OF MY CUSTOMERS . . . Pedestrians were attracted to a 1931 jalopy, gaily bedecked with crepe streamers and a posy on the radiator, and dragging a noisy cluster of tin cans along Brooklyn Avenue in Boyle Heights, but instead of the usual blissful newlyweds there was only the driver in the car. As it passed a gaudy sign on the back explained in full JUST DIVORCED. AM I HAPPY!

During the war, a test pilot at a big airplane factory told a friend "You know, people who live at the end of airport runways must be crazy" . . . A girl arrested for immoral conduct gave her name as Mrs. Emily Post alias Kathleen Norris alias Margaret Mitchell . . . Some members of the police robbery detail at the City Hall report for work through the second-story window. It's a short cut . . . A very angry woman stomped into the pottery department of a downtown store. "I've come to return that urn you sold me," she said. "It has a hole down at the base and I didn't know it until nearly half my poor husband's ashes spilled out." She was advised she had purchased a flowerpot vase.

Two old codgers came out of a building in the Wilshire Medical Center and shook hands. One said, "Well, happy gastric acidity!" . . . For a long time, the *Pasadena Independent* had in its classified-personals column, one under the other, ads headed LONESOMENESS ELIMINATED and SWEATERS MADE TO ORDER . . . An Inglewood aircraft worker was arrested in Las Vegas for flying his plane while under the influence of marijuana. He said it made him fly better . . . Orson Welles spoke on fascism in a Wilshire section auditorium and afterwards, as is the custom there, submitted to questioning by the audience. A man in the back brought down the house with "Was Rosebud in your picture 'Citizen Kane' the same as Umbriago?"

A man came into a Western Avenue drugstore and asked for a dime's worth of powdered alimony. Eventually he got his alum . . . A middle-aged man stalked out of a Seventh Street restaurant, holding aloft a plate containing a few dabs of food. He launched into a soapbox tirade against the management for charging him sixty-five cents for it . . . Beverly Boulevard store, which sells unpainted furniture, advertises FURNITURE IN THE NUDE . . . A female dachshund wears blue-denim overalls on which is embroidered *Scat, Cupid!*

A West Eighth Street restaurant listed on its menu "TURKEY—T.P.T.W.O.T.F.L."(the part that went over the fence last) . . . A tall fence at Third and Vermont bore the usual POST NO BILL notice. Under it a lovesick youth chalked EXCEPT ABOUT DOLORES . . . Sign on the avocados in a West Pico Street market: DO NOT SQUEEZE ME UNTIL I'M YOURS . . . Highway sign near Tujunga: NUDIST COLONY AHEAD. PROCEED AT YOUR OWN RISQUE . . . Disillusioned comment of old lady viewing moon through Griffith Park observatory telescope: "Why, it looks like an old worn-out golf ball!" . . . Traffic was halted on busy Valley Boulevard, near Soto Street, while a man got out of his green sedan and rescued a desert turtle which had wandered onto the highway.

A jewelry store on Cahuenga near Hollywood Boulevard has a sign DON'T LOSE YOUR CHARMS. WE WILL SAUTER THEM FOR 15 CENTS . . . A woman who left her dog with a veterinarian explained: "You know how difficult it is to get a sitter these days" . . . A dime store in Santa Monica had a sign APPLICATIONS TAKEN FOR SALESLADIES. CARE TO APPLY FOR ONE? . . . A motel on San Fernando Road is named "The Supreme Court" . . . A waitress in a Wilshire Boulevard drive-in eatery told a customer: "The reason the service is so bad, it takes so long to tell people what we haven't got" . . . A man took a visiting Midwesterner to Santa Monica, for her first view of the mighty Pacific. "Well, well," said the Midwest woman, "it isn't as big as I thought!" . . . Sign on a Pico Street Garage: I'VE GONE FISHING. IF YOU HAD ANY SENSE, YOU WOULD TOO.

A Chinese boy attendant at Grand Central Market keeps the customers in a good mood with "C'mon get your jitterbug tomatoes, solid that is!" . . . Lady to dreamy spouse at Santa Anita: "To hell with the beautiful landscape. That's my horse running last!" . . . Sign on back of a bakery truck: HIT ME EASY. I'M FULL OF PIE . . . During the noon hour on bawdy Main Street, an old man was seen ambling along wearing a truss—outside his clothes . . . Sign on a dachshund kennel on Valley Boulevard: GET A LONG LITTLE DOGGIE . . . A cash-register exchange at Olympic and Grand has for years saved the hired help conversation with the window sign YES, MADAM, THE OLYMPIC BUS STOPS HERE . . . A schoolteacher asked a fourteen-year-old boy to define "straight." "Without ginger ale," he replied promptly.

A Kansas woman, after seeing the ocean for the first time, was asked what impressed her. "Those cute seagulls," she said, "when they fly they hold their feet exactly like ZaSu Pitts holds her hands" . . . When Wallis Warfield Simpson became Mrs. Edward Windsor, a woman at the Congress of Parents and Teachers meeting in Pasadena was heard telling a companion: "You know, I've felt all along that Wally would be no help to the P.T.A." . . . A candy butcher at a bus station startles passengers with "Get your candy, magazines, crackerjack. None sold after the bus leaves the depot, and damn little before."

A lady got on a streetcar and handed the conductor a transfer. He said it was no good and explained why, at great length. She interrupted with "Well, don't bother *me* with it. It's distinctly your problem!". . . A sign on a Hill Street store front: Astro-Science. We solve all problems came and went. Apparently there was one exception: how to pay the rent . . . Asked why he moved to Flintridge, Jack Messler, ad man, replied: "It's one of the few places from which, on a clear day, you *can't* see either Catalina or the City Hall!". . . The telephone book has a listing for Confucius, CRestview 60241. Confucius is *restaurateur* Mike Romanoff's English bulldog . . . A Central Avenue drugstore had a sign Special Today. Beef stew prescription.

An oldster sitting next to the window in a streetcar was observed involuntarily twitching every few minutes. The cause seemed either alcoholic or pathological. Some blocks later a young man sat down beside him. The first time the old man erupted the youth almost jumped out of his clothes. Soon they established a rhythm: jerk, jump, jerk, jump. It went on until the old man turned to the youth and said: "For heaven's sake, stop doing that! You're making me nervous!". . . Classified ad in the *Manhattan Beach Messenger*: "wanted. This newspaper will pay 50 cents each for the first four copies of Sears large catalogue, brought to this office. Reason, paper shortage in the editor's throne room. 108 Wall St. Basement. Arcade bldg., Redondo Beach."

The city seems not like a real city resulting from natural growth, but like an agglomeration of many variegated movie sets, which stand alongside one another but have no connection with one another. Hardly anything looks as if it had struck roots under the surface.—PAUL SCHRECKER, *Harper's* 1944

UNTIL the nineteen thirties, Los Angeles had indeed an air of impermanence. It gave the feeling that a hard enough puff of wind might blow the whole thing away and that if this happened it wouldn't be missed, because maybe it wasn't there in the first place.

Many persons, in fact, adapted their lives accordingly. They had an expression: "Don't buy anything you can't put on the Santa Fe Chief."

They weren't transients but something about the city seemed psychologically unsound, even impossible. They wanted to be ready, should handsomer opportunity present itself elsewhere, to pull up stakes at a moment's notice.

They liked the place well enough, but in the ephemeral sense that they liked a circus or a Fourth of July fireworks display. Nothing about it gave any confidence that it was there to stay.

The depression, paradoxically enough, changed their minds. It hit hard in Los Angeles. The unemployment and relief rolls were in the tradition of the biggest and best; but during these bad years, while things were at half speed, people rediscovered the city. They couldn't afford night clubs, or the fancy places, so they went to the zoo at Griffith Park. They ducked Palm Springs and the High Sierras in favor of a picnic in Mint or

Bouquet Canyon, or their back yards. The economic pressure taught them a great lesson: a person couldn't have his malnutrition in a nicer place than Los Angeles.

The war was the clincher. While the All-Year Club wisely advised outlanders to stay away but to buy and save bonds for a postwar trip, Los Angeles' biggest if inadvertent public-relations job was on.

The thousands who came Westward to work in airplane factories and shipyards for the most part decided to stay. Not only that, they spread the word to the folks back home that life in Los Angeles could be beautiful, or at least prettier than in Oklahoma, Texas, New York, Pennsylvania, and Illinois.

Additional thousands of soldiers, sailors, and marines trained in California long enough to be exposed to the sunshine, the pretty girls, and possibly a movie star's tile swimming pool and made a mental note "This I got to see more of."

The big job was done by the Southern Californians sweating out the war in camps and in Leyte, New Delhi, Italy, and Iceland. They dripped their nostalgia so effectively their friends, weakened by the repetition, promised to visit the place.

By the middle of 1946, the impact of the mass migration was being felt. In October, Mayor Bowron appealed to members of the National Association of Secretaries of State to discourage their residents from coming to Los Angeles. The city could not accommodate any more new residents, he said, for at least five years.

But the flow continued. Around thirty thousand newcomers continued to crash in on the city monthly. Some found sleeping quarters by doubling or trebling up in their relatives' single-family homes, or living in stores, garages, basements, or trailers. Others came on a tentative basis, their stay predicated on getting suitable jobs and places to live.

The result was a rental and real-estate inflation more fantastic than in the early boom days. The city was 162,000 family housing units short and desperation set in, with evicted families sleeping in their cars and couples paying three dollars a day for single rooms without baths or cooking facilities. Real-estate men besieged home owners to sell at three times what they paid. One modest Westsider, told he could easily get twenty-five thousand dollars for the home that cost him eighty-five hundred to build ten years ago, was deeply disturbed. "I can't afford to live in such a high-priced place," he said.

The housing squeeze was only one of the city's irritations. The end of the war brought in focus a number of others which had temporarily been set aside.

First there was smog, so heavy it literally brought tears to people's eyes. When it first appeared in 1941 as a gloomy, forbidding cloud over the metropolitan area, it was attributed to the mammoth new war plants. Everyone anticipated that when the war ended and the plants eased up or shut down, it would be turned off. The obnoxious stuff, however, wouldn't go away and authorities, under pressure, recklessly appointed committees and sought out experts.

Honest smog is usually a combination of smoke and fog. Now, you can't do anything about fog but you can about smoke, so the experts analyzed it, investigated its sources, and on bad days cut it with a knife.

It was traced to the big industrial plants, to unusual atmospheric conditions, to fleets of diesel trucks, to back-yard incinerators, and almost to chain smokers. Some plants accepted their responsibility and spent thousands of dollars cleaning up their portion of sky. Others, for reasons best understood by politicians, didn't lift a lever.

Until eliminated, smog will remain a sensitive issue to those whose work includes selling Los Angeles as a sunshine city. Then there's the bad smell. Los Angeles' outfall sewer at Hyperion sprung a leak and due to wartime scarcity of materials couldn't be repaired. A new twenty-one-thousand-dollar job is on the way but doesn't seem to be happening very fast. Meanwhile the Santa Monica bathing beaches have become contaminated and the state has quarantined them, a matter of general disgust.

Los Angeles is hopelessly in the grip of horse-race fever and after each semester at Santa Anita and Hollywood Park the usual embezzlements and defalcations hit the papers. The degree to which the disease complicates the lives of the patrons was demonstrated at a film studio, which has its own bookie so employes won't waste too much company time telephoning their own bookmakers. A group of writers were waiting for the result of a race and one of them who had wife trouble, as well as horse trouble, decided to call his attorney. The attorney wasn't in so he asked the secretary if anything had happened in his pending divorce case. She told him the interlocutory decree had been granted.

The horse player hung up the telephone, danced a jig, and yelled: "I got the interlocutory! I got the interlocutory!"

One of his fellow writers, who had bet on something else, said sourly: "What'd it pay?"

Anyone who puts his mind to it can pin down any number of other problems. Automobile traffic has reached a point of hopelessness. Marauding gangs of delinquent juveniles lead police an unmerry chase. Downtown parking is a fantastic *snafu*. The overcrowding in schools and universities is desperate. The drunk-disposal program is a disgrace.

Until 1929, Los Angeles kept abreast of its problems. Since, it has fallen far behind in its planning. It may never catch up.

More serious menace lurks in the wings. Los Angeles has serious racial tensions and little inclination to face them has been indicated. With the influx of population, mobsters from the East and Midwest have settled here and with the right political climate might attempt to wrest control of the rackets, now relatively dormant, from the local underworld. Traditionally an open-shop town, Los Angeles has not come of age in its concept of the working man. In fact, it has shown itself susceptible to dangerous demagoguery.

With all these, one thing is certain. Since the war, particularly since the end of the war, Los Angeles has permanence aplenty. It is no longer a Hamburger town, as it used to be called derisively. Oh, you can get a Hamburger at almost every corner, but you can also buy a *filet mignon*. In short, the notion that the city is a brash real-estate development no longer is valid. On the contrary, the city has become conscious of a vague, glamorous destiny, to the point that the subject is boring.

The booster spirit has been sublimated. Now, with a cold inevitability, ex-boosters conjure a magnificent picture. Out of the present flux, they say, the most gigantic community in the world is likely to emerge. Men who have flown over the city regularly in the last few years tell of the blank spaces on the ground gradually disappearing and becoming new business centers and residence sections. They visualize one vast populated area, from San Diego to Santa Barbara, 230 miles, and from the ocean to the San Bernardino Mountains, sixty miles.

Perhaps this is a pipe dream but consider San Fernando Valley, five minutes from Hollywood. Its residents bore with weary indulgence the Hit Parade song of the same name in 1944. It had an out-where-the-West-begins note indicating the valley was cowpoke country inhabited by coyotes, rustlers, and perhaps a few demure ladies who said you-all. The part that went "Gonna pack my grip, gonna take a trip," wasn't so bad. But the line "You can forward my mail R.F.D." was a slight libel by the lyric writer. San Fernando Valley has 248,779 residents, more than three times the number recorded in the 1930 census, when the figure was 78,582. It is probably the most amazing residential and small-farm development in the nation. It is but one of many.

Furthermore, all the seeds are present for a golden era of economic and cultural greatness. Big business and industry, attracted by a new, burgeoning market, have moved in, erecting stately, modernistic castles that house garment shops, restaurants, or perfume showrooms. The motion-picture and radio industries continually enlarge their horizons. Los Angeles has always been derided for its lack of culture. The criticism seems to embody the note that culture has a pattern, or at least has a publicity man who states that it has a pattern. In Los Angeles culture does not grow in the streets like palm trees. It thrives quietly among modest but celebrated people who think publicity and organized culture groups destroy it. They constitute, in their retiring way, a crossroads of the world in literature, art, music, the dance, and education.

The seeds are also present, however, for a future of arrogant, militant mediocrity. It takes all kinds of people to make a world and Los Angeles has them all. They come in the usual assorted sizes and shapes and from the familiar big cities and wide places in the road. A few, surprisingly enough, are born in Los Angeles.

At a certain indefinite age, due perhaps to an elusive vitamin in the air, the sap within them rises or even effervesces. For some, this is bad. They turn out to be heels. They work day and night to enhance Los Angeles' already oversold reputation as a city of chiselers, phonies, and something-for-nothing boys. Just as many turn mellow and become do-gooders, but you never hear of them. Most of them, I like to keep repeating, are no different than people anywhere else.

However they act and whatever they do, Los Angeles is changing. It is not the same city it was before the war. The landmarks are disappearing and with them the Spanish heritage of friendliness and hospitality. Increased leisure remains the great goading incentive, but today you have to travel farther away from the city to find it, or learn to manufacture your own.

There is no immediate hope that Los Angeles will work itself out of its chaos. There is merely the possibility that with a little luck it will make a pattern of the chaos.

Meanwhile it's nice watching. In no other city is the simple business of living an occupational disease, from which recovery is practically unheard of.